EVANGELICALISM
AND MODERN AMERICA

EVANGELICALISM AND MODERN AMERICA

Edited by
George Marsden

William B. Eerdmans Publishing Company
Grand Rapids, Michigan

To Timothy L. Smith

Library of Congress Cataloging in Publication Data
Main entry under title:

Evangelicalism and modern America.

"Most of the chapters in this volume were initially
prepared for a conference . . . organized primarily by
Nathan Hatch and Mark Noll, on 'Evangelical Christianity and modern America, 1930–1980,' . . . held at
the Billy Graham Center at Wheaton College in April
1983"—Introd.
   Bibliography: p. 206
   Includes index.
   1. Evangelicalism—United States—Congresses.
I. Marsden, George M., 1939–
BR1642.U5E893 1984   280'.4   84-21046

ISBN 0-8028-1993-1 (pbk.)

The editor wishes to thank Calvin College for a Calvin Research Fellowship, which
provided some of the time for work on this project. The essay by Martin Marty is a revision
of "Fundamentalism as a Social Phenomenon," *Review and Expositor* LXXIX:1 (Winter
1982), pp. 19–29, and is used with the permission of the editors of *Review and Expositor.*

TABLE OF CONTENTS

v

69773

CONTRIBUTORS

MARGARET L. BENDROTH is a doctoral candidate in American religious history at The Johns Hopkins University.

JOEL A. CARPENTER is an assistant professor of history and the administrator of the Institute for the Study of American Evangelicals at the Billy Graham Center of Wheaton College.

NATHAN O. HATCH is an associate professor of history and associate dean of the college of arts and letters at the University of Notre Dame.

ROGER LUNDIN is an associate professor of English at Wheaton College.

GEORGE MARSDEN is a professor of history at Calvin College.

MARTIN E. MARTY is a Fairfax M. Cone Distinguished Service Professor of the History of Modern Christianity at the University of Chicago.

MARK A. NOLL is a professor of history at Wheaton College.

RONALD L. NUMBERS is a professor of the history of science and medicine at the University of Wisconsin in Madison.

RICHARD N. OSTLING is an associate editor who writes on religion for *Time* magazine.

RICHARD V. PIERARD is a professor of history at Indiana State University in Terre Haute.

LEONARD I. SWEET is Provost and a professor of church history at Colgate Rochester/Bexley Hall/Crozer Theological Seminary.

GRANT WACKER is an associate professor of religion at the University of North Carolina in Chapel Hill.

DAVID F. WELLS is a professor of historical and systematic theology at Gordon-Conwell Theological Seminary.

THE EVANGELICAL DENOMINATION

GEORGE MARSDEN

THIS VOLUME has two main purposes. The first is to help describe and explain the re-emergence of evangelicalism as a formidable force in modern America. This resurgence, which involves both actual growth and a striking change in public attention, is one of the remarkable developments in contemporary culture. Certainly, thirty years ago few would have predicted the solid place of evangelicalism in American life today. From the evangelical perspective, the nation seemed to be slipping into a secular dark age, a decline that spokesmen for ecclesiastical liberalism seemed all too eager to bless. Secularists, meanwhile, cautiously hoped for an age of prosperity and progress built on science and wealth. In any case, old-time religion never figured in futurist projections: theories of secularization posited that traditional religions must decline as highly industrial cultures advance. Today such theories are being revised.[1]

The second purpose of this book is to help assess the character and quality of the evangelical return to prominence. Most of the essayists represented here are evangelicals, and all of them have sympathy with evangelicalism. They realize, however, that recent evangelical successes have been mixed blessings. During the past decades the gospel has been advanced, many persons have been brought into the Kingdom, and vast numbers of institutions have funneled American abundance into diverse channels of evangelism, education, and social service. Yet success has taken its toll. The rich and successful have the hardest time entering the Kingdom. Sometimes the price paid for popularity is an adjustment of the message to what an audience wants to hear.[2] This is, perhaps, the archetypal temptation of the age of marketing. Moreover, power, wealth, influence, and honor within one's own country, although capable of proper uses, are not the goals of Christian life. So this volume, although largely descriptive, also has the purpose of taking a critical look at evangelicalism's relationship to modern America. How has the culture shaped evangelical thinking in key areas, and how might evangelicalism better challenge the culture?

The greatest conceptual challenge in a discussion of this sort is to say what evangelicalism is. The issue can be clarified by asking whether evangelicalism is not a kind of denomination. Evangelicalism is certainly not a denomination in the usual sense of an organized religious structure. It is, however, a denomination in the sense of a name by which a religious grouping is denominated. This ambiguity leads to endless confusions in talking about evangelicalism. Because evangelicalism is a name for a religious grouping—and sometimes a name people use to describe themselves—everyone has a tendency to talk about it at times as though it were a single, more or less unified phenomenon. The outstanding evangelical historian Timothy L. Smith has been most effective at pointing out the dangers of this usage. Smith and his students have repeatedly remarked on how misleading it is to speak of evangelicalism as a whole, especially when one prominent aspect of evangelicalism is then usually taken to typify the whole. Evangelicalism, says Smith, is more like a mosaic or, suggesting even less of an overall pattern, a kaleidoscope.[3] Most of the parts are not only disconnected, they are strikingly diverse.

So on one side of evangelicalism are black Pentecostals and on another are strict separatist fundamentalists, such as at Bob Jones University, who condemn Pentecostals and shun blacks. Peace churches, especially those in the Anabaptist-Mennonite tradition, make up another discrete group of evangelicals. And their ethos differs sharply from that of the Southern Baptist Convention, some fourteen million strong and America's largest Protestant body. Southern Baptists, in turn, have had experiences quite different from those of the evangelicals who have kept the traditional faith within the more liberal "mainline" northern churches. Each of these predominantly Anglo groups is, again, very different from basically immigrant church bodies like the Missouri Synod Lutheran or the Christian Reformed, who have carefully preserved Reformation confessional heritages. Other groups have held on to heritages less old but just as distinctive: German Pietists and several evangelical varieties among Methodists preserve traditions of eighteenth-century Pietism. The spiritual descendants of Alexander Campbell, especially in the Churches of Christ, continue to proclaim the nineteenth-century American ideal of restoring the practices of the New Testament church. Holiness and Pentecostal groups of many varieties stress similar emphases that developed slightly later and in somewhat differing contexts. Black Christians, responding to a cultural experience dominated by oppression, have developed their own varieties of most of the major American traditions, especially the Baptist, Methodist, and Pentecostal. Not only do these and other evangelical denominations vary widely, but almost every one has carefully guarded its distinctiveness, usually avoiding deep contact with many other groups.[4] Viewed in this light, evangelicalism indeed appears as disorganized as a kaleidoscope. One might wonder why evangelicalism is ever regarded as a unified entity at all.

Nonetheless, once we recognize the wide diversity within evangelicalism and the dangers of generalization, we may properly speak of evangelicalism as a single phenomenon. The meaningfulness of evangelicalism as such a "denomination" is suggested by the fact that today among Protestants the lines between evangelical and nonevangelical often seem more significant than do traditional denominational distinctions.

We can avoid many of the pitfalls in speaking about this single "evangelicalism" if we simply distinguish among three distinct, though overlapping, senses in which evangelicalism may be thought of as a unity. The first two are broad and inclusive, the third more narrow and specific. First, evangelicalism is a conceptual unity that designates a grouping of Christians who fit a certain definition. Second, evangelicalism can designate a more organic movement. Religious groups with some common traditions and experiences, despite wide diversities and only meager institutional interconnections, may constitute a movement in the sense of moving or tending in some common directions. Third, within evangelicalism in these broader senses is a more narrow, consciously "evangelical" transdenominational community with complicated infrastructures of institutions and persons who identify with "evangelicalism."

Since these three senses of "evangelicalism" are not usually clearly distinguished, the word is surrounded by a haze of vagueness and confusion. In part, this haze is an inescapable characteristic of just such a loosely organized and diverse phenomenon. Much of the confusion, however, arises from the widespread tendency to confuse evangelicalism in one of the first two broad senses with the more self-conscious community of the third sense, whose leaders often aspire to speak for the broader grouping. In this volume the writers sometimes look at the broader movement and sometimes at that self-conscious community. Once the reader has the distinction clearly in mind, he should not find it difficult to tell whether one or the other or both of the subjects is in view. So it may be helpful for clarifying this and future discussion to look at the broad and the narrow usages in detail.

First is the broad usage in which "evangelicalism" designates simply a conceptual unity. Evangelicals in this sense are Christians who typically emphasize 1) the Reformation doctrine of the final authority of Scripture;

2) the real, historical character of God's saving work recorded in Scripture; 3) eternal salvation only through personal trust in Christ; 4) the importance of evangelism and missions; and 5) the importance of a spiritually transformed life.[5] Evangelicals will differ, sometimes sharply, over the details of these doctrines; and some persons or groups may emphasize one or more of these points at the expense of the others. But a definition such as this can identify a distinct religious grouping. Because evangelicalism in this sense is basically an abstract concept, the diversities of the grouping may be more apparent than is the organic unity.

One way of looking at evangelicalism that has depended heavily on this definitional approach is the opinion survey. Pollsters deal best with abstractions and must reduce their topic to operational definitions. Whether or not one is an evangelical is thus tested by whether one professes a combination of beliefs and practices that fit a certain definition. Evangelicalism delineated in this way will, of course, come out to be somewhat different than if it is considered a movement—either in the broad or the narrow sense. For instance, the 1978-79 *Christianity Today*-Gallup survey classified between forty and fifty million Americans as "evangelicals," a number that accords with other estimates. However, even if the definition used to make such a determination is cleverly formulated and qualified, it will inevitably be inflexible, excluding some who would be "evangelicals" by more intuitive standards and including some whose evangelicalism is marginal. For example, such surveys have no very adequate way of dealing with American folk piety. Also, a fair number of Americans seem ready to profess traditional religious beliefs even though these beliefs for them have little substance.[6] Thus, though definitions of evangelicalism are necessary and helpful, they provide only limited ways of grasping the broad phenomenon.[7]

The other major way to perceive evangelicalism broadly is to view it not so much as a category but as a dynamic movement, with common heritages, common tendencies, an identity, and an organic character. Even though some evangelical subgroups have few connections with other groups and support few common causes, they may still be part of the same historical movement. There may indeed be an "evangelical mosaic"; though it is made up of separate and strikingly diverse pieces, it nevertheless displays an overall pattern. Thus, many American evangelicals participate in a larger historical pattern, having substantial historical experiences in common. All reflect the sixteenth-century Reformation effort to get back to the pure Word of Scripture as the only ultimate authority and to confine salvation to a faith in Christ, unencumbered by presumptuous human authority. During the next centuries these emphases were renewed and modified in a variety of ways, often parallel or interconnected, by groups such as the Puritans, Pietists, Methodists,

Baptists, nineteenth-century restorationists, revivalists, black Christians, holiness groups, Pentecostals, and others. Many evangelical groups, now separate, have common roots and hence similar emphases. Widely common hymnody, techniques of evangelism, styles of prayer and Bible study, worship, and behavioral mores demonstrate these connected origins.

Moreover, common cultural experiences have moved this broad evangelical movement in discernible directions. For instance, American evangelicals have all been shaped to some extent by the experience of living in a democratic society that favors optimistic views of human nature, the importance of choosing for oneself, lay participation, and simple popular approaches. American materialism has also provided a common environment for most evangelicals. And they have been shaped by cultural and intellectual fashions. Nineteenth-century evangelical hymnody of almost all denominations, for instance, tended to be sentimental-romantic and individualistic, following the larger culture. In addition, as a number of essays in this volume suggest, twentieth-century evangelicals have often incorporated current cultural values into their messages.

On the other hand, the common or parallel experiences in the movement may involve resisting cultural trends. Most notably, twentieth-century evangelicals all have in common a belief that faithfulness to Scripture demands resistance to many prevalent intellectual and religious currents. While many in mainline American denominations and their educational institutions abandoned their evangelical heritages during the first half of this century, today's evangelicals all hold firmly to traditional supernaturalist understandings of the Bible message. Simple love for the traditional gospel has no doubt been the chief force in this stance. But many secondary reasons also account for that resistance: because they were immigrants, because they were culturally or intellectually isolated, because they were strongly committed to evangelism and missions, because of traditions of biblical interpretation, or perhaps because of sheer cussedness. Nonetheless, the experiences were parallel, and the resulting willingness to assert the authority of the Bible against some dominant cultural values was similar. So, alongside the striking diversities in heritages, emphases, and cultural experiences are extensive commonalities that make evangelicalism discernible as a larger movement.

Evangelicalism, however, is also a movement in a more narrow sense. Not only is it a grouping with some common heritages and tendencies; it is also for many, self-consciously, a community. In this respect evangelicalism is most like a denomination. It is a religious fellowship or coalition of which people feel a part. This sense of an informal evangelical community or coalition goes back to the international Pietism of the eighteenth century. Common zeal for spreading the gospel transcended party lines. By the first half of the nineteenth century this movement had assumed something like its present shape. Evangelicalism in this more specific sense is essentially a transdenominational assemblage of independent agencies and their supporters, plus some denominationally sponsored seminaries and colleges which support such parachurch institutions. During the first half of the nineteenth century, evangelicals from Great Britain and America founded scores of "voluntary societies" for revivals, missions, Bible and tract publication, education, charity, and social and moral reforms. These voluntary agencies constituted an informal "evangelical united front." In America the expenditures of these independent evangelical agencies at times rivaled those of the federal government.[8] International revivalism, particularly that of Charles Finney in the first half of the century and Dwight L. Moody in the second, as well as efforts in world missions, especially helped foster a unity of purpose among evangelicals from a variety of denominations.

Successful techniques developed in one revival group or mission field quickly spread to others. The Evangelical Alliance, founded in 1846, was the most formal expression of this international evangelical community. Evangelically oriented denominations often encouraged or directly supported some of the independent evangelical agencies on an ad hoc basis. For a few independents, such as Dwight L. Moody, evangelicalism was, in effect, their denomination. For most evangelical leaders, however, the relationship was a bit weaker. Evangelicalism was a fellowship with which they identified while they also participated in a body such as the Methodists, Baptists, Presbyterians, or Congregationalists. Many constituents at the grass-roots level, such as those who supported a Moody revival or an African mission, might be only dimly aware of their connection with a wider evangelical coalition. They would know, however, that their Christian allegiance was wider than simply loyalty to their formal denomination.

During the nineteenth century this trans-Atlantic, transdenominational evangelical fellowship or coalition, although often strained by rivalries and controversies, was unified primarily by shared positive evangelical aspirations to win the world for Christ. In the early decades of the twentieth century the basis for unity was modified, although never abandoned, in response to a deep crisis centered around conflicts between "fundamentalists" and "modernists" in formerly evangelical bodies. Fundamentalists were especially militant evangelicals who battled against the modernists' accommodations of the gospel message to modern intellectual and cultural trends. Modernists, on the other hand, allowed little room for an authoritative Bible, traditional supernaturalism, or a gospel of faith in Christ's atoning work. In short, they had abandoned the essentials of evangelicalism. To make matters worse, the leadership in the major northern denominations tolerated or encouraged this revolution. In reaction, the new fundamentalist coalition emerged at the forefront of the conservative evangelical fellowship. In the face of the modernist threat to undermine the fundamentals of evangelical faith, a threat magnified by the accompanying cultural revolution, much of surviving evangelicalism took on a fundamentalist tone. The perennially upbeat mood of the nineteenth-century movement was now tempered by accents of fear and negativism.

The situation was complicated by the prominence of dispensationalist premillennialists in the leadership of interdenominational fundamentalism. Dispensationalists, whose prophetic interpretations predicted the apostasy of old-line churches, made a virtue out of working independent of the denominations. Accordingly, they had already built a formidable network of evangelistic organizations, missions agencies, and Bible schools. Their transdenominational orientation and their evangelistic aggressiveness, together with a hard-line militance against any concessions to modernism, put them in a position to marshall, or at least to influence, many of the conservative evangelical forces. During the 1920s leaders of this movement presumed to speak for all fundamentalists and did coordinate many fundamentalist efforts. They thus developed a disproportionate influence among conservatives in the old interdenominational evangelical movement, which during the next three decades was generally known as "fundamentalist." As Joel Carpenter shows in the first essay in this volume, heirs of this dispensationalist-fundamentalist movement, especially after 1940, reorganized and revitalized the broader and more open branches of fundamentalism. This "neo-evangelicalism," as it was known for a time, preserved many of the positive emphases of the old nineteenth-century coalition as well as some of the negativism of fundamentalism.[9]

Close connections with Billy Graham gave this new leadership national impact and attention. For the two decades after 1950, the most prominent parts of this more narrowly self-conscious evangelicalism focused around Graham. Graham's prominence and the commanding position of former fundamentalists in organizing this neo-evangelical effort, however, partially obscured for a time the fact that the movement, even as a conscious community, had many other foci and included many other traditions. Since the 1960s, and especially with the successes and growing self-awareness of "evangelicalism" in the 1970s, the diversities that had always been present in the old evangelical fellowship have become more apparent. In the 1980s the movement in fact faces a crisis of identity, evidenced by debates over "who is an evangelical?"

With this background we can see more clearly how our third meaning of "evangelical" refers to a consciously organized community or movement. Since mid-century there have been something like "card-carrying" evangelicals. These people, like their nineteenth-century forebears, have some sense of belonging to a complicated fellowship and infrastructure of transdenominational evangelical organizations for evangelism, missions, social services, publications, and education. Typically, those who have the strongest sense of being "evangelicals" are persons with directly fundamentalist background, although persons from other traditions—Pentecostal, holiness, Reformed, Anabaptist, and others—often are deeply involved as well. Sometimes the people, groups, and organizations that make up "evangelicalism" in this sense are rivals; but even in rivalry they manifest the connectedness of a family grouping that is quite concerned about its immediate relatives.

To look at evangelicals this way does require some adjustment to account for those who still call themselves "fundamentalists." By the end of the 1950s the term "fundamentalism" had come to be applied most often to strict separatists, mostly dispensationalists, who were unhappy with the compromises of the new "evangelical" coalition of Billy Graham. Fundamentalists were also adamant in condemning Pentecostal evangelicalism, while the former fundamentalist neo-evangelicals, despite some reservations, saw Pentecostals as basically allies in their preeminent task of leading people to Christ.

Since the 1970s some fundamentalists, centering around Jerry Falwell and the Moral Majority, have begun to build broader coalitions, much like the neo-evangelicals of the 1940s and 1950s. Yet even the hard-line fundamentalists, such as those at Bob Jones University, who condemn all such compromises, remain a part of the consciously evangelical movement, at least in the sense of paying the closest attention to it and often addressing it. In another sense, however, hard-line fundamentalists have formed a distinct submovement with its own exclusive network of organizations.

So with the possible exception of this extreme position, evangelicalism is a transdenominational movement in which many people, in various ways, feel at home. It is a movement as diverse as the politically radical Sojourners community in Washington, D.C. and the conservative Moral Majority. The leaders of these groups undoubtedly read many of the same evangelical periodicals and books and are familiar with much the same set of evangelical organizations and names. Institutionally, this transdenominational evangelicalism is built around networks of parachurch agencies. The structure is somewhat like that of the feudal system of the Middle Ages. It is made up of superficially friendly, somewhat competitive empires built up by evangelical leaders competing for the same audience, but all professing allegiance to the same king. So we find empires surrounding Billy Graham, Jerry Falwell, Oral Roberts, Pat Robertson, Jim Bakker, Jimmy Swaggart, and other television ministers. Card-carrying evangelicals are just as familiar with Campus Crusade for Christ, Youth for Christ, Young Life, Navigators, Inter-Varsity Christian Fellowship, Francis Schaeffer's L'Abri Fellowship, and other evangelistic organizations. Other agencies for missions or social work have similarly broad interdenominational support. Educational institutions also long have provided institutional strength for evangelicals, especially in hundreds of Bible institutes. Christian colleges, sometimes still under denominational control, help provide stability and continuity of leadership for the transdenominational movement. Wheaton College graduates, for instance, long have stood at the center of one of the most influential networks of organized evangelical leadership. A similarly central role has been played by independent theological seminaries such as Gordon-Conwell, Fuller, Dallas, and Westminster. Some more clearly denominational schools, like Trinity Evangelical, Covenant, Asbury, or Eastern Baptist, have also played direct roles in shaping the card-carrying evangelical fellowship. Evangelical publishers also contribute importantly to the sense of community, both in major periodicals such as *Christianity Today, Eternity,* and *Moody Monthly,* and in the flood of books that keeps the community current with the same trends.

We can see, then, that a decisive factor in distinguishing evangelicals in the more narrow sense from evangelicals in broader senses is a degree of transdenominational orientation. So, for instance, many Missouri Synod Lutherans, Southern Baptists, Wesleyan Methodists, Church of the Brethren, or Mennonites whose religious outlook is channeled almost exclusively by the programs and concerns of their own denomination, are hardly part of the card-carrying evangelical fellowship, even though they may certainly be evangelicals in the broader senses. A few denominations, such as the Evangelical Free Church or the Evangelical Mennonites, have been so entirely shaped by twentieth-century contacts with organized transdenominational evangelicalism as to be virtual products of that movement. Most ecclesiastical bodies, however, offer more distinctively denominational orientation, and "evangelical" would not be a primary term which members would use to describe themselves. Yet still others in these same bodies are clearly evangelicals in the narrow sense that they orient themselves substantially to the transdenominational movement. Thus Billy Graham and Harold Lindsell, for instance, are more "evangelical" than they are Southern Baptist. Similarly, John Perkins and Tom Skinner are black evangelicals because they identify in part with the general evangelical community. The vast majority of black Bible-believers, however, although evangelicals in the broader senses, are only distantly part of evangelicalism as a narrower movement. Nor do they *think* of themselves as "evangelicals."

Evangelicalism, then, despite its diversities, is properly spoken of as a single movement in at least two different ways. It is a broader movement somewhat unified by common heritages, influences, problems, and tendencies. It is also a conscious fellowship, coalition, community, family, or feudal system of friends and rivals who have some stronger sense of belonging together. These "evangelicals" constitute something like a denomination, although a most informal one. Some from the tradition of the original fundamentalists and their neo-evangelical heirs, who indeed have been the strongest party in this coalition, have attempted to speak or to set standards for evangelicals generally. To perceive the difficulties in such artificial efforts to unify the diverse movement by fiat should not, however, obscure the actual unities of the movement, whether broadly or narrowly conceived.

*　　　*　　　*　　　*

The essays in the two parts of this volume are arranged so as to address the two principal questions of our inquiry. Part One deals in rough chronological order with the rise of American evangelicalism since World War II. Part Two, arranged topically, explores various ways in which evangelicalism has challenged or reflected the prevailing cultural ideals of the day. Despite this arrangement, many of the observations in each part bear on the central topic of the other.

Part One presents a variety of ways to account for the evangelical resurgence in modern America. The distinction between organized evangelicalism and evangelicalism as a broader tendency is useful here. Joel Carpenter looks particularly at the forging of a new evangelical coalition designed to rescue America spiritually during the World War II era. One of the keys to this evangelical resurgence was the effective leadership and organizations which revived evangelicalism as a movement in the narrower sense. Grant Wacker, from the other perspective, approaches evangelicalism as a more generalized cultural phenomenon, and he provides some astute and striking suggestions as to why it has been so resilient and why it has assumed its recent direction. His approach is complementary to Leonard Sweet's brilliant depiction of the dilemmas of mainline Christianity in the 1960s. Certainly one factor in evangelical growth has been the dramatic decline during the past two decades of the old mainline denominations. Wacker shows that liberal decline is not a sufficient explanation for evangelical growth, nor does Sweet intimate that it is. Sweet, however, finds a lesson for evangelicals in investigating his own mainline tradition. Accommodation to a dominant culture may help religious groups, but only to a point; soon in such an accommodation a church's members begin to sense that it has nothing distinctive left to say.

Sweet thus not only sets the historical-religious context for understanding evangelical growth, but also offers a warning that underscores the explorations in the second part of the volume.

Richard Ostling, viewing recent evangelicalism from his vantage point as a leading journalist of American religion, also compares evangelicals with liberals. Whereas Sweet looks at the vital difference in terms of the message, Ostling concentrates on the media. Much like Carpenter, Ostling sees a key to evangelical strength in its effective network of organizations. Martin Marty, with an approach closer to Grant Wacker's, adopts a cultural-historical approach to his subject. But where Wacker looks at the broad evangelical phenomenon, Marty concentrates on the most prominent of its subgroups, the new fundamentalists of Jerry Falwell and the Moral Majority. Drawing on his vast knowledge of American religion, and paralleling Wacker's analysis in many respects, Marty concisely sets the new politicized fundamentalism in both its religious and cultural context.

Part Two looks more specifically at the evangelical message, or, more precisely, at the culturally defined traits that have given the traditional gospel a peculiarly American shape. In a pivotal essay for the volume, Nathan Hatch brings together the themes of the two sections. His argument parallels Wacker's by suggesting that recent evangelical successes arise from its adaptation to the American setting. Hatch, however, stresses the democratic character of the movement that has shaped not only the evangelical message but also the structure of its organizations and the ways it uses the media. Hatch here shows why evangelicalism operates as a seemingly unified movement on a broader scale than the direct connections of the card-carrying fellowship would account for. The most diverse elements in the broader movement have been shaped by the same cultural forces. Hatch, however, also builds an effective critique of evangelicalism's characteristic reliance on the allures of democracy. Often the democratic audience has dictated the message, and too often evangelical intellectual life has been impoverished accordingly.

Mark Noll picks up the latter theme by exploring the area where evangelicals have produced the most scholarship: biblical studies. Noll specifies some of the ways that the specific ethos of evangelicalism, both as a broad phenomenon and as a conscious community, has shaped even its most scholarly enterprises. David Wells's sequel to this, on theology, raises what must be the most ironic question in this book. How is it, Wells asks in effect, that evangelical theology still claims to be so timeless when we are now so aware of the pervasive power of cultural influences? His prescription points to the value of cultural-historical analysis for the theologian and theological students. Evangelicals, says Wells, must contextualize their theology, not by letting the culture determine what the Bible says but by directly relating its timeless truths to a sophisticated understanding of the American culture to which we speak.

My essay on evangelicals and history provides a counterpart to Wells's message. Twentieth-century evangelicals generally have had little sense of history as an ongoing process shaped by cultural forces. Christianity's central doctrine, the Incarnation, however, can provide a model for understanding the way in which God works in real historical circumstances. Therefore, we ought to take human cultural forces seriously in evaluating our own tradition. Roger Lundin's essay on evangelicals and the arts suggests a similar theme. The ahistorical and culture-denying tendencies of the evangelical tradition have disposed evangelical literary critics, once freed from fundamentalist constraints, to accept uncritically the prevailing romantic aesthetic of the surrounding literary community.

Evangelical scientific inquiry, as characterized by Ronald Numbers, provides an interesting comparison. Because of the evolution controversy, evangelical science has been politicized and sharply divided between fundamentalists, who insist on "creation-science," and moderate evangelicals, who attempt to reconcile contemporary science with God's workings in the natural world. Challenging the accepted cultural canons has indeed been difficult for the moderate evangelical scientists, since their fundamentalist colleagues are satisfied with nothing less than a full-fledged assault.

The role of women in the movement has more recently been politicized but follows closely the pattern that Lundin describes for the arts. Because of inadequate definitions of the "women's role," Margaret Bendroth argues, both sides in the new politicized atmosphere have too readily embraced the extreme alternative views of women that prevail in the culture at large.

Richard Pierard, while concentrating on the more prominent phenomenon of the evangelical political right, suggests a similar pattern of cultural accommodation as he surveys the seemingly overwhelming literature on this subject. Pierard's account, which includes the literature on evangelicalism in general, also serves as a bibliography for this book.

Most of the chapters in this volume were initially prepared for a conference, made possible by a generous grant from the Lilly Foundation and organized primarily by Nathan Hatch and Mark Noll, on "Evangelical Christianity and Modern America, 1930–1980." This conference, held at the Billy Graham Center at Wheaton College in April 1983, inaugurated the Graham Center's Institute for the Study of American Evangelicals. The volume that has emerged, however, is designed to be a unified account of recent evangelicalism rather than the proceedings of a conference. For this reason, in fact, several fine conference papers do not appear in this book, though they certainly will be published elsewhere. Two other papers, Martin Marty's and Richard Pierard's important essays on the New Right, were added here to place that theme of high current interest in one of its most illuminating but neglected contexts, the recent history of broader evangelicalism. Of course, not every topic on evangelicalism and modern America is covered in this volume. We hope, however, that we have explored enough of evangelicalism's important facets to provide a balanced picture that will advance understanding of this fascinating yet elusive denomination.

The dedication of this volume is a token of our high esteem for a mentor and a friend to many of us.

Part One

THE SHAPING
OF
CONTEMPORARY EVANGELICALISM

Chapter 1

FROM FUNDAMENTALISM TO THE NEW EVANGELICAL COALITION

JOEL A. CARPENTER

THE RESURGENCE OF AMERICAN EVANGELICALS since the rise of Billy Graham has been one of the most striking developments in contemporary culture, but surprisingly little is known about its origins. Evangelicals themselves have faithfully chronicled this resurgence, and a few perceptive church histories have noted the trend as well;[1] but its roots have remained obscure. Part of the problem, no doubt, has been a theoretical one: social scientists have been prone to equate modernization with secularization and to discount the worth of studying supposedly moribund traditions. The continued vitality of evangelical Christianity, however, casts doubt on this perspective and has forced a greater burden of proof on those theorists who continue to insist that evangelicalism is a passing reaction to the rapid transformation of society.[2]

Few should be surprised to find that Billy Graham and the evangelical renaissance he has embodied are the products of earlier developments within fundamentalism and other evangelical traditions; historical common sense dictates as much. Yet the history of fundamentalists and other evangelicals in the second quarter of this century has remained hidden, for the most part. There is nothing like dramatic conflict to inspire the interest of journalists and historians, so the cessation of overt conflict, as in the winding down of the fundamentalist-modernist controversies, usually marks the end of the story. Yet that was merely the closing of a chapter. As subsequent history has made so obvious, it is a mistake to interpret the fundamentalists' public defeats as the mark of their passing and the decline of evangelical piety in general. Evangelical Christianity is doing rather well. Its continued vitality and reborn activism in recent years have forced the pundits to take it seriously once again. But one can hardly fathom the evangelicals' postwar surge without understanding their experience in the crucial years preceding it.

Unfortunately, the stories of the varied evangelical traditions that contributed to the resurgence of recent decades have scarcely begun to be told. With so much historical spadework still to be done, I will not presume to give a comprehensive picture. Rather, I will trace the experience of one prominent evangelical group, the fundamentalists. One should not presume, as the fundamentalists and their modern heirs have, that their tradition represented the normative, vital center of modern American evangelicalism. But the fundamentalists did initiate and set the terms for the new evangelical coalition that has sought to bring revival to America. Thus the career of fundamentalism in the 1930s and 1940s provides a good starting point for probing the roots of the revival of evangelicalism.

How was it, though, that the fundamentalists, who seemed to be outcasts from respectable religious life, were able to play a prominent role in the new religious vitality of the postwar years? Was fundamentalism not a dying force after its exposure to defeat and ridicule in the 1920s? These are complex questions that can be answered only by examining the career of fundamentalism in the 1930s and early 1940s, a period which has comprised a hidden part of its history.

As we shall see, fundamentalists did recoil from the antimodernist and antievolution controversies in defeat and disarray. Some of the coalitions they had formed splintered into contending factions, and many fundamentalist leaders despaired of ever again mounting a public campaign before the return of Jesus. There was more to fundamentalism than crusading against modernism, however. During the 1930s fundamentalists struggled with competing desires: they wished to separate themselves from a culture they thought was on its way to Armageddon, yet they still wanted to win that culture for Christ. Fundamentalism was built upon an older evangelical movement with deeply rooted concerns for evangelism, popular religious education, and both personal and communal righteousness. Fundamentalists' commitment to these concerns and their pursuit of them through a thriving network of institutions marked them as anything but a dying movement. During the 1930s the fundamentalists weathered defeat and ridicule by shifting their energies to evangelism and religious community-building. Fundamentalism had the popular support, structural strength, innovative flexibility, and reproductive potential to maintain its vitality during the Depression years and by the 1940s to seek once again to win America—this time by revival. And although it used discredited intellectual equipment, the fundamentalist movement produced a message that attracted many at a time when Americans were searching for a heritage to remember and conserve. Thus the movement was prepared to play a leading role in the postwar evangelical revival. Three dominant motifs, then, pervaded fundamentalists' thought and action in these years: separation, the Second Coming, and revival.

One of the most important tasks for fundamentalists in the 1930s was finding their bearings. Their movement had been raised up, they were convinced, to be a testimony to Christian truth and against the scourge of apostasy. Fundamentalist congregations and agencies thrived everywhere, but their campaigns against liberal religion and the teaching of evolution in the schools lay in shambles. So what was left for them to do? The movement began to take on an alienated "faithful remnant" stance toward the culture. So what if orthodox Christians were often the laughingstock of the secular press? The world hated our Lord, Presbyterian fundamentalist Donald Grey Barnhouse recalled, so "if the world loves us it is because we are not following Jesus Christ."[3] According to Melvin G. Kyle, editor of the *Bibliotheca Sacra,* "'Come ye out from among them and be separate' is the program . . . for a devout people."[4] Indeed, this sentiment fairly summarizes much of the fundamentalist enterprise in the 1930s.

Fundamentalists could not agree, however, on what separation meant for their denominational relations. Many, like Presbyterian dissidents J. Oliver Buswell, president of Wheaton College, and J. Gresham Machen, founder of Westminster Seminary, believed that any denomination that refused to discipline theological liberals and harassed conservatives was no longer a true church and was not worthy of true Christians' loyalty. This separatist impulse spawned the Independent Fundamental Churches of America in 1930, the General Association of Regular Baptist Churches in 1932, the Orthodox Presbyterian Church in 1936, and the Bible Presbyterian Church and the Fundamentalist Baptist Fellowship in 1937, while scores of congregations became independent of any denominational ties.[5] Those who demurred from ecclesiastical separation were deemed cowards and compromisers.[6] Other fundamentalists disagreed. Baptist editor John W. Bradbury charged separatists with deliberate divisiveness in order to practice "religious racketeering . . . under the cloak of Fundamentalism." He thought that it made neither good sense nor good Christianity to abandon or wreck the denominations, that fundamentalists should instead work from within to fortify the churches.[7] Probably the majority in the movement accepted this advice and tried to prevail over the long run by building up congregations and multiplying the number of fundamentalist pastors and missionaries. Said the old Baptist warrior William Bell Riley, "I have learned to labor and wait."[8] Yet the issue was not resolved and would re-emerge in the 1940s with new virulence.

The separatist impulse had other manifestations as well. Fundamentalists' separate sense of identity and loyalty would invest itself in a growing network of nondenominational institutions. The controversies of the 1920s had exposed the extent to which liberal theology and its priorities for the life and work of the church had permeated the old-line denominational and interdenominational institutions. Hillyer Straton, a young Baptist pastor from Philadelphia, expressed the complaint of many when he said in 1927 that "many denominational colleges that pretend to hold to the fundamentals have been tarred by the Modernist stick," and that "you could take the 'C' out of the YMCA and nobody would ever notice the difference."[9] He and others wanted institutions that they could trust, and the fundamentalist movement was well prepared to provide them. Indeed, while the old-line denominations' programs were depressed in the 1930s, the fundamentalists' network of Bible schools, summer Bible conferences, religious magazines, evangelistic and missionary agencies, and leading urban congregations prospered.[10]

These institutions readily became substitutes for denominational agencies, advertising that they were worthy of their new constituents' loyalty. Fundamentalist Bible schools and liberal arts colleges, for example, advertised that they would fortify the young against dangerous ideas. "Perhaps your son graduated from high school and you are uncertain as to his future," a *Moody Monthly* editorial read. "Have you considered sending him to the Moody Bible Institute for at least a year?" Even if the lad was planning to go to the state university, he could use some steadying first to become a well-equipped "militant type of Christian youth."[11] Wheaton College, claimed its promotional material, was "a safe college for young people." They would learn no dangerous ideas there, not only were "communism and modernism . . . not in vogue" and their theories "conclusively disproven," but the school could be trusted to teach only "conservative social and economic views."[12] Such claims appear to have been very attractive, for Wheaton led all liberal arts colleges in growth nationwide for three years in the 1930s.

Fundamentalism's institutional envelopment helped to provide the plausibility structure, as Peter Berger has put it, to protect fundamentalist views from a hostile environment.[13] In the face of disturbing modern relativism, fundamentalists held out for old landmarks: the absolute authority of a verbally inerrant Bible, a world view based on Enlightenment science and philosophy, and evangelical mores.[14] Modern skeptics such as Walter Lippmann and H. L. Mencken might look with wistful unbelief at such certitude,[15] but in America's segmented culture many could and did find fellowships in which they could rest their faith on the Rock of Ages rather than on the age of rocks.

During the Depression years, however, much more elemental forces struck at people's equilibrium. Society itself seemed to be hurtling out of control. Americans found the simple and familiar aspects of their daily lives altered by the grim facts of the Depression. Robert S. and Helen M. Lynd's second Middletown study reported that "for the first time in their lives, many Middletown people have awakened . . . from a sense of being at home in a familiar world to the shock of living . . . in a universe dangerously too big and blindly out of hand."[16] The uncertainty of one's daily bread and the mystery of that uncertainty magnified all human problems. Political upheavals in Europe and Asia now seemed more threatening. Could it happen here? Was this the end of the American Dream? Was American democratic capitalism dead? Should the nation seek radically new alternatives?[17] While intellectuals wrestled with these questions in the 1930s, Americans everywhere struggled to find security and values to which to commit themselves.[18]

While fundamentalists offered a potentially attractive package of security and values, people might have considered its answers irrelevant if they did not address the present situation. But, in fact, fundamentalists, like Marxists, confirmed their position from the apocalyptic developments of the era. The overwhelming majority of fundamentalists were premillennialists, and among these the dominant position included a dispensational view of history. In the last days, said the dispensationalists, the institutional church would apostatize, warfare and oppression would increase, and the Jews, facing persecution, would flee to Palestine to reestablish their nation. True Christians would be evacuated from earth in an event called the Rapture, as the anti-God political and religious forces began to consolidate. The leader of this conspiracy, the Antichrist, would seek to wipe out the Jews. His power would be tested by the Red Dragon of the North, and as these great powers engaged in battle on the plains of Armageddon, Christ would come to slay all the wicked, redeem the Jews, and establish his millennial kingdom.[19] The world might have been stunned and bewildered at the rise of totalitarian and neopagan regimes, the persecution of the Jews, and the beginning of a Second World War; but fundamentalists got the news in advance by reading the Bible.[20] "While the prophets are at work in many a secular magazine and newspaper telling us what is to happen," Donald Barnhouse observed, "Ezekiel knew more about it than the *Saturday Evening Post*."[21] The daily news, he was convinced, confirmed the timeliness and trustworthiness of his Bible.

Their millenarian vision also allowed fundamentalists to critique some aspects of modernity and the American way of life. In this sense fundamentalism at times became a plain person's parallel to the "realism" of the neo-orthodox movement. Most fundamentalists believed that civilization and its institutions would experience a decline in the last days.

Thus no ultimate security, no peace or order, could be based on social and political reforms. Faith in progress was naive and unfounded. The Depression meant, said the editor of the *Sunday School Times,* that "man is increasingly a failure." The notion that "civilization . . . moves onward and upward," he said, "leaves out God, leaves out sin, and closes its eyes to the hopeless and helpless condition of man when left to himself."[22]

Fundamentalists greeted New Deal politics and the revived social gospel impulse with hard-boiled pessimism. The New Deal, most thought, was a futile exercise. It presumed to offer materialistic cures to a spiritual problem. Thus the fundamentalists were not surprised that the New Deal failed to bring lasting recovery.[23] Likewise, as one minister put it, the social gospel was an "ill-conceived, naive scheme" to bring the Kingdom of God on earth by social reform when only the Second Coming of Jesus Christ could bring it.[24]

World War II brought further fundamentalist critiques of modern values. The Nazi onslaught, thought Will Houghton of the Moody Bible Institute, had been created by a materialistic concept of progress.[25] The universities owed the world an apology for their "fat-headed conceit," he insisted, since they had produced the techniques and ideologies of destruction.[26] He was not about to let repentant liberals off with their "mild reversals" of recent days, either; their disparagement of the Bible's authority and the gospel message had opened the way for these ideologies. "You denied the blood of the Cross," he accused, "and as a result you had shed the blood of a million."[27]

These critiques formed a striking parallel to those of the neo-orthodox movement. But while Sherwood Eddy, Reinhold Niebuhr, and other religious radicals sought to identify with the poor, bring judgment on the nation for its social sins, and fight against the demonic forces unleashed overseas,[28] fundamentalists resorted to an individualistic view of the gospel. Donald Barnhouse said he could find no verse in the Bible "that tells [the Christian] to go out and crusade for political righteousness."[29] Thus, while the millenarian perspective placed fundamentalists at a critical distance from some of the age's cherished nostrums, it also tempted them to respond passively while injustices abounded, sighing that nothing could be done until Jesus came back. Fundamentalists' retreat from social and political activism seemed nearly complete.

The only political tendencies the millenarian perspective seemed to encourage were those the fundamentalists possessed already: conservative individualism and a penchant for conspiracy theories. Their prophetic scenario suggested an increasing consolidation of world power just before Antichrist appeared. The signs of the times readily validated such an interpretation. People had turned to collectivist schemes to restore prosperity and order, while neopagan state-and-ruler worship, replete with graven images and insignia, anticipated the "mark of the Beast" prophesied in Revelation 13.[30] America was not exempt from these signs; the NRA Blue Eagle, for example, paralleled the swastika and the fasces.[31] If big government was part of Satan's plan for the end times, then obviously, as *Moody Monthly* editor James M. Gray put it, "Individualism . . . forms the warp and woof of the Bible."[32]

Since their prophecy presented an intensely conspiratorial version of Christ's warfare against Satan, fundamentalists were always tempted to believe conspiracy theories.[33] Subversion of biblical and American individual freedom could come from either the Antichrist, who was generally linked to fascist, capitalist plots, or the Red Dragon of the North, which signified, of course, communism.[34] Only a small contingent of militant separatists became obsessed with anticommunism.[35] Yet fundamentalists' apocalyptic foreboding about the Soviet Union and the American Left would contribute to the Cold War climate.[36]

The "hope of His appearing," as they fondly referred to Christ's return, had one other effect on the fundamentalists. It brought comfort and assurance at a time when many felt bewildered and helpless. Charles G. Trumbull, editor of the *Sunday School Times*, lamented that the biblical prophecy of "perilous times" was being fulfilled: "Everywhere men's hearts are failing for fear." What could the people do in the face of great trials? "Shall we not . . . listen once more," he pleaded, "through the stress of anguish and tears, and hear His sweet Word of comfort . . . 'Be ye not troubled . . . your redemption draweth nigh.'"[37] God was still in control, still shaping things to his good purpose. Much as Marxists drew hope from what Malcolm Cowley termed "the long view," fundamentalists were cheered by seeing events in the light of Bible prophecy.[38]

The picture of fundamentalism thus far is of a movement drawing in upon itself, separating from the rest of the Protestants and from the world. Yet this hardly explains the expansive, fellowship-seeking, revival-promoting movement one sees expressed in the Youth for Christ movement, the National Association of Evangelicals, and Billy Graham. Thus we need to understand what George Marsden calls "the paradox of revivalist fundamentalism." On one hand, the fundamentalists drew much of their militancy and separatism from dispensationalism and Princeton theology. But they had deep roots as well in the warm-hearted and irenic piety and revivalism of Dwight L. Moody. Another paradox: fundamentalists saw themselves as "insiders"—heirs of the virtual evangelical establishment of nineteenth-century America.[39] Their outcast condition by the 1930s, however, had prompted strong "outsider," separatist tendencies. Yet the fundamentalist movement never lost these two opposing self-images. From the darkest days of the 1930s, and with increasing confidence and success over the following years, fundamentalists restored revivalism as a major public force in American life. Here is how it happened.

Much of fundamentalists' driving force came from their belief that their movement had been raised up by God to preserve the evangelical foundations of American civilization. So, in tension with their separatist and millenarian impulses, they felt compelled to save America. Their failed crusades in the 1920s, however, had soured them on politicized reform. And multiplied crises at home and abroad during the 1930s, seen from a millenarian perspective, reinforced their cultural pessimism. Yet they could not simply give up all responsibility for their neighbor while waiting for the Second Coming. Reform crusades had failed, but perhaps a great national revival would turn America around. America seemed bound for Armageddon, but perhaps, if Americans repented, God would stay his judgment. Editor Will Houghton of the *Moody Monthly* conveyed this ambivalence when he commented at the end of 1938: "We are a year nearer the coming of the Lord. That is our hope. But we are also a year nearer the dissolution—apart from revival—of the type of government established by our fathers. . . ." The only recourse for America, he said, was to "go back to the Bible."[40]

Houghton and other moderate fundamentalist leaders recognized, however, that this would happen only if they reached the masses once again. These nonseparating, "progressive" fundamentalists, many of whom had strong connections with the new mass media and the business world, were doggedly working, praying, and hoping for revival. Their innovative leadership would help bring about a resurgence of mass evangelism by the 1940s, supported by the fundamentalist institutional network and new techniques, especially radio broadcasting and an emphasis on young people. Two important trends would appear in fundamentalism as a result of this initiative, as we shall see: a new surge of panevangelical cooperation and a growing rift between fundamentalist separatists and progressives.

At a time when an increasing number of people had no contact with evangelical churches and the old methods of evangelism appeared hackneyed and culturally irrelevant, enterprising fundamentalists looked to a new measure, the radio. As radio listening was becoming the nation's favorite pastime, fundamentalists were making radio broadcasting a major fixture in their network. In May 1931 a *Sunday School Times* reader-contributed list of radio ministries included over 100 different programs by seventy broadcasters, including Philadelphia Presbyterian Donald Grey Barnhouse's CBS network program on Sunday afternoons.[41] Some of these attracted large and loyal audiences. A *Kansas City Star* poll in 1932 named the "Morning Bible Hour," taught by Dr. Walter L. Wilson of the city's Central Bible Church, the area's most popular radio program.[42]

Radio proved a potent aid to fundamentalist outreach and institutional growth. Broadcasts brought the fundamentalist gospel to the general public, giving them the most audible evangelical voice of the day. Radio instructed and encouraged the movement's adherents and helped to make new friends among nonfundamentalist evangelicals. The programs gave their sponsors broad publicity and contact with an intimacy that print media did not have. Radio made preachers and gospel musicians public figures once again. No other fundamentalist radio venture illustrates this potential better than station WMBI of the Moody Bible Institute. Station WMBI, inaugurated in 1926, aired a variety of programs, including a weekly Radio School of the Bible, devotionals, the "Know Your Bible" (or "KYB") Club for children, MBI campus activities, guest preachers, and plenty of gospel music.[43] By 1930 the station had become a fixture in Chicagoland and Midwestern fundamentalism; it received over 20,000 letters annually.[44]

The evangelistic potential of radio was not lost on MBI president Will Houghton. In the pages of the *Moody Monthly* he called for a revival to cure the nation's ills.[45] While preaching in Toronto during the D. L. Moody Centenary celebrations of 1937, he predicted that a revival would soon break over the land. The next year he launched a new evangelistic broadcast, "Let's Go Back to the Bible," on which he preached twenty-six sermons over eleven major Mutual System stations.[46] Houghton called for national repentance. He believed, he said, that "God has a stake in the nation, and He is concerned that His word of warning and invitation shall be given forth."[47] All told, the Institute received 40,000 letters of response, and Houghton initiated a second series the following fall, hoping once again that the broadcast would help spur revival.[48] Another venture began in 1940, a transcribed weekly program entitled "Miracles and Melodies," which featured baritone soloist George Beverly Shea. By early 1942 the program was heard on 197 stations in forty-three states.[49]

These new measures had not yet restored the mass revivalism of earlier days, but the fundamentalists' evangelistic thrust was gaining momentum. Among the scores of fundamentalist broadcasters, one man in particular was demonstrating how radio could help generate the interest and support needed to bring the crowds to the evangelist. Charles E. Fuller's "Old-Fashioned Revival Hour," founded in southern California in 1931, had reached a national audience on the Mutual Network by 1938, and crowds filled great public arenas wherever and whenever he spoke. He was invited to Boston by the New England Fellowship in the fall of 1941, and in two evangelistic meetings at the Boston Garden he spoke to a total of 32,000.[50] Such events prompted new vision and anticipation. In February 1942 the Founder's Week Conference at the Moody Bible Institute featured Houghton, Fuller, and other revival promoters, and its theme was devoted to "America's God-Given Opportunity for Revival Today."[51]

This evangelistic quickening encouraged many fundamentalists to reassess their place in American Christianity. Fundamentalists' zeal for separation had made them insular and defensive, but now their desire for revival was leading many of them to seek fellowship and cooperation with other evangelicals. Revival would come, many thought, only as evangelicals put aside their quarrels and formed a great united front to accomplish the task. J. Elwin Wright of the New England Fellowship predicted that an association of those who had rejected a "merely militant fundamentalism" would arise in the next decade.[52] From 1939 to 1941, Wright repeatedly toured the country, romancing evangelicals of every variety with the vision of national revival made possible by a new evangelical coalition.

Others sought cooperation for a different purpose. In September 1941 fundamentalist separatists led by Carl McIntire of the Bible Presbyterian Church formed the American Council of Christian Churches to attack the Federal Council of Churches.[53] Wright's nascent group now faced a dilemma: should they join forces with the McIntire organization or continue their own plans, even if it meant a damaging rivalry?[54] Fundamentalist leaders met at the Moody Bible Institute in Chicago on October 27, 1941 to consider this matter.[55] After a lengthy discussion with the American Council men, Wright, Houghton, and other moderates decided that they could not unite with the American Council because of differing objectives. Any new association, they believed, should be organized on a positive basis and not primarily to attack the Federal Council.[56] The moderates wanted all evangelicals to help found the organization, so they believed that no small, unrepresentative group had the moral right to start a national organization.[57]

Wright and his colleagues invited representatives from every evangelical sector to a national conference in St. Louis on April 7–8, 1942. They asked for no detailed doctrinal statement, and they avoided belligerent tones and volatile labels like "modernist" or "fundamentalist." From this meeting came the National Association of Evangelicals, a fundamentalist-initiated but genuinely inclusive fellowship that signaled the formation of a new evangelical coalition.

From the very start, however, McIntire and other separatists led a chorus of denunciation against this new organization, claiming that it had betrayed the fundamentalist cause by refusing to attack and expose all error and by not requiring its members to separate themselves from the Federal Council.[58] Thus began a bitter new debate that eventually split the fundamentalist movement, put the moderates on the defensive, and hampered the cause of evangelical unity and pluralism for decades to come.[59]

This controversy would provoke the separatists to an even more antiworldly and conspiratorial outlook. The liberal poison, they believed, had invaded the fundamentalist camp, and the most dangerous enemy was now "neo-evangelicalism."[60] They retreated into their own religious communities, especially in the sunbelt states, where political conservatism and Protestant hegemony better suited their outlook. Separatists would be split by internal rivalry but in their own way would contribute to the evangelical resurgence with rapid growth and vigorous new spokesmen such as Jerry Falwell and Bob Jones III.[61]

Despite these problems, the NAE soon developed into a major symbol and coordinating center of the evangelical resurgence. By 1947 it represented thirty denominations, totaling 1,300,000 members. It spawned several evangelical interest groups such as the National Religious Broadcasters and the Evangelical Foreign Missionary Association.[62] These evangelicals now saw that they were not so weak and isolated as they had supposed. Encouraged by the prospects of revival through united efforts, they saw that their support could make the Youth for Christ movement and the Billy Graham crusades more successful than their fundamentalist founders could have by themselves. And encouraged by this first flowering of a new evangelicalism, a younger generation of university-trained scholars, most of them having come up from fundamentalism, moved into leadership positions, where they sought to define and speak for evangelicalism in America.

The new evangelical coalition was made possible to a large extent because fundamentalism, as the era's most vocal and visible evangelical movement, had influenced many other evangelical groups. For example, many people in immigrant-based Protestant denominations found that fundamentalism offered an appealing way to sing Zion's songs in a strange land.[63] Fundamentalist beliefs and emphases penetrated these varied traditions with uneven success. Some communions with close previous affinity to American evangelicals, such as the Swedish Baptists, became thoroughly part of the fundamentalist movement.[64] Others, such as the Mennonite Church and the Christian Reformed Church, had both affinities and strong antagonisms toward fundamentalism.[65] Strict Lutheran confessionalists, such as the Missouri Synod Lutherans, vigorously shunned fellowship with the movement.[66] Still, the fundamentalist tension between an expansive, revivalist impulse and a sense that "this world is not my home" appealed to many immigrant people who were torn between making good here and preserving the faith of their parents.[67]

In addition to influencing immigrants, fundamentalism penetrated Anglo-American denominations other than those in which it was rooted.

The movement's role as public champion of orthodoxy introduced them as allies to other conservatives, such as the Southern Baptists and the southern Presbyterians. While both of these communions felt threatened and compromised by interdenominational cooperation, they both developed fundamentalist contingents, much to the chagrin of denominational leaders.[68]

Likewise, both the holiness and Pentecostal movements, which shared roots with fundamentalists in the revivals of the 1870s and 1880s, felt the influence of fundamentalist perspectives and emphases. By the 1930s holiness-oriented denominations such as the Church of the Nazarene and the Evangelical Friends emphasized premillennialism and antiliberal protest more than they had before.[69] Many Pentecostals considered themselves "fundamental" and held their own variety of dispensational premillennialism.[70] Yet they were estranged from the movement by the fundamentalists' abhorrence of their tongues-speaking and reputation for emotional extravagance.[71] When J. Elwin Wright and others proposed a national evangelical fellowship, they insisted that Pentecostals be invited. This surprised Pentecostal leaders, but they were glad to be so recognized.[72]

The new evangelical coalition represented by the National Association of Evangelicals came from all these sources and more. Fundamentalists' presumption of national evangelical leadership, their position as an interdenominational movement, and their penetration of other traditions led them to envision and successfully call together this broad, cooperative alliance. Yet cooperation under the NAE rubric had its limits. These other traditions did not all simply become fundamentalists; they had reasons of their own for joining or not joining the NAE. Each tradition's story reveals unique considerations and deserves extensive treatment not possible here. Suffice it to say that several major groups, including the Southern Baptists, sensed that despite the NAE's inclusive intentions, its leaders presumed that the fundamentalist doctrinal heritage formed the norm for American evangelicalism.[73] Thus the "progressive" fundamentalists' long hard work at building evangelical solidarity bore mixed fruits. The first major outpouring of a nationwide revival of religious interest would come not so much from official NAE channels as from a group of enthusiastic "Youth for Christ" evangelists from whose ranks came Billy Graham. In attacking a nationally acknowledged problem with a bold, innovative approach, Youth for Christ would attract support from a much wider base than the National Association of Evangelicals could provide.[74]

The Youth for Christ movement's phenomenal success in the mid-1940s shows that a remarkable convergence of events and moods in the war years underlay the resurgence of evangelical Christianity. The American public was showing more interest in things religious than they had for at least a decade. It was as if every reservoir of spiritual strength was being tapped for the war effort.[75] Religious fiction like *The Robe* and *The Song of Bernadette* became best sellers, and *Going My Way,* a mildly inspiring movie tale of two priests in Brooklyn, won several Academy Awards. Church attendance in all faiths was up sharply, and the press regaled its readers with stories of foxhole epiphanies.[76] At the same time, however, family disruptions and the enticements of wide-open industrial and military-base boom towns brought disturbing reports of public licentiousness and teenage crime.[77]

As spokesmen ranging from Robert S. Lynd to J. Edgar Hoover called for something to be done to save America's youth,[78] the Youth for Christ movement was primed for the task. Pioneered by radio preacher Percy Crawford and former jazz band leader Jack Wyrtzen, and led everywhere by young pastors and businessmen with mass media experience,[79] Youth for Christ understood the "language of youth" and the younger generation's tensions. The result was an astonishing public response. Youth for Christ became an overnight sensation with the "bobbysoxers" and armed forces young people in 1944 and 1945.[80] Under the organizing genius of Chicago pastor and broadcaster Torrey Johnson, Youth for Christ International was formed in 1945 and in its first year grew from about 300 regular rallies with 300,000 to 400,000 youths attending to nearly 900 rallies and about one million constituents.[81] By following up the efforts of its G.I. promoters with evangelistic "invasion teams," Youth for Christ had reached forty-six countries by 1948.[82]

This Saturday night sensation passed its innovative energy on into the broader new evangelical movement as its young evangelists founded other ministries. In addition to providing almost the entire original staff of the Billy Graham Evangelistic Association,[83] Youth for Christ evangelists also formed the Far East Gospel Crusade, Greater Europe Mission, Trans-World Radio, and World Vision International.[84] Youth for Christ also translated the Allied offensive and victory into a mandate for world evangelization. Consequently, the growth of the evangelical foreign missionary force in the following twenty-five years would be unprecedented in the history of the church.[85]

Meanwhile, public receptiveness for the evangelical message continued and encouraged postfundamentalist evangelicals to feel like part of the "establishment" again. As the threat of confrontation with the Soviet Union intensified, national leaders such as President Harry S. Truman and General Dwight D. Eisenhower called for national spiritual renewal to meet the challenge.[86] The new evangelists eagerly picked up and quoted such jeremiads,[87] and when they were praised for their efforts by public officials, a new civic and religious alliance began to take shape.

The fundamentalists' retreat from social and political activity was being turned around.

Thus the new evangelical coalition looked at a promising future at the beginning of the postwar era. The National Association of Evangelicals signified a new desire for fellowship and united action. The Youth for Christ movement showed that urban revivalism on a massive scale was again possible, since it had captured the public's interest and a broad base of support in city after city. The surge of commitment to foreign missions was prompting new agencies, the rapid growth of older ones, and a backlog of thousands of young people demanding Bible school and seminary training.[88] And stirrings of an evangelical intellectual renaissance issued in the formation of Fuller Theological Seminary in California and at least one attempt to found a new Christian university. At the same time, a group of fundamentalist graduates of Harvard Divinity School were moving into positions of leadership in the movement.[89] Everywhere the new evangelicals looked forward to a fresh start, a chance to become respectable, responsible contributors to the American way of life.

Yet the new religious landscape of the postwar era would be colored by the past. The paradox in the fundamentalist character that prompted a wavering between "establishment" and "outsider" self-images would come back to haunt the new evangelicals, and success would have its own perils.

Chapter 2

UNEASY IN ZION:
EVANGELICALS IN
POSTMODERN SOCIETY

GRANT WACKER

ONE OF THE FASCINATING QUESTIONS facing students of American religion is why Protestant evangelicalism has flourished so remarkably since World War II and especially since the mid-1960s. Evangelicals themselves often say that the movement has prospered because people are fed up with secular humanism, which has led to, among other things, drugs in the public schools, sex on television, liberalism in the government, and weakness in foreign affairs. Historians and social scientists phrase it differently, but frequently they too end up saying pretty much the same—namely, that the evangelical surge has been a direct reaction to a long series of provocations in the external culture. And when we think about the developments of the last quarter century, it is difficult to doubt that there is a measure of truth in this interpretation.[1]

Even so, this stimulus-response model of explanation, which poses real or perceived secularism as the efficient cause of the evangelical revival, is inadequate for several reasons. In the first place, it does not account for the apparent vitality of what might be called (albeit very loosely) the "Evangelical Left." Although all evangelicals would dissociate themselves from "secular humanism"—if that term is defined as the ideology of human automony—many cherish the benefits of secularization, or what Richard Lovelace has called "Common Grace humanistic values," such as "freedom of inquiry, the open market of ideas, cultural and artistic liberty, and humane technologies." Further, many evangelicals approve of, or at least are not dismayed by, the trajectory of American politics during the last half century. They understand that an increasingly integrated political system—represented by the evolution from the New

Deal to the Great Society—is necessary in order for them to enjoy the benefits of modern technology and democratic process. It is extremely difficult to know how large the Evangelical Left is, or even if it is growing or shrinking. Nonetheless, there are quantitative and impressionistic reasons to believe that most black and perhaps a fourth of white evangelicals fall into this category.[2]

A second and more serious flaw in the stimulus-response model is that it does not very well explain the expansion of the Evangelical Right, where, presumably, most of the numerical growth of recent years has been concentrated. The main difficulty is that the correlations between cause and effect are not very persuasive. This is a complicated problem, the kind that sociologists love to tinker with. Here it must suffice to say that the evangelical surge started in the early 1950s, long before external provocations like the death-of-God theology or the Vietnam debacle had started to rattle evangelical nerves, and the surge has continued without abatement ever since. Or to put it a bit differently, neither wars nor recessions nor Watergate nor Reaganomics nor fluctuations of the hemline have had discernible impact on the rate of evangelical expansion.[3] Moreover, there is no hint in the scanty poll data that is available that a significant number of persons have become evangelicals because they were appalled by the way things were going in the nonevangelical world.[4] And no one should really be surprised. The general history of movements of collective behavior, religious and otherwise, suggests that they are generated not by discrete provocations in the cultural environment but by fundamental realignments in the social system that create new needs and stir new aspirations.[5]

The magnitude and durability of the postwar evangelical movement seems to require, in short, a more systematic interpretation of its causes. By this I simply mean that in order to understand why the movement has swelled in the last quarter century, we need to look beyond the immediate and transitory swings of contemporary culture and seek, instead, to set evangelicalism in the longer and broader contexts of American history and society. We need to see, in other words, how the movement fits into larger historical and structural dimensions of the American experience.

Fortunately we have not been left high and dry, as Perry Miller once said, in "a parched and barren land crying for deliverance from the hold of ideas that have served their purpose and died." Recently several historians have in fact fashioned impressively systematic interpretations of the sources of the postwar evangelical surge. In one way or another most have claimed that the distinctive structure of postmodern or postindustrial society, which arrived in the West in the 1920s and 1930s, and became an overwhelming force in American life after World War II, brought with it distinctive cultural forms, and the evangelical revival has been one of them. This is to say, in other words, that the roots of the revival must be sought in fundamental social transformations such as mass communications, high technology, and the triumph everywhere in American life of "impersonal structure[s] of expertise."[6]

With these developments in mind, some analysts of contemporary evangelicalism have taken an essentially reductionist approach, arguing that the evangelical upswing has been a negative reaction, not just to recent liberalizing trends in government and secularizing trends in the culture, but to the whole thrust of postmodern society itself. They have assumed, in short, that the revival has been an artifact, or epiphenome-non, of modern society, and that the fate of the former has been and will continue to be determined by the direction of the latter. Other analysts, on the other hand, have taken a more positive functionalist approach, arguing that the evangelical upswing has been an integral part of modern-ization, neither separable from nor reducible to the larger process. Both of these approaches have been construed and applied in various ways, but here it will suffice to look briefly at the work of two historians whose thinking illustrates the strengths and, I believe, the pitfalls of each ap-proach.[7]

Perhaps the most distinguished representative of the view that the evangelical renaissance is essentially an artifact of postindustrial modern-ization is William G. McLoughlin. In his 1978 study *Revivals, Awakenings, and Reform,* which is, in a way, a distillation of several books and many years of research in evangelical history, McLoughlin distinguishes between evangelical revivals and cultural awakenings. In the eighteenth and nine-teenth centuries, he argues, these were pretty much the same. In the early years of the twentieth century, however—and again and more clearly since World War II—evangelical revivals have been by-products or "efflu-via" of cultural awakenings that followed fundamental transformations of the social system.[8]

In order to see why, in McLoughlin's estimation, this has been the case, we must first understand how he (and many students of religious history) sees the underlying social process. Drawing upon the work of anthropologist Clifford Geertz, McLoughlin contends that in a healthy society an awakening takes place whenever the society's ethos—its behav-ior, values, and attitudes—wobbles out of synchronization with its world view—the principles that ultimately undergird and legitimate the society's ethos. An awakening, then, is a long transformation, often lasting a generation or more, in which the core myths of a society are redefined or reformulated to legitimate new patterns of behavior. Thus McLoughlin contends that "great awakenings are periods when the cultural system has had to be revitalized in order to overcome jarring disjunctions between norms and experience, old beliefs and new realities, dying patterns and emerging patterns of behavior." Yet how does all this come about? What are the social mechanisms that trigger an awakening?

Guided by a model of cultural revitalization formulated by anthropologist Anthony F. C. Wallace, McLoughlin argues that when the tension between ethos and world view becomes sufficiently severe, individuals, then larger and larger groups, begin to crash through the old habits of thought and establish new legitimations for new patterns of behavior. Others, by contrast, invariably try to alleviate the tension by calling for a revival of traditional legitimations and behavior. This pressure to turn back is intense but futile. Like a nova, it is a flare-up that signals the demise of the old and the beginning of the new. In McLoughlin's view, this is precisely the role that evangelicals played in the 1900 awakening, and it is the role that they have played in the awakening that started to unfold again in the 1960s. They are the custodians of a tradition that was born long ago when the stable values of a predominantly rural society were normative. But in the increasingly pluralistic culture of postindustrial society that tradition is destined to become an anachronism at best, and an impediment to progress at worst.

Evangelicals are not likely to find McLoughlin's interpretation of their recent good fortune congenial, but unquestionably he has done his homework and offered a serious analysis of the way that the movement fits into the larger picture of American history and society. Nonetheless, McLoughlin's reductionist model creaks with problems. In the first place, if the postwar evangelical surge is essentially a backward-looking by-product of a more fundamental social transformation, it is worth noting that that transformation has been going on for several decades but the evangelical revival shows no signs of sputtering, much less dying out. More significant is the fact, noted at the beginning of this essay, that a large minority of evangelicals—the Evangelical Left—are remarkably in tune with the rhythms of social and cultural change. And among those who are not, or who claim that they are not, are many who have exhibited an uncanny aptitude for adapting to modern life. This is one of the reasons why a more flexibly functionalist interpretation of the wellsprings of the evangelical revival merits consideration.

Perhaps the most notable exponent of this approach is Martin E. Marty. In several books and articles Marty has thoughtfully argued that contemporary evangelicalism is best understood not as a negative reaction to, but as an integral part of, the modernization process.

> Because Evangelicalism is the characteristic Protestant . . . way of relating to modernity, it has recently experienced a revitalization concurrent with the development of a new stage of modernity.

> This does not mean that Evangelicalism is epiphenomenal in relation to modernity, or that the modern condition predestines the outcome for passive religious adherents. . . . But there has been a symbiosis between unfolding modernity and developing Evangelicalism.[9]

In Marty's view, the first phase of modernization, the industrial revolution of the eighteenth century, was marked above all by structural differentiation. Life was chopped up into state, home, and job. By emphasizing worldly success, free church polity, and the values of domesticity, Protestant evangelicals sensitively registered these and other aspects of the transformation. The second phase, which overtook Western nations in the middle third of the twentieth century, has been marked by uniquely mobile and affluent styles of life and by a new sense of entitlement among large segments of the population. Again, Marty contends, evangelicals have been in the vanguard. Thus he points to their dextrous use of the media, their aptitude for forming cohesive cell groups, their facility for creating firm psychological boundaries, their fondness for born-again celebrities and authoritarian ministers, and, alas, their perennial willingness to confuse Christian faith with the accouterments of a tastefully appointed suburban lifestyle.

While most evangelicals are not likely to find Marty's interpretation much more palatable than McLoughlin's, Marty's is, I think, preferable because it is richer—because it takes seriously the subjective intentions as well as the objective consequences of evangelical faith. Or to put it more plainly, Marty's flexibly functionalist scheme, more than McLoughlin's rigorously reductionist scheme, ascribes causal, instrumental power to evangelical ideas. Marty's work suggests that evangelical religious and theological notions, though outmoded in the mainline seminaries and leading universities, have nonetheless been an indispensable part of the evolution of modern society. Indeed, when we use a model of this sort, other reasons for the movement's growth begin to appear. One thinks, for example, of the way evangelicals in the 1940s and 1950s instinctively responded to the distinctive youth culture that emerged in the United States between the world wars.[10]

Even so, any attempt to account for the evangelical renaissance by linking it to the development of modern society, even in a positive and functional way, is complicated by the fact that evangelicalism is relatively localized,[11] while highly modernized societies obviously are not.[12] Evangelicalism, securely tied to its Wesleyan and Edwardsian roots, has always been a largely Anglo-American phenomenon, and the recent surge of evangelical fervor seems to have been a distinctively American phenomenon. I am not suggesting, of course, that the movement has been uniquely American, but its numerical magnitude and cultural influence do appear to have been measurably greater in the United States than in Canada or in the historically Protestant regions of Europe. (Journalistic hoopla notwithstanding, there is little reason to believe that the rise of religious traditionalism in nations like Iran is truly comparable, either religiously or socially.)[13]

Consequently, we need to search for distinguishing forces in the American experience that will explain, or at least help explain, evangelicalism's singular strength in the United States since World War II. While many ingredients might be profitably factored into the analysis, I suggest that two traditions, deeply rooted in the American past, have particularly influenced the relationship between evangelicals and modern society. The first is the peculiar structure of church-state relations, and the second is the religious legacy of the American South.

The peculiarity of the American church-state tradition arises from the fact that it embraces two ideals which are, and always have been, essentially adversarial. One is what might be called the custodial ideal. It assumes that society is organic and that civil authorities have a custodial responsibility for the spiritual as well as the physical well-being of the organism. The custodial ideal was articulated with timeless eloquence in John Winthrop's *A Modell of Christian Charity*, which he wrote in 1630 aboard the *Arbella*. While other societies are expected to uphold only the usual ways of justice and mercy, Winthrop observed, we are an exceptional society, in covenant with each other and with God to live by the higher requirements of the gospel. Thus "we [dare not] think that the lord will beare with such faileings at our hands as hee dothe from those among whome wee have lived." The rolling cadences of Winthrop's prose should not obscure the blunt truth that the establishment of one or another form of Protestantism in most of the colonies was the legal articulation of this sense of corporate liability. The founder of Pennsylvania disdained an established church; "penal laws for religion," he wrote, "is a church with a sting in her tail." Nonetheless, Penn insisted that all citizens of the commonwealth were members of the realm of nature and therefore subject to the moral prescriptions of "General and Practical Religion." Even Virginia's Thomas Jefferson assumed the existence of universally normative moral absolutes; what he doubted was the expediency of trying to coerce lip service to these absolutes through legal sanctions. Throughout the nineteenth century, in the wake of disestablishment, the great tradition of the American churches was not unbridled freedom but "the coercion of voluntarism"—to use Winthrop S. Hudson's arresting phrase—the "compulsion to fulfill a distinctive and specific vocation in society," to nurture the common and enduring spiritual values and life of the republic. And even in the mid-twentieth century, the call for a transcendent civil religion or a refurbished religion of the republic has been, I suspect, a contemporary translation of John Winthrop's conviction that in a healthy society the cultivation of private and public virtue is the legitimate concern of government.[14]

Yet always handcuffed to the custodial ideal has been another tradition, which might be called the plural ideal. This notion assumes that there is a critical difference between public interests and private concerns, and religion, for the most part, is a matter of private concern. The roots of the plural ideal stab just as deeply into the subsoil of American culture. Again, the primitive documents of Massachusetts are instructive. In the *Cambridge Platform* of 1648 the ecclesiastical and civil jurisdictions of the Commonwealth were separated. While it is undeniable that the clergy influenced civil affairs, it is also undeniable that the civil foundations of the colony were set not in Scripture but in the common law, which was notoriously susceptible to the ferment of cultural and religious pluralism. The outcome is evident in the Constitution and First Amendment. Whatever the framers "really meant" when they stipulated that "Congress shall make no laws respecting the establishment of religion or prohibiting the free exercise thereof," it is clear that in the twentieth century the Supreme Court has progressively enlarged the proscriptions against government aid to organized religion. From time to time, of course, constitutional judgments have veered in a different direction. But the tendency has been to give nontraditional faiths equal standing with Judaism and Christianity and, concurrently, to make civil support of religion increasingly problematical. Besides these constitutional trends, the plural ideal has been undergirded by social changes such as the Eastern European immigration in the 1890s, the northward migration of American blacks in the 1920s, the democratization of higher education fostered by the G. I. Bill in the 1940s, and by the perennial leaven of nature religions involving magic, astrology, and shamanism. Taken together, these changes have differentiated American life, gradually transforming raw social diversity into a positive ideal of cultural and religious pluralism.[15]

When the Constitution and Ten Amendments became the normative charter of the land in 1791, the custodial ideal was formally subordinated within the plural ideal. Still, both traditions have persisted as integral parts of American civilization. Indeed, the venerability of each is one of the reasons why the current debate between spokesmen like Jerry Falwell on one side and Norman Lear on the other is not readily resolved. Each has a firm foundation in American history, and each has broad support at the grass roots. And this is the critical point. The doubleness of the church-state tradition has prestructured the relationship between evangelicals and modern society, making that relationship inherently adversarial.

23

The structural nature of the tension between evangelicals and modern society becomes evident when we remember that over the years evangelicals have been the chief spokesmen for the custodial ideal. Their commitment to legal separation of church and state has been genuine, yet, as George Marsden and others have demonstrated, all but the most radically alienated of fundamentalists have embraced the notion that Christians, and especially evangelical Christians, ought to be the moral custodians of the culture. Some aspects of this self-assigned responsibility have been more commendable than others; but that is another matter. Here the important point is that since the early years of the nineteenth century, and more clearly and sharply since the 1920s, evangelicals have been locked in an adversarial relation with the dominant pluralistic tradition.[16]

Let us now return to the question of modernization. We are now able to understand why evangelicals in the United States, in particular, have been so restive and aggressive during the past quarter century. Although many scholars believe that modernization—and especially postindustrial modernization—has spurred secularization, some analysts, such as Talcott Parsons, have argued that modernization has simply forced people to express their religiousness in new and different ways. Whatever the exact nature of the relationship between modernization and secularization, it is clear that modernization has decisively benefited the plural rather than the custodial tradition, and it is not difficult to see why. The differentiation of the public and private spheres of life, the elaboration of occupational specialization, the triumph of technological rationality, and so forth, have forced religion in general—and Protestant evangelicalism in particular—to evacuate one public outpost after another. As a consequence, in Peter Berger's words, "different sectors of social life [have] now come to be governed by widely discrepant meanings and meaning systems."

> Not only [has] it become increasingly difficult for religious traditions . . . to integrate this plurality of social life-worlds . . . but even more basically, the plausibility of religious definitions of reality [has been] threatened . . . within the subjective consciousness of the individual.[17]

This, then, is the heart of my argument: an essentially ahistorical, transcultural structural development—namely, advanced modernization—has collided with and upset the historic balance between two immensely powerful traditions. The result has been that evangelicals, along with Mormons, conservative Catholics, orthodox Jews, and countless others who believe that American society cannot survive unbridled pluralism, have been aroused, like the proverbial sleeping dragon, to protect their place in the sun—and in the process to aggrandize as much enemy territory as possible.[18]

Most evangelicals probably do not have a very clear sense of the way in which the evolution of modern society has collided with and upset the precarious balance their values have long enjoyed in American culture. But the results have been serendipitous, for the modernity crisis has placed them in a surprisingly auspicious situation—the position of a young man or woman on the make who has not made it yet. In all sectors of society they have moved into positions of power, but they are not yet fashionable. They have pretty well learned how to fit into the rest of the culture, but in most places—at least most places outside the South—they are still a bit angular. Borrowing John Murray Cuddihy's terms, evangelicals have become civil enough to enjoy most of the trappings of the good life, but they are still uncivil enough to profit—and profit handsomely—from the psychic tension of the struggle.[19]

This advantageously adversarial position includes all or virtually all evangelicals who comprise the Evangelical Right. It probably includes the majority of evangelicals and evangelical sympathizers who are not particularly self-conscious or literate about economic and political matters, but who find themselves increasingly ill at ease in the Zion of postindustrial society. And to tell the truth, it also undoubtedly includes many within the Evangelical Left who consider themselves culturally sophisticated and politically liberal, yet who cannot countenance the loss of Jewish-Christian values in the public discourse and in the "reality defining" institutions of the land.[20]

There is, however, another important reason why evangelicals have survived and even won some major beachheads in their contest with modern society. They have been sustained, I think, by traditions deeply rooted in the American South—not the Old South, but the New South that came into existence in the 1880s and 1890s and that haunts the pages of writers like Flannery O'Connor and Erskine Caldwell. To be sure, I am not suggesting that Carl F. H. Henry begins each day by dipping into the works of Robert Lewis Dabney, nor that Confederate bumper stickers are likely to become hot items in the Wheaton College bookstore. Moreover, it is clear that the cultural diaspora of Southern evangelicalism has been facilitated by social changes such as the development of the interstate highway system in the 1950s and the unprecedented movement of folk into and out of the South during and after World War II. Yet measurable social changes help make less measurable cultural transformations possible. So the point simply is this: since World War II, and especially since the early 1960s, ordinary evangelicals in the North and West—mainstream evangelicals, they might be called—have been increasingly predisposed to accept perceptual patterns and interpretations of reality long established in the Baptist and Methodist empire of the South.[21]

One indication of the growing coalescence of mainstream and Southern evangelical outlooks is the extent to which the former have accepted the public leadership of persons who have been associated with the evangelicalism of the New South. The most obvious example is, of course, Billy Graham, reared in Charlotte and for many years a resident of tiny Montreat, North Carolina, tucked in the Southern highlands. Although Graham's ministry is global, it is, as William Martin and others have shown, still profoundly Southern in style. Other superstars betray similar connections. A short list would include Jim Bakker, based in Charlotte; Pat Robertson in Virginia Beach; Jerry Falwell in Lynchburg, Virginia; James Robison in Fort Worth; Jimmy Swaggart in New Orleans; Oral Roberts in Tulsa; Bob Jones III in Greenville, South Carolina. Rex Humbard, though situated in Akron, Ohio, was reared and started his ministry in Arkansas. Most of the big-name independent faith healers of the last quarter century—A. A. Allen, William Branham, LeRoy Jenkins— have been, like Oral Roberts, rooted in or especially associated with the South. Among evangelical celebrities (or celebrities lionized by evangelicals) Southerners again predominate: Anita Bryant, Johnny Cash, Marabel Morgan, Tom Landry, Bobby Jones, Jesse Helms, Jeremiah Denton, and at one time, Jimmy Carter.[22] Moreover, many of the leaders and celebrities not based in the South are clustered at the other end of the sunbelt. Here one thinks, for example, of Southern California luminaries like Bill Bright, Robert Schuller, Chuck Smith, and Pat Boone.

The prominence of these personalities is only the most obvious manifestation of the cultural diaspora of Southern evangelicalism. Less obvious but more influential is Southern evangelicalism's habitual involvement in "secular" politics—the myth of the spiritual church notwithstanding. From the late nineteenth century to the present, Southern evangelicals have been mired up to their hip boots in every major question of public policy, and their moral scorecard is more complex than most people think. Some fought—and some supported—Jim Crow codes and child labor regulations in the 1890s, alcohol prohibition and textbook censorship in the 1920s, civil rights laws and textile union restrictions in the 1950s, prayer in the schools and the Equal Rights Amendment in the 1970s. The point is, in short, that even in the "Christhaunted" South, in Flannery O'Connor's marvelous phrase, evangelicals, seeking to be the moral custodians of the culture, have always known how to play political hardball when the prayer meeting let out.[23]

There is, moreover, a deeper dimension to all this. Southern evangelicals' propensity to vote their faith has grown from a distinctly premodern, if not antimodern, determination to fuse the public and the private, the legal and the moral.[24] Jimmy Carter's willingness to share his Southern Baptist faith with foreign heads of state appalled the Washington press corps, but it was perfectly natural for a Southern evangelical. This inclination to fuse (or confuse, depending on one's perspective) the public and private realms has led Southern evangelicals over the years to insist that the cultivation of expertness cannot be divorced from the cultivation of character. The ramifications of this conviction are not minor, for it means, on one hand, that the virtuous amateur is fit to judge the scientific merit of a biology textbook, or the economic merit of Keynesian fiscal theories, or the strategic merit of the SALT II treaty. On the other hand, Southern evangelical leaders, working from precisely these assumptions, have often exhibited a capacity for social realism and ethical growth that is difficult to criticize. One thinks, for example, of Billy Graham's longstanding position on race relations, his matured awareness of the dangers of ill-informed political involvements, and his recent courageous moves to alert evangelicals to the staggering moral implications of nuclear and environmental destruction.

Another characteristic of Southern evangelicalism that has become more visible in mainstream evangelicalism in recent years is the Southern white evangelical notion of history. Throughout the nineteenth century, evangelicals everywhere were prone to identify evangelical destiny with America's destiny. "If you converse with these missionaries of Christian civilization," Alexis de Tocqueville observed 150 years ago, "you will be surprised to . . . meet a politician where you expected to find a priest."[25] But there was a difference between Northern and Southern assumptions. In the North the coalescence of evangelical and American interests was tempered by the universalism of millennialism; in the South, white evangelicals took the opposite turn. There the identification of religion and soil was hardened by the humiliation of defeat. It was chastened by the necessity of extorting from Scripture a warrant for the segregation and subordination of half the population. And it was enriched by common memories, as Wilbur J. Cash said long ago, of the region's extraordinary natural beauty—"extravagant colors . . . proliferating foliage . . . the rich odors of hot earth and pinewood and the perfume of the magnolia in bloom." In a land where, in short, "the past is never dead, it's not even past," as one of Faulkner's characters puts it, critically verifiable history has imperceptibly blurred into a mythical history of sacred origins. And in the land of sacred origins, God's unique favor rested upon this soil, upon this band, upon these heroes. For the typical Southern evangelical, the land of cotton became the "last great bulwark of Christianity," "the defender of the ark, its people . . . the Chosen People."[26]

The enduring significance of this religious Cult of the Lost Cause is that it bears an uncanny resemblance to the myth of sacred American origins that is heralded every day in the broadcasts of the Electronic Church and in evangelical bookstores across the land in tracts like Francis Schaeffer's *Christian Manifesto*. Scholars who hope to understand how these fictions emerge and what functions they serve may find the historiography of the Lost Cause instructive. Both myths have been tokens of a partly justifiable siege mentality, which is to say that in both instances the threat has been real: Yankee materialism and secular humanism have been palpable facts of life. Yet in both cases the threat has swelled to outlandish proportions, like night shadows on the walls of a child's bedroom. And the result has been a kind of Manichean dualism that has temporarily protected the familiar—this Christian American land, these Christian American schools—from the dangers of an alien world and a perplexing future.[27]

In summary, then, if we hope to understand the relationship between evangelicals and postmodern society, we need to scuttle the assumption that the contemporary revival is a direct reaction to the real or perceived encroachments of secular humanism. Instead, we must try to see how long-range processes have worked. Toward this end I have suggested that in the United States, especially since World War II, vast structural changes common to most Western societies have collided with and upset the historic balance between the custodial and the plural visions of American life. Not so much in reaction to, but as an integral part of this immense process of social and cultural readjustment, evangelicals have been aroused to fight for their accustomed place in the sun. But history works in unpredictable ways: this process seems to have driven evangelicals into an advantageously adversarial relation with the larger society. At the same time, for good or ill, they have been increasingly disposed to draw upon the tradition of cultural custodianship preserved in the religious subculture of the American South.

This last point is especially important. Now, more than ever, historians of evangelicalism need to understand the ways that this regional subculture has overflowed its sectional boundaries and permeated the mainstream. Long ago the prophet Amos foretold a day when many would "wander from sea to sea, and from the north even to the east," seeking the Lord in vain. "In these latter days," Southern sociologist John Shelton Reed has written, "the wayfaring stranger would be well-advised to forsake the secular North, abjure the mysterious East, and check out the South." Good advice, for the South, like the Second Coming, may be closer than most people think.[28]

Chapter 3

THE 1960s:
THE CRISES OF LIBERAL
CHRISTIANITY AND THE PUBLIC
EMERGENCE OF EVANGELICALISM

LEONARD I. SWEET

ALMOST EVERY DECADE IN THE TWENTIETH CENTURY seems to have been given its own emphatic adjective. One thinks of the Roaring Twenties, the Trying Thirties, the Forlorn Forties, the Fabulous Fifties, the Stormy Sixties, and the Narcissistic Seventies. Futurists like Herman Kahn already have spoken of the Sobering Eighties. While each adjective fails to express the essence of the decade to which it refers, the adjectives do conjure up pictures that image that essence. Through the "storm" of the sixties, for example, we see the swirl of violence—both domestic (the three assassinations and Kent State) and exported (Vietnam)—Haight-Asbury, Woodstock, SDS, participatory democracy, the "Great Society," acid rock and gospel rock, Selma and Watts, black power and flower power, the Free Speech Movement and filthy speech movement, sit-ins and marches, topless theology, unkempt hair, unshaven faces, unbuttoned minds. Deep in our souls we have established a love-hate relationship with this wild decade that drew out the best and worst: we may love its idealism, its youth, its activism, passion, and optimism; but we may also hate its violence, its turgid rhetoric, its self-righteousness, irrationalisms, faddishness, and promiscuous embrace of social change.

A generation of Americans traveled posthaste and often "postchaste" into a decade dominated by "a sense of endings":[1] postmodern, post-Freudian, postindustrial, posthistorical, post-Puritan, post-Christian, post-God—with new endings always arising (post-Vietnam, post-Watergate, etc.).[2] Sixties art led the movement from the ebullient "Age of Aquarius" into the brooding "Age of Narcissus." From the sixties to the seventies, fiction went from engagement to escape; music went from protestation to recreation; drug use veered from LSD mind-expansion to Valium mind-massage; religious belief traveled from a death-of-God theology to a "Burger-King theology" (a "have-it-your-way" Whopper faith); and religious behavior shifted, as Martin E. Marty has pointed out, from buffeting to ballasting.[3]

The 1960s is both the easiest and most difficult of periods to assess critically. Easiest, because what could one say about the sixties that would be wrong? Hardest, because America's religious repertoire was never so full, allowing for a quiverful of different interpretations. A bewildered Diana Trilling has even declared the generation to be a strange new mutation.[4] One of the major reasons historians have so much difficulty making sense of the 1960s is that there were really two "sixties."[5] The first sixties is harder to understand, since its revolutionary passions have faded, and its symbols no longer communicate with their original power. But the first sixties, which lasted roughly from 1960 to 1967, were bursting with belief, fresh hope, and high ambition. A millennial movement of tremendous force gripped many of America's churches as they sought to bring the kingdom of God to earth through such modern instruments as social activism, technology, science, the arts, and the Democratic party. The phrase most characteristic of the spirit of this first sixties was the civil rights slogan "We shall overcome," as a "new optimism" (William Hamilton) expectantly labored for what some called a "greening of America" (Charles Reich) and others a "new Pentecost" (Harvey Cox), a "new millennium" (Gibson Winter), a "new world come of age," wherein could be found a "new morality" (Joseph Fletcher), a "new theology" (radical theology), a "New Frontier" (John F. Kennedy), a "new religion" (Dietrich Bonhoeffer's phrase), a "new humanity" (Thomas Altizer), and new cultures (youth, drug, and counter-). Ironically, the death-of-God movement did not represent one of Christianity's more funereal moods; it constituted one of the decade's most high-spirited youth demonstrations (the average age of its four theologians in 1960 was 34.5) against selfishness, hatred, injustice, and entrenched authority. In the words of the youngest person ever elected to the presidency of the United States, "the torch has been passed to a new generation."[6]

The spirit and mood of the second sixties, which ran roughly from 1967 to 1971, were the polar opposites of the first sixties. Even words like "hysteria," "panic," "chaos," "disarray," "demoralization," and "disintegration" fail to do justice to a Humpty-Dumpty world of broken dreams, worn-out emotions, shattered institutions, fragmented selves, and failed communes. In the second 1960s America came the closest in its history to suffering a national nervous breakdown, as witnessed by the mindless destruction perpetrated by the Weathermen and the madman Charles Manson, who picked his blossoms from among the flower children.

Similarly, many Christians, especially the ones who bought into the "expressive ethic" of impulse, self-realization, and self-actualization,[7] developed spiritual pathologies of alarming dimensions. A worried Peter Berger in 1971 chose the metaphor of an earthquake to describe the religious situation of the day: "The ground on which we are standing has been profoundly shaken, and most of us feel it in our bones."[8] The second 1960s inaugurated what Benton Johnson has called the "second great depression of the mainline churches," a depression "far worse than the one they experienced 50 years ago."[9]

Historians have not been inattentive to either the "crisis of authority" or the "crisis of identity" that pervaded American religion during the 1960s. But the umbilical connection between authority and identity has not been sufficiently elucidated. While some historians bracket the authority issue as most decisive for shaping the course of American Protestantism in the 1960s, others find themselves constantly bumping into identity matters in analyzing the decade.[10] By failing to reconcile these two issues, scholars have missed what some sociologists have begun to call the "complementarities of authority and identity"—the fact that the "comprehension of the one requires the simultaneous invocation of the other."[11] If religious developments in the 1960s are to be fully understood, an historical thematization that links issues of authority and identity must be forthcoming. While this essay can only present a preliminary framework for such an understanding, I hope that it will make a useful beginning.

At the beginning of the 1960s the "mainline" (soon to be old-line) tradition helped to define the "vital center" of American religious life. It was this center that was pulled at from too many directions in the sixties, causing immense pain, frustration, and a questioning of authority. The ways in which old-line churches came to terms with the question of authority in the sixties led to a profound loss of Protestant identity and consequent evacuation of meaning, confusion of purpose, and frustration of mission in American religious life. As Robert E. Fitch warned in the middle of the decade about the "Protestant Sickness," the funeral procession gathering in the churches was not for God. Rather, "the real candidate for interment is a lesser chap by the name of Liberal Protestantism."[12] In the first sixties there was a rebellious questioning of old authorities and an embracing of new ones. For the first time in American religion, the authority of the church was widely discredited. Many Christians abandoned an understanding of the church as an institution that sets standards for society in favor of an institution that meets the needs of society, a change in definition that had shuddering consequences for the formation of religious and personal identity. In the second sixties, when no distinct identity arose out of the new cultural authorities, confusion abounded, ambiguities and uncertainty became positive values, and inner sources were affirmed as the ultimate authorities.

As theological dry rot worked its way through the edifice of old-line religion, people began to go elsewhere for edification, mainly back to old-time religion. Although evangelicals took some bodies from liberals, the reshaping of American Christianity appeared even more severe than it was because liberal abdication allowed attention to be fixed on groups that were there more or less all along. In the floundering around that ensued from the loss of their own self-confidence, liberal media once again discovered the conservatives. Not all who remained members of old-line churches allowed themselves to be caught up in the developments outlined in this essay. While they would not escape the effects of what was happening to their churches, to their altered worship life, and to their leaders, many waited patiently until the bad dream would pass or plodded on by serving the church in the same old-fashioned ways.

By way of contrast to the theological avant-garde of the early 1960s, conservative Protestantism looked like a theological dead duck. Yet by the mid-1970s it had emerged with more vitality and resources than at any time since the Second Great Awakening 150 years before. The rise of evangelicalism in the second sixties must be seen against the backdrop of a dispirited and ailing conventional Protestantism that had little to declare theologically and was seldom able to answer even the simplest questions about the faith, to say nothing of answering them with a distinctive or a strong voice. Into the vacuum created by this liberal "mainline" Protestantism stepped a more conservative Protestantism that would become the "mainline" religion of the 1970s. In short, evangelicalism came to function as a primary carrier of affirmations for an American culture otherwise in disarray.

I

One of the popular bumper stickers at the University of California at Berkeley during the 1960s said "Question All Authority." The questioning of all authority in the first sixties, however, led less to a breakdown of authority than to a redistribution of authority. It was not the absence of authoritarian claims that gave the sixties its chaotic, antinomian appearance[13] so much as the thumbing of the nose at old authorities and—for the churches—the turning from ecclesiastical to cultural authority. We can see this most clearly in the development of a "situation ethics" for moral decision making. While Joseph Fletcher did not like to think of the "new morality" as in any way authoritarian, and indeed spoke of the "polarities of law and love, of authority and experience, and of fixity and freedom,"[14] the new morality appealed as much to authority as did the old. The authoritative referent of "situation ethics" was the cultural situation, which determined the course of action in times of moral crisis. Where absolutes and traditional moral codes had once presided over situations, the new morality reversed categories so completely that Christian ethics collapsed into ethical relativism. Christians could bring little that was distinctive or even relevant to moral decision making, except possibly a "love" that was itself more culturally than biblically defined. By slivering life into a series of autonomous units, situation ethics made it virtually impossible to fashion even a secular philosophy of life, much less a Christian one.

The wildest miscalculation of many churches in the 1960s was their belief in the basic inhospitality of the "modern mind" to traditional religious symbols and doctrines. Why religious leaders and theologians misread the situation so badly, as even the evidence of the times revealed,[15] would take another essay to explore. But old-line religion widely assumed that resisting the forces of secularization was like standing up to a steamroller. Since progress dictated that people become completely secular, this reasoning went, one must minister to them in secular ways. This meant "the loosening of the world from religious and quasi-religious understandings of itself," Harvey Cox wrote as he advocated "wasting little time thinking about 'ultimate' or 'religious questions.'"[16] Thus being secular was not a way of acknowledging defeat but a way of being authentically Christian in the new age. Churches willingly relinquished their creeds, rituals, pieties, and beliefs to accommodate new social attitudes. And many Christians began to downplay the Christian label and made being "truly human" and being a Christian the same thing.

First of all, then, it was primarily for apologetic reasons that there arose the desperate yearning to be "with it," the fear of being "out of touch," and the modish concern for "relevance"—whether social relevance for the church or intellectual relevance for theology. "The modern world will not allow us" was a phrase so excessively used it became almost a kind of religious chant. Whatever seemed alien to the modern mind had to go. As a nervous Bernard Meland put it critically, "Their ways must be our ways. What is not meaningful to them or useable by them must be discarded."[17] Christians felt deeply the tone of disparagement in such comments as Norman Kemp Smith's "belief in God is no longer possible for any really enlightened mind." While most resisted giving up belief in God, the most conspicuous leaders willingly pulled up the anchor of absolutes so that the church might sail alongside "enlightened" minds. The concern of the "new morality" was to provide, as the back cover of *Situation Ethics* (1966) put it, "a meeting place for Christians and existential agnostics." Christians who had taken this path applauded as whole structures of institutional Christianity were secularized, fervently hoping that now disbelievers would see that religion was taking the ideals of the contemporary world seriously.

Whereas an older liberalism had capitulated to the authority of a modern scientific world view, the liberalizing trend that characterized religion in the first sixties capitulated to the authority of a broader and more encompassing phenomenon of cultural secularization. The sixties cliche that "change is the only constant" got thrown around rather thoughtlessly, especially by those whose tradition of intellectual hospitality, in times of cultural drift or revolution, can make them go unthinkingly agog before whatever is new. "New" was the pet word of the first sixties because cultural developments were so exciting and promising. Avant-gardism itself often became the authority for religion. Not wanting to offend the secular mindset or be left behind by the forces of modernity, denominations and individuals opened wide their doors to the winds of change, completely forgetting how recurrent the change of winds can be. For if the cliche is indeed true, then change itself changes, there is no stable ground anywhere, and those who seek relevance face defeat from the start.

A second reason why religious authority in the first 1960s began to defer to cultural relativities and "turn toward the world,"[18] as Harvey Cox put it, was less a compliance in the face of steamrolling modernity (or a fear of being implicated in an antediluvian resistance to change) than an enthusiastic embrace of secularity. In this view, secularization was made to mean all things bright and beautiful: the real world could only be unlocked by the techniques of natural science, and there was nothing beyond what could be apprehended by the modern mind. To the extent that one relied on traditional authority one was not only being antimodern; one was opposing the coming of the new age, an emerging world culture marked by exclusively secular paradigms. Only when Christians became theologically cold-blooded and realized that this world is all there is, that meaning must be found here or nowhere, could they take charge of history and get it in shape. The dethroning of traditional religious authority and the brandishing of Christianity's secular connection were thus seen as incitements to social action.

A third reason for the dismantling of religious authority in favor of cultural authority was a belief that the old theological mold had cracked beyond repair. Certainties to which people had clung were undermined by the forces of relativism and pluralism. A loosening of authority from the traditional centers accompanied the positive, almost festive emphasis on diversity, as the first sixties rewrote the Golden Rule to deal with pluralism: "Do not do unto others as you would have them do unto you. Their tastes may be different." The concept of "tolerance," which once denoted openness and fairness, often deteriorated in the first sixties from neutrality to indifference and finally to an "anything-goes" flaccidity. A word once enterprising in the face of pluralism had now become supine. Pluralism now meant egalitarianism, which could be seen in the revolt against traditional fashion by the flaunting nonconformity of blue jeans, bell-bottoms, army fatigues, and handcrafted skirts—which made everyone look pretty much alike[19]—and by the attacks on "elitism" in all sectors of American life—which was essentially an assault on the traditional concepts of authority, the claims of expertise, and the presence of standards and distinctions.

The first sixties also learned to deal with relativism by putting everything "in its context," a context that revealed the collapse of the American episteme—the "sacred canopy" upon which hung our common visions and aspirations. For the first time in America's history, its people were without a sense of transcendent, certain, demonstrable truths that gave purpose to the nation's history as well as shared meaning and confidence to its citizens. A host of respected intellectuals and scientists lectured Americans on the meaning of relativism, arguing that, in the words of the British archaeologist Jacquetta Hawkes, "nearly all the really important questions, the things we ponder in our profoundest moments, have no answer."[20]

Religious leaders could with equanimity obliterate traditional standards of reference, even to the point of bidding God good-night, because they sensed that radical problems required radical responses. After the superficialities of religion in the 1950s,[21] which had done little more than apply rouge and powder to the face of sagging dogmas and protruding injustices, some people found in "radical theology" a way of getting at the depths of issues and structures. Here finally was a gospel without gloss, a theology that "tells it like it is," a way out of moldy versions of the old, old story. Whereas past theologians had struggled with the "problem of evil," in the 1960s God became the "problem," and not just for necrotheologians or process theologians.[22] The comedian George Carlin captured a popular mood when he joked, "God can't be perfect; everything he makes dies." Radical theologians ostensibly found Jesus less of a "problem" than God, and so when God died, Jesus took on new life as a model for humanity, a "man for others," a "place to be" alongside those in the struggle—in short, a functional christological embodiment of all those virtues heralded by the emerging modern world.[23] To deny God and affirm Jesus was like saying, some critics pointed out, "There is no God, and Jesus is his prophet." But with the exception of Harvey Cox, whose attachment to Jesus seemed downright evangelical, the emphasis on Jesus by secular and radical theologians basically served as a kind of theological chaser, making it all go down easier.

35

A final reason why theologians of conventional Protestantism and many of their bureaucratic fellow travelers largely abandoned appeals to moral absolutes and churchly authority was that they saw the church itself as irrelevant to modern life and an impediment to social change. Throughout the 1960s people lashed out at institutions that had allegedly failed them, and the devaluation of organized religion that was pointedly focused in the house-church movement was a part of this antiestablishment sentiment. The church's noninvolvement in the world during the 1950s meant for many that the church was a disgrace to religion. The debate over "Is the local church obsolete?" swirled around books like Peter Berger's *The Noise of Solemn Assemblies* (1961) and Gibson Winter's *The Suburban Captivity of the Church* (1962), which showed how the local church was out of step with modern society and did little more than baptize all that was wrong with society. Other widely read thinkers like Erich Fromm contended that religion did not need the trappings of theology, authority, and organization.[24] In fact, both Fromm's support of a churchless religion and Dietrich Bonhoeffer's call for a "religionless Christianity" revealed an acute disregard for institutional ties and an intense concentration on subjective relationships.

Religious leadership, both institutional and theological, reflected the tendency to discount the church either as a locus for authority or a focus of concern. Of all the special interest groups that formed in the first 1960s to streamline and improve the structures of major denominations, not one had any special interest in the local church. Norman Pittenger characterized the sixties as a time "when most young people preparing for the Christian ministry appeared to assume that the best way to do this was to engage in action but to abstain from worship."[25] Van Harvey demonstrated how theological education switched its authority during this period from the church to a theological method. And others argued that theology must be done outside of traditional frameworks, thus enforcing the divorce of theology from the church.[26] The mandate of a theologian was not loyalty to the church but loyalty to the experience of love in the totality of human experience. Theologians absorbed in speculative theology became more and more abstruse in their vocabulary and abstract in their concerns. Indeed, to many Christians it appeared as if these theologians, who would make no concession to the ordinary believer, had contracted the gift of tongues. Similarly, the theological and biblical scholarship that adopted the religious studies model of inquiry operated, by very definition, outside of a faith commitment. Just because one took the Bible apart did not mean one had to put it back together.

Not surprisingly, the Bible in many conventional Protestant churches became a closed book. Few theologians gave signs of deep feelings about the tradition to which they belonged, and according to

James D. Smart's study, the blame for *The Strange Silence of the Bible in the Church* (1970) rested on scholars and pastors. William Hamilton's controversial essay "Thursday's Child" characterized the theologian in America as someone without faith, someone who did not go to church, read the Bible, or even believe in God.[27] Jeffrey Hadden's analysis of this growing rift between clergy and laity carried with it the ominous title *The Gathering Storm in the Churches* (1969).

II

In the second 1960s the crusading spirit of the first sixties vanished. The gruesome dramas of the decade repeatedly knocked the spectacles of optimism off our eyes, and much of a generation lost faith in everything human and divine. Instead of "the golden sixties," as Winthrop S. Hudson put it, "the 1960s turned out to be a decade when almost everything went wrong."[28] In his widely used textbook, William E. Leuchtenburg fittingly titles his section on the sixties "The Travail of Liberalism," and Henry F. May argues that the failure of liberalism was less the "greening of America" than the "souring of Progressivism."[29]

The side effects of success as well as failure contributed to this tremendous upheaval of spirit. The alienated of the second sixties were not just the poor and the oppressed but the sons and daughters of the affluent,[30] the children who had been led to believe that a new world would come from these new sources of authority. A new world did begin to come, but it was a vacant universe, a world where a living faith seemed remote and inaccessible and where people were left feeling abandoned and empty. The success more than the failure of authority structures created the profound loss of confidence in the American experience, in American institutions and leaders, and in "anyone over thirty." "Theology of hope" was a natural successor to "God is dead" not only because it posited a God unavailable in the present (God is becoming, awaiting us in the future), but also because it provided a way for discouraged Christians in the second sixties to wash their hands of history and take up the cause of the future or flee to the regions of the metaphysical and the occult.

Albert Einstein's comment that the only fundamental certainty in the universe is entropy summarized the feelings of those betrayed by excessive expectations. An era of diminished dreams and bare expectations set the tone, as people began to be entranced with hobbits, elves, and the beauty of smallness. The second sixties wanted nothing to do with things big, whether giants, heroes, or visions. And all too often the second sixties, having learned from the first sixties to devalue organized religion, wanted nothing to do with the church. When people stopped looking to the church for answers, the hemorrhaging of the church's membership rolls began.

The second sixties was a time of search for new bases of authority other than culture, although in many cases the search for authority was confused with a mere search for authorization. One promising prospect was the self. The shifting away from external sources of authority toward internal, subjectivist insights spelled a crumbling of the superego and a reinvigoration of the ego ideal.[31] Thus in the second 1960s there was a sharp veering off in an inward direction and an upsurge of narcissism. Erich Fromm's *The Art of Loving* (1956) started the attack on the notion that self-love was bad.[32] Paul Tillich helped Christians to feel more comfortable about "loving themselves" by replacing "self-love" with words like "self-affirmation" and "self-acceptance." But it remained for Harvey Cox in his *On Not Leaving it to the Snake* (1967) to remove pride as the primal sin and to replace it with *acedia*—self-assertion and the failure to be "responsible."[33] With self as the ultimate authority, one did not treat others unkindly because that was treating oneself unkindly.

Expressions of the self as a new source of authority could be seen in the simpering self-exhibition of Christian authors and celebrities, the various movements for "self-help," "self-discovery," and "self-realization," the "show-and-tell" style of evangelism, and the "let it all hang out" countercultural styles where people were encouraged to "do your own thing." People began to journey with anyone who promised them either some new insight about the self or some escape from the burden of building a self, and Americans pursued a variety of religious options from A(rica) to Z(en). In different ways both the Jesus movement and later the charismatic movement were variants of that subjectivist search for authority. Both movements were obsessed with feeling and exhibited the strong desire to romp spiritually through new forms of consciousness and new dimensions of experience,[34] although within each there were wide fluctuations in authoritarian leadership patterns going all the way from an almost anarchical "participatory democracy" to "shepherd submission." With the self as the author of authority, one's feelings became the ultimate criterion for everything. Indeed, even the church became a place where people went to feel good about themselves.

Others sought a new basis for authority in human relations. Psychology became the ruling discipline in all areas of life, with one of the more exciting intellectual events of the 1960s being Noam Chomsky's declaration that grammar was a branch of psychology. In the world of religion, "therapeutic Christianity"[35] and "pastoral psychology" sought to help people who had been released from the compulsions of tradition to regain order, stability, and purpose in their lives through various kinds of small groups where people "hugged" and "shared." The grounding of authority in human relations was especially evidenced in the new theories of management or styles of organization that surfaced in the 1960s and began to be adopted by the churches in the second sixties. Guy E. Swanson has convincingly demonstrated that participation management and "management by objectives" are attempts to circumvent the constraints of traditional ecclesiastical authority by rooting authority in the objectives to which people commit themselves by participating in a process of goal selection and definition.[36] Many found in "goals" and "objectives" a way of recovering the authority of religion without having to accept the arbitrariness of that authority. The attempt to redirect ecclesiastical authority from the creeds, traditions, and offices of the church to human relations through a "theology of church administration" governed all the structural retooling that conventional Protestantism underwent in the beginning of the second sixties. The "church management" movement constituted the most significant call to order issued by conventional Protestantism after the institutional bedlam and vandalism of the faith caused by culturalist Christianity.

The attempts to establish a new foundation for authority in the self and human relations only increased the identity problems experienced by individual Christians and the church at large. The worst kind of slavery has self as master, and people had difficulty trying to maintain an identity when nothing protected them from the rampagings within. Thrusts against identity were also exacerbated by the new management styles and their processes. People were rallied around goals to which they had committed themselves, but after they had reached a consensus, people were reminded that the objectives they had set today could be overturned tomorrow with a different set of people. Guy Swanson has described the ways in which this perception of the zigs and zags of goal setting gradually incubates in the psyche until it assaults one's personal identity:

> People working in this way cannot help but realize that their skills, and even their personalities, could become irrelevant—or at least in need of change. Since no one is infinitely changeable or creative . . . he will find himself objectively condemned by the very standards and authorities that he espouses. He will constantly encounter and evaluate himself, be asked repeatedly to express his thoughts and feelings and to make choices on his own behalf and on behalf of the organization, be expected constantly to uphold whatever will promote the collective task, but be constantly aware that he is inadequate or irrelevant or that, with the next turn of change, he may become so. In sum, what modern organizations and societies in principle eschew is a steady defini-

tion of the relevance—the meaning—of any of their participants: of their skills, their personalities, and, certainly, of their life careers.[37]

Issues of identity surfaced repeatedly throughout the entire decade of the 1960s in a variety of ways. On one level, groups based on sex, ethnicity, and age began discovering and asserting themselves, and a whole slew of new consciousnesses were raised. But on a deeper level the second sixties witnessed a phenomenon unique in history—the belief in a "right to identity." Ralph Turner has elucidated this new development: "The urgent demand that the institutions of our society be reformed, not primarily to grant man freedom of speech and thought, and not primarily to ensure his essential comforts, but to guarantee him a sense of personal worth is the new and recurrent theme in contemporary society."[38]

Matters of identity became so important because the new bases for authority were destructive of identity. Erik H. Erickson has insisted that there cannot be any identity without an ideology (theology) to which one gives oneself fully and completely, being captivated by it (faith commitment). When a family, church, or nation loses its sense of identity, when its traditional ideology becomes diffused and dispersed rather than reinterpreted, the fabric that binds it together is weakened and destroyed. And when this happens, the individual is also in trouble: one's "ego identity" may collapse or one may strike out aimlessly and heedlessly in frustration.[39] Lacking natural boundaries and a frame of reference within which individuals find their niche—a conception of self that corresponds roughly to the particular community's perception of self—a person becomes the victim of a diffused self-image and suffers the sense of confusion that leads to personality dissolution and disintegration. In sum, problems of authority collided with problems of identity in the second sixies, and cult communes and psychiatrists' couches were strewn with the casualties of such collisions.

Christians in such an ethos often discovered that they did not love themselves—nor did they love their country, nor did they love their church. Whereas the Bible presupposes that you love yourself—that is the promise and peril of the human condition—in the 1960s self-acceptance in relationship to a group identity or ideology had dwindled to a point where a sense of self-love was a difficult part of one's personal identity. The act of asserting self-love, a new phenomenon characteristic of the sixties, testifies to the radical nature of the attack against individual identity caused by the lack of an inner solidarity with a group's ideals and authority.

In an expansion of Erickson, Vytautas Kavolis contends that the establishment of identity depends on three things: coherence, commitment, and continuity. The acceptance of cultural authority meant that in one way or another the church sniffed at all three. The result was that no one knew any more what it meant to be a Christian. When a member of a conventional church said "I am a Christian," one did not know very much. From the perspective of 1972, two observers of American religion wrote about "the profound crisis in Christian self-identity. It is not at all clear what it means to be a Christian."[40]

One reason was that many churches no longer provided coherence for their people. People need to feel put together, individually and collectively. In the first 1960s, religion happily deferred to scientific rationalism to do this for people. But it seemed meaningless. While at first many may have found a world without religion gripping, the grip soon began to choke meaning and sense from existence. It was not enough to admonish people to find "meaning in meaninglessness." By allowing the arbiters of cultural fashion to do its thinking, the conventional church's mind and spirit began to grow stale and dull. The world of modern secular experience had become liberal Protestantism's only world at the same time there was a slow turning of the *Zeitgeist* at its back. A resurgence of pantheism, metaphysics, and a "turning Eastward" testified, for example, to a growing revolt against scientific rationalism.[41] By renouncing a religious understanding of the world and through the emptying of religious symbols, culturalist Christianity had written itself into a corner, unable to shape or contribute to public debate or even define the issues at stake in the moral and political questions of the day. Forced to follow the leads and definitions of others, even when local churches got directly involved in social meliorism, many did so by becoming landlord to various groups and agencies already involved in social outreach.

As trust in culture became less easy to maintain in the face of growing emptiness and estrangement, conventional religion found itself unable to make sense of people's lives. A theology based on topicality, like yesterday's news, quickly fades. With a vocabulary and a grammar that was predominantly secular, a large segment of American Protestantism found itself speaking a foreign language, one that was increasingly alien and alienating to the ordinary believer. To the hurting eyes of a weary world, the church had lost sight of the one thing it needed most—the spiritual dimension. People did not turn to the church for coherence, because the church now seemed more part of the problem than the solution. There was the feeling that somehow the church had been tainted. When a church could take seriously the celebration of the death of God, it was obviously not on the side of the angels.[42]

The commitment component to identity formation was also difficult to engender because old-line Protestantism by and large showed itself empty of affirmations to which one could be committed. To be sure, relativism made the "truth question," as it came to be called in theological circles, a difficult one—and not just for liberals. Yet the problem of truth was more acute for liberals because of their romanticist attitude toward culture. In fact, many gave up the concept of "truth" entirely for the concept of "values." Those who did not, inspired by Heidegger's notion that questioning is the piety of thinking, often seemed more dogmatic about doubt than about faith. E. M. Forster pointed the way in 1941 to the reduction of liberal affirmations to negatives when he prophesied: "What the world will most need is the negative virtues; not being huffy, touchy, irritable, revengeful. I have lost all faith in positive militant ideals; they can so seldom be carried out without thousands of human beings getting maimed or imprisoned."[43] Conventional Protestantism abandoned evangelism less because of a tight-lipped faith than because its faith was devoid of declarations. In the words of one prominent church leader, the best strategy for evangelism was honesty and kindness: "I'm as lost as you are. But I promise not to leave you alone in your search."

Without anything much to say, liberal Protestantism made listening into a religious value. Sunday School curricula, for example, taught teachers how to listen and children how to talk. And all too often listening was not toward the end of knowing how best to respond, but it was the response itself. The only way religion can rest its claim to legitimacy and thus exert authority is on the basis of its unique relationship to or embodiment of a concept of truth. When a church's authority was no longer derived from its being a witness to the truth, people had little other than political values to which to make a commitment. There was little reason for evangelism.

The most serious problem, however, was less the churches' lack of interest in evangelism than their lack of interest in their own traditions. Continuity is at the very heart of identity. What a religious tradition does with its past has everything to do with the establishment of a distinctive identity. The preservation and transmission of the tradition is an ineluctable obligation of the church. But culturalist Christianity discarded the cultivation of religious belief and the preservation of the heritage for social engagements in changing national and international society. The avowed aims of Christian education in the 1960s became less transmissive than transformative: the goal was not to prepare a new generation for the church but to promote social and personal values among the young and to translate religious symbols into ethical and political imperatives among the adults. There was little sense of the necessity of putting oneself under a tradition because what was important was the intrinsic worth of values themselves, not their Christian pedigree. Thus Protestantism raised a generation of kids who were robbed of their history and without inheritance.[44] Church members fared little better, as few efforts were put forth to make them feel at home in their tradition in any more than a rhetorical way. Without a claimed tradition, theology was reduced to an endless succession of "nows"—which helps to explain why modern liberal theology became so porous, with every new fad sinking in.

A tradition cannot long survive without a living memory. By failing to generate among church members a sense of living out of their past, much of Protestantism cut the cords of community in the present and endangered its survival. In an article on the state of Protestantism entitled "From Somewhere Along the Road," Barbara Hall and Richard Shaull observed in 1972 that "koinonia has all but disappeared. Again, we are not speaking about the normal lack of love in congregations, but about the apparent inability to create and sustain the Christian community where we once expected it."[45] "Koinonia" and "community" became trendy items in the 1970s, even to the point that local churches complained of "koinonitis." But the labor of liberalism to give birth to "community" failed in that era because of no tradition of meaning to build around. Just as one learns a language by living in community, so one learns the language of faith—what it means to live and think the Christian story—by living in Christian community. One of the main reasons for the widely lamented illiteracy about the language of faith in the churches, and the lack of consensus among the faithful about doctrinal matters, was this decline in Christian community due to the demise of the past.

III

Against the background of hopeful secularization that characterized the first sixties and the disillusioned identity crisis of the second, evangelicalism emerged as the dominant religious force in the American 1970s.

Evangelicalism's affirmative disposition and sense of identity provided the primary reason for the ascendancy of evangelicalism in the 1970s. Billy Graham closed one of his early books with lines that capture the evangelical spirit: "I know where I've come from, I know why I'm here, and I know where I'm going."[46] When many churches found the going hard, those who still saw the face of God had a tremendous appeal. But even more than this "any port in a storm" reason was the fact that evangelicalism's life of the mind was rigorous in its appeal to reason and its denunciations of irrationalism. Of course, this is contrary to evangelicalism's popular stereotype as a faith which distrusts the intellect and prospers in ignorance. But whereas culturalist Christianity allowed modernity to do its thinking for it, evangelicals had engaged modernity in intellectual combat and even created a Protestant scholasticism that built elaborate historical props and logical supports for faith. Evangelical scholasticism with its sense of absolute truths, moral standards, and evangelistic passion proved attractive to a culture adrift in the shallows of uncertainty, relativity, and boredom. Those within the conventional churches who deemed uncertainty unbecoming to a Christian founded raspy, recoil organizations to prod the denominations into a more evangelical direction.

Two other reasons why religious liberalism lost its power at the expense of evangelism were the consequences of liberal successes rather than its failures.[47] In fact, these successes opened the way for important evangelical preoccupations of the 1970s. Evangelicalism adopted much of the liberal program but integrated it into a different system of authority. Just as Dennis Voskuil has recently argued that the "neo-orthodoxy" of the 1930s and 1940s might be better called "neo-liberalism," so one could make a strong case for seeing certain segments of the "neo-evangelicals" as really "neo-liberals." First, liberal theologians won the battle against evangelicals on the use of higher criticism in the interpretation of Scripture, although liberalism had become so insular it did not realize it. The difference was that, whereas liberal biblical scholarship side-stepped questions of authority, evangelicals faced the issues of biblical authority— although evangelicals were as guilty as liberals of not addressing the issue of *church* authority. Partly because of the liberal default, evangelicals became increasingly preoccupied with problems of authority, until today evangelicalism possesses an authoritive theology to its credit, but an authority-identity crisis to its discomfort.

Liberalism also triumphed in its assertion that a social witness stood at the center and not the periphery of the faith (as the evangelical Chicago Declaration of 1973 made clear). The 1960s in a liberal mode—primarily the first sixties—contributed much that is in keeping with what the Christian faith demands in terms of coherence, commitment, and continuity: specifically, care for the earth, peace, civil rights, concern for the poor, renewal of the cities, and generally the notion that the gospel calls the church to a perpetual criticism of the state and society. Unlike evangelicals, for example, conventional church leaders in the 1960s showed great courage in following racial policies that they knew would cost them dearly in church membership and support. While liberals themselves did not follow through on these matters, since they became privatized in the second sixties and seventies, the liberals' contribution in the first sixties did get picked up by some evangelicals. In the second sixties and the seventies evangelicals discovered that religion and politics do mix, and they restored a social dimension to the faith that had been missing in conservative Christianity for many years.

By the 1970s, however, more and more evangelicals could be found trying to engage in the same kind of "me too" that had become so disastrous for liberalism in the 1960s. It seemed as if the evangelicals were as busy following the course of the liberals as offering an alternative to it. Sensuality, for example, became rampant, with Sam Keen and Marabel Morgan cut from the same cloth. Evangelicals followed the liberals in forms of cultural accommodationism, which found expression in a growing "subjectivization" that James Davison Hunter has located within a "new Evangelical theodicy." Like the liberals of the sixties, many of the evangelicals of the seventies became preoccupied with the self, selling self-adjustment, self-fulfillment, "psychological balance," "emotional maturity," Christian hedonism, and success. As Hunter demonstrates, much of evangelical theology has been culturally edited to remove views that are not positive and upbeat. The implicit theme of civility is "No offense, I am an Evangelical."[48] The liberal accommodation to culture in matters of doctrine and ethics was replicated among many evangelicals in matters of politics and economics.

Evangelicals have also followed the liberals in defining the church according to social science categories, issuing in a managerial style that Richard G. Hutcheson, Jr. finds especially pronounced in the church growth movement.[49] After virulently criticizing liberals over the years for their Bible translations, especially the RSV, evangelicals did an about-face in the late 1960s and became very busy turning out biblical paraphrases and amplified versions, each one a rewriting of Scripture (the one basis on which evangelicals had stood up to modernity) in the writers' own image.

But the most dangerous similarity that developed between evangelicals and liberals occurred in the realm of popular religion, where both could be found answering the question that stands at the heart of evangelism—"Why should I become a Christian?"—in the same way. The evangelistic techniques of many conservatives answered with stories of healed bodies and minds, ships coming in, prospering businesses, saved marriages—in short, a life where the shadows flee away. Liberals were more prone to tell about greater purpose and meaning to existence, enhanced appreciation of creation, the growing of an authentic, integrated, whole soul—in short, a life where the sun shines brighter. But both liberals and conservatives were answering the question in the same way: both were offering inducements to the Christian faith that were pragmatic, with differences primarily psychological and aesthetic. Neither were prone to provide the answer to the question that substantively engages issues of authority and identity, "Why should I become a Christian?" Because it is true.

Chapter 4

EVANGELICAL PUBLISHING
AND BROADCASTING

RICHARD N. OSTLING

HISTORIANS OF FUNDAMENTALISM AND EVANGELICALISM have chronicled how the conventionally orthodox and revivalist Protestants who once predominated in American religion began losing control of the major denominations as well as the broader culture. This process was most dramatic in the 1920s. A group made up of fundamentalists and what we now call evangelicals went into exile within both church and culture. But instead of gradually withering away, as so many expected, these groups began creating a complex of new parallel institutions through which they could express their religious convictions, seek recruits, and carry out their common work.

The evangelical and fundamentalist empire as it exists today includes large numbers of local congregations and individuals in the "old-line" or "mainline" Protestant denominations, and also many conservative denominations, some of them quite large and notable for rapid growth at a time of "old-line" decline. However, the movement is most distinctive not in terms of congregations or denominations but of its many "parachurch" organizations which serve the Christian populace but remain outside denominational control. This independence produces creativity, flexibility, anarchy, divisiveness, and sometimes irresponsibility. A substantial portion of parachurch agencies' income, personnel, and prayer support comes from within the old-line denominations. Meanwhile, the national agencies, schools, and mass media programs sponsored by the old-line denominations remain substantially in the hands of nonevangelicals. This old-line leadership party is often called "liberal," although especially in the conservative 1980s it resists that label.

Whatever the labels, we have a two-party system of sorts, or perhaps more accurately, a two-movement system. If fundamentalism is a separate movement from evangelicalism, and in many ways it is, then America has a three-party Protestant system. The stakes in this spiritual contest are rather high. The *Yearbook of American and Canadian Churches* lists fewer than seventy million conventional Protestants on the church rolls in the U.S. But in its 29,000 interviews conducted through 1982, the Gallup organization found that 59% of adult Americans consider themselves Protestant, which extrapolates to a populace of ninety-eight million. Thus Protestant culture or vague Protestant impact is apparently far broader than formal Protestant membership. (The existence of many churches which do not baptize infants also explains part of the statistical gap.) Evangelicalism and fundamentalism have an impact on this large segment of nonchurchly, cultural Protestants.

The evangelical Protestants, to summarize, have put together a quite remarkable network of denominational and parachurch agencies to promote their beliefs and programs. The communications media to which we now turn have been at the core of this successful effort. In fact, they are the very matrix of survival for evangelicals who exist within semievangelical or nonevangelical denominations. We will look at various of these media in turn.

The independent evangelical book publishers have carved out a tremendous market, even though their competitors in the (nonexpanding and more liberal) denominational book houses often enjoy advantages of tax exemption. Obviously, the conservative publishers have shown a knack for appealing to the mass market, which is evident in both individual titles and overall retail sales. The Christian Booksellers Association, which does not encompass all of this market, estimates that its 3,200 member stores make gross sales worth $179 million per year. The CBA, formed in 1950, is strictly a trade association for anyone selling Christian literature. It has a minimal code of ethics and no doctrinal standard at all for membership. Nonetheless, it has remained thoroughly evangelical in spirit. The CBA meetings, periodicals, and programs have become a far more vital factor in the publishing industry than anything the old-line denominational houses have been able to sponsor. We have even reached the point that one house, Wm. B. Eerdmans, publishes not only some of the bread-and-butter scholarship from the conservatives but some of the more important works of "liberals." A curious feature of the immense evangelical publishing phenomenon is that it is overlooked in the broader culture, in part because religious bookstores are excluded from the best-seller surveys in the *New York Times* and *Time*.

In Sunday School curricula as well, the independent conservative publishers have made major inroads, even within the old-line denominations that promote their own officially sanctioned texts. If this were a truly free market, with pastors and congregations under no pressure to use the denominational products, the inroads would doubtless be greater. Again, tax advantages for the denominational houses make the comparison of their performance with that of the independents all the more noteworthy. Some of the conservative materials are of high quality and show increased sensitivity in such matters as race relations.

The same pattern appears in church journalism: considerable growth among the conservatives and independents and a marked stagnation or decline in official old-line circles. Despite their national fundraising capacity, the old-liners have had difficulty producing a vital voice for their views. This is not to say that many particular articles in their periodicals have not been highly effective. But members of the Presbyterian Church, for example, often look to well-distributed, polemical, conservative publications to learn certain information about Presbyterian affairs. In the huge United Methodist Church, the great journalistic success is the *United Methodist Reporter* chain, which is independent of national agency control. While not evangelical, this group of newspapers is more friendly toward the old-time evangelical religion than the official media are.

The Evangelical Press Association, founded in 1949, has grown to include 275 member periodicals with a claimed total circulation of more than twenty-two million, roughly the same as the combined weekly audience of the much-discussed television preachers. In contrast with the mainline journalistic doldrums, the EPA announced eighteen new members in December 1982, some of them newly established. One of the latter, Jerry Falwell's *Fundamentalist Journal,* is of interest in terms of bridging the two conservative movements. Members of the EPA must sign a rather generalized code of ethics and a rather precise statement of doctrine.

Having twice served as a judge for EPA contests, I can report that many of these periodicals are dreary—but by no means all of them. While old-line denominations offer one predictable brand of politics, the EPA and the evangelical network provide vigorous social views ranging from the right-wing to conservative to moderate to left-wing (e.g., Falwell's publications, *Christianity Today, Eternity, Reformed Journal, Other Side, Sojourners*—and *Wittenburg Door* for some comic relief). *Christianity Today,* which began self-consciously as a competitor to the liberal *Christian Century,* rather quickly left it far behind in paid circulation. Among the subsidized publications, *Moral Majority Report* boasted a bigger circulation than any of the old-line denominational magazines right from the start.

Despite all the attention friends and foes of the fundamentalist and evangelical movements have given to television, daily and weekly radio shows are probably still the backbone of evangelical broadcasting, complemented by largely or wholly religious radio stations. Radio is still a powerful medium, most obviously in the Third World but also in the United States. It is also more open to strict preaching and teaching than its newer competitor, television.

Significantly, the evangelicals' fear of losing access to purchased time on radio was a major factor leading to the formation of the National Association of Evangelicals, and subsequently to the National Religious Broadcasters as its official radio arm. The NRB is tied to the NAE's conservative doctrinal statement but maintains its own loose code of ethics. In more recent times the broadcasters' group has appeared to outshine its parent, and it has also attracted support from conservatives who remain outside the NAE as such.

In 1966 the NRB listed 104 member organizations; today it has 1,000 stations or producers. Most of the 922 radio stations, 65 TV stations, 535 radio producers, and 280 TV-film producers in the NRB directories are NRB members and staunchly evangelical. The claim of Executive Director Ben Armstrong that religious broadcasting draws a cumulative weekly audience of 130 million may well be inflated, but critics sometimes miss that he relies heavily on radio audiences rather than TV in that claim. In the endless wars over TV ratings, Arbitron data have been cited to prove both a rise and a decline in TV preachers' audiences since 1978. The NRB cites a 1980 Gallup survey to the effect that half of U.S. adults tune in to religious broadcasts at least occasionally.

It is the TV component of evangelical communications that provokes much of the discussion—and hostility. Consequently, TV receives inordinate attention in this survey as well. (But it should not be forgotten that the Billy Graham organization, not the mainline churches, has figured out a way to get quality, wholesome inspirational films onto the screens of commercial movie theaters.) A lot of the criticism of evangelical TV smacks of transmitter envy, or in terms of current technology, let us call it transponder envy. The more liberal Protestants are ever ready to criticize the TV preachers, and often enough they have good reason to criticize. But they appear far less able to acknowledge the important experiments and achievements performed by conservatives on behalf of Christianity in a secularizing and media-prone culture. Nor have they shown any ability to appropriate the strategies and enthusiasms of the evangelicals and apply them to the religious messages and motifs they might prefer. Some of the envy stems from a very understandable fear that religious TV undercuts the local church. The NRB, the National Council of Churches, and the U.S. Catholic Conference have cooperated in a study of this important matter by the Annenberg School of the University of Pennsylvania and the Gallup Poll.*

Following the pattern originated by evangelical radio, evangelical TV operates almost wholly on a system of buying commercial air time. This tactic was necessary because the free time was given largely to the more liberal Protestants and purchasing time was the only way the evangelicals could get their piece of the airwaves. The independents such as Charles Fuller, whose struggle for outlets influenced the birth of NAE and NRB, lacked the established character of the denominations and church councils, so the commercial networks' hesitations were understandable. However, when the profit interest all but submerged the lingering commitment to the "public interest" in commercial TV, the evangelicals were ideally equipped to seize the initiative.

The results have been well documented by the Rev. William Fore, Assistant General Secretary for communication with the National Council of Churches and an articulate leader of the old-line Protestant establishment. The three commercial TV networks produce shows in cooperation with the National Council and other groups, but it is up to local stations whether or not to broadcast them. By Fore's figures, the ABC show "Directions" reached a peak of 114 stations in 1975 and has since declined to 67 stations. More importantly, the audience estimate is only one-fourth what it was in the mid-1970s. The CBS series "For Our Times," formerly "Look Up and Live," declined since 1974 from 94 stations to 33. On the NBC network, the eighteen hour-long religion specials per year were carried on 144 stations in 1973, but only 52 in 1982, and the audience has declined by more than half. Note that this decline has occurred quite rapidly, and only within recent years.

Fore prefers to see his cup as being half or one-third full rather than half or two-thirds empty. He points out that those three "mainline" religion series together have an average audience of at least three million a week, considerably more than the 2,275,000 average audience in Nielsen rankings for the apparent top-rated independent preacher, Oral Roberts. Fore also notes—could it be happily?—that Roberts (a United Methodist) is suffering a ratings slide. However, those three mainline series enjoy only about *one-fourth* the cumulative audience of the top eight independent evangelists. Also, these data overlook the prime-time occasional specials by Roberts and others, and the all-important cable TV audiences.

In a report to the board of the NCC Communications Commission

---

*This major study was released a year after this article was prepared, in April 1984.

in September 1982, Fore accurately characterized the evangelical complaint about mainline TV religion: "Since our programs are dependent on the networks for production facilities and free public service time, our message has been compromised and lacks distinctive gospel content." Fore grants that there is an element of truth in that analysis, but he considers the program philosophy to be a matter of principle:

> We have never believed that through television we could truly evangelize or communicate the core of the gospel. Certainly we could never want to proselytize or engage in sectarian attacks. All that we could expect on network television was to help prepare people for the gospel, by showing the church at work, by offering models of hope, by helping the audience become aware of and sensitive to pressing national and international moral and ethical issues, and finally by suggesting that individuals might be able to find answers and a fuller life in and through the local church.

That is an excellent summary of what mainline religious TV is and of what evangelical TV is not. In the NCC promotional newspaper Fore states that all the program series running on the three networks deal with the National Council of Churches' "priorities, which currently include peace and nuclear disarmament, economic justice, human rights and the stewardship of natural resources." This constitutes a TV triumph for the social gospel. Note that the following are not listed as program priorities: the recruiting and training of new disciples of Jesus Christ, Bible instruction, worship, prayer, spirituality, church tradition and history, doctrine and theology. However, many of these venerable evangelical interests get short shrift on evangelical TV as well. In this context it is amusing to recall that the most frequently heard criticism of the TV evangelists is that they are "too political"! The liberal Protestants are vocally upset when the conservatives begin to "meddle" in politics over the airwaves, which they have been doing for many years. And the conservative Protestants, who used to preach that the church had no business "meddling," have suddenly fallen silent as their cobelievers meddle via TV and other means.

The other most common mainline complaint about TV evangelism concerns the constant pleas for money. TV has a voracious appetite for funds, and it takes huge amounts to produce shows and buy time to put them on the air. In an interview, Fore told me that the mainliners are unwilling to go beyond free over-the-air time, and they are slow to jump into cable and satellite distribution because "we do not seek money from the audience. In fact, the criterion for really faithful religious programming is whether you ask for money or not." In time, Fore's principle could mean that there should be no religious programming at all on American television. Certainly, conventional denominational budgets have shown no ability to provide the kind of financing that is required.

While the mainliners maintain their commercial purity, the independents are intent on expansion, not retrenchment. The outstanding example is Pat Robertson's Christian Broadcasting Network and ancillary organizations. Robertson's impact is especially strong in cable TV, which has often been neglected in articles on TV religion. Robertson was shrewd enough to get CBN on cable satellite as early as 1977 and now, according to the *New York Times* survey, is in solid third place in access to subscribers to standard non-fee cable systems, behind Ted Turner's "super station" WTBS and the ESPN sports network. CBN is now fed to 3,200 local cable systems with a claimed access to twenty million homes, and it offers programming twenty-four hours a day. The majority of CBN shows are wholesome secular entertainment, while about 40 percent are religious. CBN owns four over-the-air stations on a profit basis, and it produces a number of its own shows, including gospel music specials, news capsules, and the soap opera "Another Life." Robertson's own talk show, the "700 Club," runs both on cable and on purchased time on 150 over-the-air stations.

Everyone who treats TV religion is fascinated with money, and here Robertson's performance is impressive too. Based on previous patterns, he expected to receive contributions of $110 million or more in 1983. Some $40 million of that was pledged in his January fund-raising telethon, double the amount pledged in January 1982. That $110 million is vastly larger than the entire national program budget of even the largest denominations. For evangelicalism as a movement, this expenditure of hundreds of millions of dollars on American television programs raises important questions about both stewardship and strategy, given the churches' great needs in education, social welfare, and other ministries. Within that big problem are the little ones, the nagging news stories about free-lance preachers in trouble with federal government monitors, or refusing to come clean about their finances, or living the high life on their proceeds. Robertson has kept himself free of such encumbrances.

In addition, Robertson is pioneering a new method for personalizing TV. He operates eighty phone counseling centers around the United States while the "700 Club" is on the air. These centers logged two million calls in 1982, 400,000 alone during a two-week series on family problems, according to the CBN staff. Besides spiritual counseling with a Pentecostal flavor, the TV volunteers also participate in "Operation Blessing." Persons who phone in with material needs are matched up with church members willing to help. It is fascinating that his attempt to move beyond the alleged narcissism of TV evangelism into social outreach has been subject to fearful criticism: Robertson has been charged with using this program as a means to build up his political hold on the American public. Instead of transponder envy, we now have blessing envy. Another tack might be to be thankful that 8,800 conservative congregations are willing to help people, or else to outdo Robertson in doing good. To attack this scheme is to yearn for a simpler form of small-town neighborly assistance that, alas, is passing away in our urban and electronic culture.

In other words, Robertson, for one, has taken a hard look at modern American culture and media, and has tried to figure out how his version of Christianity can make its way there. Those who dislike Robertson's theology, his high-pressure fund-raising telethons, his telegenically smiling manner, or the sometimes relentless slant of his political and economic comments, should stop carping and start getting to work on their own projects.

As it happens, the two largest U.S. Protestant denominations have done just that, deciding not to surrender the tube to the parachurch agencies. Once again, there is an illustrative contrast between the United Methodist Church effort, from what is without doubt a liberal denomination, and that of the Southern Baptist Convention, which is resolutely evangelical. (The SBC remains aloof from the interdenominational evangelical movement in many ways, though it should be noted that its radio-TV commission cooperates in the NRB.)

In 1978 the United Methodist communications agency began talking about a church breakthrough on TV. The Methodists would own and operate a commercial station where they could produce quality religion shows, train staff, and obtain a reliable source of income for funding future TV penetration. The 1980 General Conference of the denomination approved a $25 million fund-raising effort, over and above normal quota budgets. But, as Jean Coffey Lyles observed in *Christian Century,* nobody ever paused to consider what sort of content or theology Methodism would convey, given its pluralism in doctrine.

The kickoff for the fund drive was a special Sunday afternoon show from the Grand Ol' Opry in Nashville, beamed to 144 satellite receivers, mostly on the Holiday Inn hookup. But many Methodists were upset that the festivities relied on the inevitable showbiz style the mainliners have criticized in the evangelical TV productions. One star was Carol Lawrence, a regular guest on the "700 Club." The show cost $175,000 to produce, and just before it was broadcast the denominational planners confused things by dropping the original centerpiece of the whole project, the purchase of a commercial TV station. After the first four months of the campaign, $200,000 in cash or pledges was listed, but at a fund-raising expense of $1 million. It was costing five dollars to raise each dollar, and that million dollars was a loan that had to be paid back to other church agencies. Understandably, the whole business collapsed of its own weight, and the church decided to revamp a new TV proposal for the 1984 General Conference.

The Radio and Television Commission of the Southern Baptist Convention was like unto Robertson, not the Methodists. It spotted a target of media opportunity, tied in the national campaign to a solid local base of funding and Christian outreach, and had a confident and cohesive idea of its religious message and purpose. Under President Jimmy Allen, the commission hoped by the end of 1984 to be one of the major operators of the newly authorized low-power over-the-air TV stations. The Baptist network is called American Christian Television System, or ACTS. (Incidentally, its five-member governing board includes three minority representatives.) It hopes eventually to have stations and cable outlets, both urban and rural, with a schedule of sixteen hours a day. Most of the shows will be produced by the Southern Baptists themselves on a budget of $3.3 million a year, a more realistic sum than the lower Methodist estimate. William Fore will be pleased that ACTS will not plead for funds over the air. Instead, it will rely on church offerings, direct mail, commercial "recognition" such as public TV is now using, and sale of shared delivery costs to users of its satellite hookup. The local churches and stations in the system will share costs at the reasonable rate of ten cents per month per member. Like Pat Robertson, the Baptists plan counseling phone banks for viewers who respond to broadcasts. Based on his track record as a pastor in San Antonio, Jimmy Allen will help the network find a way to foster social concern along with the soul-winning appeals. Of course, the Methodists may still get their act together and make a major splash on TV, and the Baptist operation may fizzle. But as of this writing, it looks as if the Methodists are confused in message and programmed for failure, while the Baptist evangelicals know what their gospel is and are preparing for success.

One can sympathize with the Methodists' quandary, however. Program content has proven to be such a difficulty, on both the left and the right, that one wonders whether TV will ever be able to master the transmission of spiritual truths and values. The stereotypical liberal show is aptly described by Jean Lyles as "panel discussions of Great Issues featuring three Naugahyde chairs and a Boston fern." The stereotypical evangelical show would be a glossy entertainment format with testimonial chit-chat, enthusiasm and smiles, lots of money-raising, and some right-wing political motion—but barely any education in the Bible. In their own way, evangelicals are endorsing the philosophy of the National Council of Churches: you can't do much good Bible teaching on the air. Since TV culture is so pervasive, this tendency toward shallowness is beginning to infect even the local churches. Or at least it had infected the Wednesday night prayer meeting I recently attended at Jerry Falwell's church in Lynchburg, Virginia. The evangelicals, who for decades prided themselves as the keepers of a doctrine, now appear to have acquired all the latest hardware but to be uncertain what to teach with it. Nor do they seem much concerned about the situation.

Where, then, does the amazing broadcasting and publishing empire fit within evangelicalism? Years ago I commented that the councils of churches are a bureaucracy without a constituency, and that the evangelical movement was a constituency without a bureaucracy. That is still true. But inchoate popular movements inevitably produce their own style of institutions. While old-line denominations do their "liberal" business at national conventions and meetings of numerous church agencies, the evangelicals also have their national get-togethers. But the important meetings are not necessarily those of the National Association of Evangelicals, or even the important one-shot evangelism rallies.

On an ongoing annual basis, the movement in effect gathers during the conventions of National Religious Broadcasters and the Christian Booksellers Association. It always intrigues me how many evangelical bureaucrats and pastors with only tangential connections with radio, TV, or books make their way to these conventions in order to hobnob. These are the occasions where the movement leaders are selected out, showcased, and ratified; where the comers preen; where the implicit ideologies, politics, and limits of discourse are set; where alliances are struck and dissolved; where tips or jobs are traded; where enemies are identified and flayed; where a conservative social gospel is transmitted. One might well add other parachurch gatherings to those two, for instance the seminars that cluster around the annual Presidential Prayer Breakfast in Washington.

There is something both fitting and unsettling about the idea that evangelical religion, having been driven from the denominational fleshpots into the parachurch wilderness, has seen the desert bloom and now conducts its strategic planning, on the fly, at commercial trade shows. I wonder, what might John Calvin, John Wesley, Jonathan Edwards, or Jonathan Blanchard make of all this?

Chapter 5

FUNDAMENTALISM
AS A SOCIAL PHENOMENON

MARTIN E. MARTY

FUNDAMENTALISM, involving as it does some ten to twenty million Americans,[1] is obviously a social phenomenon and demands interpretation as such. But the observer who isolates the social dimension has to take special care to be fair-minded, to give something of the participants' point of view. To descend on fundamentalism from the outside with too many presuppositions about social movements may mean to lose the necessary sense of what animates the movement and inspires loyalty to it.

INDIVIDUAL RELIGIOSITY

Fundamentalists for the most part would not see themselves as members of a "social phenomenon." Almost all observers have agreed with participants that fundamentalism is in many respects a highly individualized version of Christian faith. The fundamentalists for the most part are church members, but they are not "churchly" in a sacramental sense. They make little of an ontological reality that calls them to communal existence, a church that exists in the mind of God or the structure of things before it manifests itself as voluntary local associations.

To the fundamentalist, participation means being saved. It begins with a separation from the world in the form of being "born again," though there are fundamentalists in, say, the Presbyterian tradition who find that term less congenial than do the majority in the Baptist traditions. From this separation follows a deeper desire to be separated also from sin and from half-faithful or even apostate people who call themselves Christians but who waver on certain fundamentals. The believer wants to be with Jesus in the Rapture, the millennial reign, and finally in the new heavens. The terms for the eschaton vary somewhat, but no one should ever forget the otherworldly or next-worldly dimension in this faith.

So it comes down to an individual search and a personal reception of grace. To take fundamentalists seriously and to see their faith as a matter of integrity, we must, in any fair analysis of the social phenomenon, listen to the participants' description. In the deepest sense of the term, people who are religious cannot help but be religious. They cannot be beguiled out of their vision, distracted from their passion, diverted from what consumes them. Members of lackadaisical mainline churches who have to be cajoled into the pew and seduced toward the tithe may forget the power of such engrossing religious appeals. But the fundamentalist does not forget. He or she is out to "get saved," and little else matters.

VOLUNTARY ASSOCIATION

Holding constantly to that understanding, however, the observer moves on. Fundamentalism, like all modern faiths—and this one is nothing if not modern, born in the face and challenge of modernity and taking advantage of its mixed technical offerings—involves the possibility that the believer will keep religion a "private affair."[2] Yet one will notice that the majority of the saved do form social organizations. The most powerful of these, of course, is the local church, which in the technical sense is the only church fundamentalism knows. However, there are voluntary extensions of this local reality: these take the form of clienteles for religious radio and television; power movements within moderate denominations like the Southern Baptist Convention; constituencies that support Bible institutes, crusades, and publishing ventures.

A SPACE IN THE SOCIAL WORLD

By this point of organization the individual fundamentalist can no longer hide from the awareness that a social phenomenon has developed. Even as an ecclesial reality of a nominalist sort, fundamentalist church life takes institutional form and thus takes up space in the world. Wary of receiving government aid and insisting as fundamentalists do on separation of church and state, they still for the most part do accept tax exemption of properties used for specifically religious purposes. This exemption, which can be argued as a "right" or "good policy" or "public benefit," is a fiscal boon to American churches that far exceeds the subsidy established churches receive in Europe. And as tax-exempt by the public, the churches enter the public realm.

The move from individuals' "being saved" to their being part of a social phenomenon goes far beyond the physical space of fundamentalist properties and the indirect public support through tax exemption. Fundamentalism wants to win converts, and this means moving door to door in public communities, passing out tracts in pluralist settings, and using air waves that are conceived as "belonging" to everyone. In this sense, in many parts of the country at least, nonfundamentalists become aware of the social dimensions of a voluntaryist religious vision.

THE POLITICAL DIMENSION

A third stage of presence, however, moves fundamentalism further in the public eye as a social phenomenon. This is its political aspiration. Most fundamentalists do not see themselves as political, and their own witness about themselves has to be taken seriously. Through most of their history, most members have tended to be passive about connecting religion and politics. Their social class, often upper-lower or lower-middle, had kept them from the kinds of colleges, support funding, or aspiring that brings people to Congress or executive mansions. Intensely patriotic, they would vote or accept the call to military service, since fundamentalist pacifism is extremely rare. They paid their taxes and probably had a lower crime and delinquency rate than the general public or some more relaxed religious forces could boast.

Fundamentalism as a social phenomenon has often been hard to isolate on the political level because voting tends to follow partisan and regional lines. Most fundamentalists insist that they do not wish to organize political parties. Although many analysts see ties between theological and political "conservatism," that term itself is problematic when dealing with fundamentalism. When the movement was born, it did not "conserve" much of what Roman Catholic, Eastern Orthodox, and mainline Protestant churches—which must make up nine-tenths of Christendom—would have regarded as the tradition worth preserving. It was quite radical in its primitivism, insisting that it was reproducing biblical-era belief and organization. More than it knew, the movement did draw on traditional thirteenth- and seventeenth-century scholasticism, Catholic and Protestant. Often in its more open Calvinist forms, it also paid respects to the sixteenth-century Protestant Reformation. But the movement makes no sense except as a very modern reaction to modernism,[3] a highly selective selection of the "fundamentals" of faith, a fresh patterning of the presumed "essences" of Christianity, one that makes little sense to the sacramental churches, whose "essentials" seldom come up. Fundamentalism in many senses, including the best ones, was not "conservative" but radical.

Yet the public and liberal religionists type the movement as theologically conservative and assume that this conservatism carries over symptomatically into politics. Certainly there are predispositions of this sort; yet examinations of voting records often show that fundamentalists of the South and the Plains States allied themselves with populist movements that were anything but conservative. In the 1930s true political conservatives often thought of the Tennessee Valley Authority as socialistic or communistic. Appalachian fundamentalists who wanted their farms electrified voted for such a program, whatever socialist images it carried. It would be a mistake to picture all fundamentalists as political reactionaries at all times.

DEFENSE AND AGGRESSION

Sometimes fundamentalism as a social phenomenon shows up politically in a defensive way. Before the Democratic Convention of 1960, fundamentalists and other Protestant conservatives sometimes made ephemeral common cause with the Protestant liberals to raise criticisms of Catholicism in American life in connection with the candidacy of John F. Kennedy.[4] They regularly hurry to Washington with the best of liberals to protect themselves from real or presumed intrusive threats on the part of the Internal Revenue Service or the Federal Communications Commission.[5] They may not see these defensive gestures as being political, bringing them into the zone of "social phenomena," but in the process of building coalitions and making alliances, testifying in Congress, lobbying, or seeking votes on specific issues, they have to be seen as far removed from individualist, nonpolitical life.

Beyond automatic participation in social life and defensiveness, much fundamentalism has moved into more aggressive endeavors to be a social phenomenal presence. This occurs whenever its leaders, backed by visible followers, assert themselves in efforts to reshape social life in America. This is almost always done in the name of "morality" in putative distinction from or even opposition to "politics." Fundamentalists have cared deeply, as is their right, about gambling, alcoholic intemperance, and accessible pornography. These are, of course, moral issues: they are issues congenial to that strain of Protestantism that had long before become expert at dealing with individual "virtue" and "vice," as opposed to social and structural reworking of society.

The problem with keeping fundamentalism an individual religiosity as opposed to a social phenomenon is that one cannot move far beyond simple personal voluntaryism without bumping into contravening political forces that have their own interests. The bumper sticker that says "Against Abortion?—Don't Have One!" illustrates an approach that would allow fundamentalism to remain withdrawn from the political order and to be seen less as a social phenomenon. Studies in the summer of 1981 that revealed fundamentalists to be represented almost as regularly in audiences of sexy-and-violent TV shows as was the general public might have inspired another set of bumper stickers: "Don't Like 'Em? Shut Them Off!" "Don't like intemperance? Don't drink." Let us take in good faith the fundamentalist claims that members do restrain themselves in the matters of abortion, pornography, and alcohol. They thus make a contribution to a moral America on their terms.

LEGISLATED MORALITY

Fundamentalists would not be satisfied, however, with only that measure of contribution. Nine-tenths of America is not fundamentalist, and if it continues in immoral practices, America will still not be "moral." So a moralist vision does and must move into politics again, let us keep insisting, in a process that is fully legitimate. Fundamentalism has its rights. It is at this point, however, that a blind spot develops, one that matches the blinders liberals wear when *they* sometimes say that fundamentalists should not enter the political arena. To the fundamentalist, religious liberal support of the civil rights or antiwar movements a dozen years ago and more was political, not moral. Liberal opposition to capital punishment is political; fundamentalist support of it is moral. Saving lives through poverty programs in the public sector is a political act; saving fetal life by prohibiting abortions is a moral venture. This distinction has not been compelling to any nonfundamentalist.

Fundamentalist leaders in 1980 and 1981 began to see the anomaly, indeed the bad faith, implied in this distinction. The best known of them, evangelist Jerry Falwell, very frankly and openly admitted that he had been "wrong" when he previously inerrantly followed his inerrant Bible in opposing clerical involvement in the politics of civil rights. He speaks with some measure of repentance for his old stand—perhaps prudently, possibly with deep conviction after a "conversion" and some measure of admiration for people like Martin Luther King, Jr.; perhaps it was a ploy, but here we should also grant the possibility of good faith, as a latter-day recognition of King's effort for human good. In either case, Falwell makes no secret of his having led part of fundamentalism overtly into that moral-political realm.

To work for constitutional amendments, to seek passage of certain specific legislation, to attempt to prevent this or that international treaty— all these are marks not of individualist religiosity but of a social phenomenon of considerable power. The leaders justify their about-face on the grounds that America has grown so immoral that they must engage in a "teleological suspension of the ethical." Intemperance was and abortion is such a gross immorality in the sight of God and such a hazard to the civil order that one must take extraordinary means to address them as problems. Then one can lapse back into political passivity. This would mean that fundamentalism is only *sometimes* a social phenomenon.

A POWER AMONG POWERS

Once the policy of separation, passivity, and even withdrawal is broken, however, much else follows. Today's fundamentalist leadership has spotted a power vacuum and has enjoyed beginning to fill it. "How're ya goin' to keep 'em down on the farm after they've seen Paree?" How are you going to keep fundamentalists off in individual religiosity after they have seen how easily they can effect some parts of their social vision? To seek power is not necessarily an evil: without power one cannot achieve good. But to seek power on present terms is to recognize that fundamentalism, whatever its historic voice, today overtly seeks to be a social phenomenon with political dimensions.

If political fundamentalism inconveniences other people, people who support the Panama Canal Treaty, abortion clinics, the Department of Education, or cocktail lounges, it has to understand that its jostling of the social fabric will inspire criticism and counterorganization. Legitimately wounded by a few unfair attacks on their rights as they intruded into the political order, some of the leaders overstepped or showed naïveté by creating the suggestion that the idea of counteraction, even if only in the form of criticism, was always out of line. But there are no exempt spaces for people who enter the political order. Politics, however unready fundamentalists may be to recognize it, is an order that involves conflict and compromise.[6] It is an assertion of power amidst other powers, an attempt to make moves that step on the toes of others who, thus alerted, stop wincing and start marching or arming or organizing. The social phenomenal character of fundamentalism, then, has become patent. Attempts to disguise it are to be short-lived. Efforts to hold out against the move on the part of fundamentalist minorities are not likely to protect the movement as a whole from a public perception that sees its social presence.

Fundamentalism, then, has become a political force among the forces. Politicians reckon with it as they do with labor unions and senior citizens' action agencies. Television critics regard it as a social phenomenon for its presence in "the electronic church." *Publishers' Weekly* gives an accounting of its book sales. There is no place to hide, and the majority of fundamentalist leadership does not wish to. Far, far removed seem the days when the individual search for salvation was the encompassing feature of fundamentalism.

A TWO-PARTY SYSTEM CHANGING?

Seeing Fundamentalism as a social phenomenon today makes most sense when viewed against the past. Some years ago, in *Righteous Empire*, I made a distinction within Protestantism.[7] It had a "two-party" system, one termed "public" and the other "private." In 1857-58, at the time of the "laymen's revivals," whose social consequences Timothy Smith has so well chronicled in *Revivalism and Social Reform*,[8] one could view revivalists also as social movement leaders for reform, welfare, and political purposes. Before them Charles Grandison Finney's generation of revivalists engaged themselves with issues that ranged from dueling to slavery.[9] But by 1908, when the old Federal Council of Churches was born, it was organized chiefly around certain more liberal social purposes and had left evangelism pretty well behind. By then, also, evangelists in the train of Dwight L. Moody through Billy Sunday, for all their casual and even sometimes forceful social comments, were seen as specialists in soul-saving, rescuing people from a world of shipwreck into salvationist lifeboats, to use Moody's celebrated metaphor.

POLITICAL NOT PUBLIC

Has the picture now changed? In some respects, yes. Fundamentalism allows for development, indeed development of doctrine, if one listens to the Falwell apologia, and what was once wrong can now become right, on biblical grounds—the only grounds fundamentalists will finally admit to taking seriously. But I believe that public/private distinction remains appropriate for the most part, at least with respect to the evangelistic-evangelical tradition. The fundamentalist move into politics in the 1980s is of a somewhat different character. Not to put too fine a point on it, its theological assumptions are now "political" but not "public." A public theology, as numbers of us have set out to define it, allows for the integrity of movements that are not conservative Protestant, Christian, or Jewish-Christian at all. God can work his "order" through the godless, in secular-pluralism. A public theology allows for a positive interpretation of that secular-pluralist order with its religious admixtures, even as it recognizes all the while the way the demonic pervades the orders of existence. The political theology of privatist fundamentalism does not do so. It is born of separatists who do not regard nonfundamentalists with any positive ecumenical feelings. The fundamentalist political scope may recognize Catholics and Jews or "traditional theists" as belonging in the civil order, but then insists that nontheists are outsiders, to be tolerated at best. Let it also be said that not all fundamentalists have made the overt political move, and not all conservative Protestantism is fundamentalist.

This public/political distinction is not a hard and fast one, and its nuances, now apparently fine, may easily elude us. Yet through the years we shall need some handle to separate the two, for there are vastly different consequences in civil life. Admittedly, one can approach the subject in Humpty-Dumpty's way: "When I use a word, it means just what I choose it to mean—neither more nor less." And when one comes to study "public" in the *Oxford English Dictionary*, there is a growing sense of elusiveness: "The varieties of sense are numerous and pass into each other by many intermediate shades of meaning. The exact shade often depends upon the substantive qualified. . . ." Yet in thirty and more *OED* definitions, the word "political" never appears to explain public. The first definition of "political" does need the word "public," however, which suggests that "political" in some ways can be a species of a genus called "public."

In the sense that I here use the word political, it refers to the activity by which interests—in this case, the fundamentalists—seek their way, though they must finally compromise (or retreat) and be conciliated by receiving a share in power in proportion to their weight in the political community. While politics is not exhausted by self-interest, it is moved chiefly by it. In the present case, the interest group seeks to protect its turf, to extend its mission, and to have its way at the expense of other ways.

On the other hand, the public is pre-, para-, and postpolitical. It allows to other interests a full integrity. In its sphere strangers meet and overcome their fears; conflict occurs and is to be resolved; life is given color, texture, drama, a festive air; mutual responsibility becomes evident, opinions are heard and countered; visions are tested. Crucial again in this second sense: religionists in the public sphere have a theological accounting of the validity of those who do not share their final outlook. Politically minded church bodies need have a positive explanation of only their own and their allies' causes; all the rest may be neutral or negative. Thus it is that one can seek one's own way in politics without taking on a public mien, guise, or intention.[10]

EVANGELISM AND PENTECOSTALISM

The evangelists from Moody through Graham tried to "work" the private realm. When Billy Graham moved beyond it, as he did frequently in the 1950s through the 1970s, he saw this as casual extrusion from his evangelist calling or part of his responsibility as a citizen, without connecting the activity to his evangelist movement. Many evangelists are even less expressive than he was about positive political points. Their evangelism makes up a social phenomenon to them, but of a largely ecclesiastical character. That is, it takes up social space, but in the modern division of labor that space is sequestered in the bloc called "religion," not "culture comment" or "social impact" or "political pressure."

It is similar with Pentecostalists, who are also often confused with fundamentalists. Taking rise early in this century concurrently with fundamentalism, this Pentecostalism could make common cause with the scholastic-minded intransigents over against modernism. But the two made an uneasy partnership because not all Pentecostalists accepted fundamentalist-scholastic views of biblical inerrancy, and the Pentecostal claims of a kind of "enthusiasm" in connection with Spirit-baptism and speaking in tongues threatened many fundamentalist dogmatists. Pentecostals may often have been populists, and they did their voting. But it has always been more difficult to get them into focus, not as a social phenomenon but as a social movement with discernible political bents.

One could add other groups that are conservative but not part of the fundamentalist social phenomena: black Protestant, whether Methodist or Baptist or Pentecostal; the Southern Baptist Convention, which has a fundamentalist wing but also has a quite separate history and existence; conservative Reformed and Lutheran movements like the Christian Reformed Church and the Missouri Synod. These are examples of groups whose social-political careers differ widely from that of fundamentalism.

A LONG POLITICAL TENDENCY

Fundamentalism almost from the beginning, then, was more ready to be overtly political than were these cohort groups at the side. If we see fundamentalism as a conservative Protestant force born of reaction to liberal-modernism that fused premillennialism with (Princeton-style arguments for) inerrancy, began to make a protostatement in *The Fundamentals,* got named in 1920, and was the aggressor in efforts to sway major denominations in the mid-twenties, we must realize that even in the first generation fundamentalism had a political posture. This was focused chiefly on the issues of Zionism. There were Protestant fundamentalist Zionists in America before Jewish Zionism took hold. This derived from the peculiar reading of biblical prophecy which was popularized in the *Scofield Reference Bible* and which in a series of prophetic biblical conferences led to a virtual takeover of proto-fundamentalism by dispensational premillennialists. Thus, as early as 1891, the tireless agitator William E. Blackstone gathered the names of over 400 prominent

Americans and presented to President Harrison a petition asserting the political right of Jews to rebuild the nation of Israel.[11]

In the second generation fundamentalism was an organized force in the political realm, as was evident from its participation in the most celebrated religious event of the 1920s, the Scopes trial. This had to do with antievolution legislation and school book policy and was thus overtly political. Through the thirties the fundamentalists were busy rebuilding their institutions after the denominational defeats around 1925. They did this very effectively through the war years, as various fundamentalist fronts were organized around 1942.[12]

Then in the fifties, during the Cold War era, fundamentalists like Carl McIntire and Billy James Hargis and any number of anti-Communist crusaders began their program for a fortress America. Then as now, part of their chauvinism grew from the conviction that Falwell still announces. Even if the Second Coming is imminent, Christians are to "occupy until Christ comes." And they are to see America as a new Zion, its people as a chosen people. America must remain free, through fundamentalist efforts, since it is the last training ground for evangelists who will rescue individuals elsewhere before the Rapture. This is far from a developed "public theology," but it is certainly a nationalist-political one.[13]

So the New Christian Right of the 1980s, which has fundamentalism at its core even as it picks up some Pentecostalists, evangelicals, Southern Baptists, and conservative Protestants from confessional denominations, has precedent chiefly in the scholastic-millennial "hardline" tradition that took shape almost a century ago and was formally organized in the 1920s. What had been latent is now patent; the covert became overt, but there has been less switching and more "development" than spokesmen like Falwell allow for in their apologiae.

WHY SOCIAL–POLITICAL NOW?

If fundamentalism is a social phenomenon with a political cast, and if it has been so in some ways from the beginning, it remains only to ask why it has become so visible, explicit, and belligerent *now.* The answer is too complex to be reduced to a few paragraphs, but several main features of a response to the question will throw light on the phenomenon today.

First, there is a worldwide reaction against many of the mixed offerings of modernity.[14] Fundamentalism, as part of it, both ministers to the victims of modernization and exploits them. Iran is the prototype. Technology and affluence swept the scene there, but the benefits were for the few. The shah's family, the Iranian elites who studied in America, and the oil sheiks reaped the benefits. The rest of the population did not have its physical circumstances improved and only saw its traditions threatened. In reaction, ayatollahs preached the old scriptures, women returned to wearing the chador, and there was a fundamentalist-based religious revolution. Something similar is going on in numbers of underdeveloped nations. American fundamentalism cannot be dismissed as a lower-class aspirant economic cohort, though some dimensions of social class are apparent in its movement. But it is clearly a force of resentment against "intellectuals," "elites," "the media," and the like, people who are at home with modernization and care little for the presumed traditions.

Second, there is a worldwide movement, which we might call "tribalism," that is obvious in African nations, Israel, Iran, Lebanon, Ireland, the Asian subcontinent, and elsewhere.[15] In this movement people retreat from modernity by withdrawing into their ethno-religio-cultural-tribal bonds. This retreat was easier to begin in Lebanon, where there are spatial separations between such groups, than in America, where there is more intermixing. But in America too, one might see fundamentalism as the latest in the two-decade movement of groups, be they black, Chicano, Jewish, Catholic ethnic, homosexual, young, feminist, or whatever, to find and assert symbols. These, then, are designed to assure a group's power, place, and pride—over against the real or presumed threats of others. For example, there are not many blacks in formal fundamentalism, though most blacks would be typed as belonging in the conservative revivalist tradition. Fundamentalists are visible as a social phenomenon because they are now getting their tribe together and finding ways to be assertive about their place.

Third, there was an ecological niche or cranny to be filled, a void that had room for a new growth. There has been, no one can deny, some sort of "values crisis" in America, a shift in understandings and practices having to do with family life, sexuality, and expression. Those who are devotees of pluralism and who believe that transmittable values can emerge from public debate and conflict somehow tolerate ambiguity and pick their way through the confusions of the decades. The fundamentalists, however, can appeal to the impatient. Theirs is an almost Manichean world of black/white, God/Satan, Christ/Antichrist, Christian/"Secular-Humanist." On these terms it is easy to invent and expose "conspiracies" of the forces against good—good America, good fundamentalists. People who seek authoritarian solutions are likely to follow charismatic fundamentalist leaders in such a time.

Finally, fundamentalists, though they may lack a positive view of certain scientific and technological processes, are uninhibited in their use of the products. Radio, television, computers, direct-mail technology—all of which remain practically mysterious and inaccessible to mainline Christianity—seem made for the world of fundamentalist splinter groups.

Speakers on radio and television can portray clear choices with great simplicity. They have found ways to raise paracongregational funds to make possible opinion-surveying and pressure-grouping. They have "borrowed" the technology of modernization with all its bewilderments and used it substantially to promote nostalgic and simplistic visions of the past as models for the future.

THE FUTURE

Will they win? The fundamentalist message and pattern of meanings appeals to a rather definite class and personality type. Leadership has to content itself with making the most of its market potential within conservative Protestantism. America is not "turning fundamentalist." It has become aware of fundamentalism, and fundamentalists have seen a great growth in morale and visibility. They will not soon slink away. But their interpretations, grounded in one kind of biblical inerrancy and premillennialism, are not the choice of the many.

This means that fundamentalists have to build some coalitions, as they have done on the abortion front. It is also likely that some leadership will adapt and modify itself to become more smooth, ingratiating, and palatable. It has begun to do this and, in the process, has already alienated huge sections of "nonpolitical" fundamentalism on one hand and "hyperfundamentalism" on the other. But the American *Danegeld* is too rich for these leaders not to be bought off, and the political lures are too strong for them to resist. Fundamentalist clienteles will also become ever more pluralistic. Their interests have to be met. Hence, for example, the exclusion of deadly tobacco from its usual place alongside deadly alcohol in the program. Leaders admit that they cannot make an antitobacco plank part of a crusade because too many followers smoke or make their living off raising and treating tobacco. Such waverings make fundamentalism more compromising, more assimilable, more capable of being conceived as one more element in the republic.

Only if the "formal system" should break down and the economic order collapse would it be likely that fundamentalists could break out of their current cohort in the competitive market. If there has to be a whole new social contract some day, it is likely that there must be in it a state religion, compulsory in character, authoritarian in tone, "traditional" in outlook. America would be "socialized" not in the name of Marx but of Jesus, not in the name of communism but of Christian republicanism.[16] To mention all this is not to hint at a self-fulfilling prophecy but to sketch the terms by which fundamentalism could ever "win America" as a social phenomenon. Until then it must pick its shots, build alliances, and make skillful use of the edges that technology and dedication give it in close

American elections. Until then, fundamentalists have to rely on the evocative power their often inaccurate images induce whenever they talk about the Jewish-Christian stipulations of "Enlightened" founding fathers, or the "traditional theism" of once-Unitarian deist public schools, as transmitters of the Founding Fathers' values.[17] Until then, they can also do their best service by making nonfundamentalists think about values and their transmission, pluralism and its problems, American public faith and individual religiosity, in their always changing conjunctions.

Part Two

CHALLENGING OR REFLECTING THE CULTURE?

Chapter 6

EVANGELICALISM AS
A DEMOCRATIC MOVEMENT

NATHAN O. HATCH

> But in a democracy organized on the model of the United States
> there is only one authority, one source of strength and of success,
> and nothing outside of it.
>
> Alexis de Tocqueville

THE VENGEANCE WITH WHICH RELIGIOUS ISSUES have reentered the public
arena in our time draws attention to what samplers of public opinion
long have known: the United States stands at the top of Western industrial
societies in the importance religion plays in the lives of its citizens. After
surveying much of this evidence, historian Laurence Veysey has concluded that at least two out of three adults in America still maintain fairly
bedrock religious beliefs. In a recent Gallup Poll that asked how important religion should be in life, 41 percent of young Americans (ages 18–
24) answered "very important." In France, Germany, and Great Britain,
fewer than ten percent of young people gave the same response.[1] On any
given Sunday morning, over 40 percent of the population in the United
States attends church. In Canada and Australia this number tails off to
about 25 percent; in England to about 10 percent; and in Scandinavia to
around 5 percent—despite the fact that 95 percent of the population is
confirmed in the church.[2]

How does one begin to explain the religious continuity and vitality
found in America? What kind of long-term cultural mores have allowed

the roots of Christianity to sink so deeply within popular culture? It is certainly not that Americans have developed a genius for ecclesiastical organization. While the United States Army or General Motors may attribute their success to a well-honed bureaucracy, centrally directed and tied together from top to bottom, American Christianity has muddled along in a state of anarchic pluralism, a sort of free-market religious economy. Dietrich Bonhoeffer once commented that it had been granted to America, less than to any nation on earth, to realize the visible unity of the church of God. Nor can the success of American Christianity be attributed to the prestige of its clergy. While some religious leaders such as Billy Graham or Theodore Hesburgh may *win* respect, American clergymen as a group enjoy less prestige than do their colleagues in other Western democracies.[3] The shadow of Elmer Gantry still lingers. Neither can Christianity here attribute its strength to an agility in making faith plausible to the modern world. European Protestant churches for at least a century have made it possible for their parishioners to embrace modernity without a twinge of conscience, while American churchmen who attempt to make peace with this age may be surprised to find parishioners still fretting about issues such as evolution, secular humanism, prayer in the schools, and the kinds of books that libraries should own.

What then is the driving force behind American Christianity if it is not the quality of its organization, the status of its clergy, or the power of its intellectual life? I would suggest that a central dynamic has been its democratic orientation.[4] In America the principal mediator of God's voice has not been state, church, council, confession, ethnic group, university, college, or seminary; it has been, quite simply, the people. American Christianity, particularly its evangelical varieties, has not been something held aloof from the rank and file, a faith to be appropriated on someone else's terms. Instead, the evangelical instinct for two centuries has been to pursue people wherever they could be found; to embrace them without regard to social standing; to challenge them to think, interpret Scripture, and organize the church for themselves; and to endow their lives with the ultimate meaning of knowing Christ personally, being filled with the Spirit, and knowing with assurance the reality of eternal life. These democratic yearnings are among the oldest and deepest impulses in American religious life. Given this fact, what is surprising is not the continued dynamism of evangelical Christianity in this century. What is surprising is that analysts such as ourselves have paid so little attention to its democratic foundations and thus too readily assumed its demise.

What do I mean when I say that American Christianity is characteristically democratic? I mean that in the century and a half from the Great Awakening to the dawn of the twentieth century America underwent a profound Christianization. Describing this culture as an "Evangelical

Empire," Martin Marty has written that "the first half century of national life saw the development of evangelicalism as a kind of national religion."[5] While many factors contributed to this "Golden Day of Democratic Evangelicalism"[6]—to use Sydney Ahlstrom's phrase—none is more striking than the impulse to rework Christianity into forms that were unmistakably popular. Noting in 1840 that the United States appeared to be more religious than European nations, the Frenchman Alexis de Tocqueville reasoned that in Europe the spirit of liberty and of religion had marched in opposite directions. In America the two had become "one undivided current," so much so that people had trouble distinguishing between them.[7] The style of Christianity which Tocqueville described was democratic in at least three respects: it was audience centered, intellectually open to all, and organizationally pluralistic and innovative.

THE SOVEREIGN AUDIENCE

The genius of evangelicals long has been their firm identification with people. While others may have excelled in defending and elaborating the truth, and in building institutions to weather the storms of time, evangelicals in America have been passionate about communicating a message. The enduring legacy of the first Great Awakening, Harry Stout has suggested, was a new mode of persuasion.[8] Defying a church callous to its common folk, John Wesley thundered that he would preach nothing but "plain truth for plain people."[9] The primary emphasis of Wesley and George Whitefield was not orthodoxy per se, as important as both thought theology to be. The end of religion was that each person would know for himself a profound experience with God. This required an idiom in touch with people. By the time of the American Revolution, the warmth of such evangelical appeals and their ability to draw the unchurched into cohesive fellowships made evangelicalism a major social force on both sides of the Atlantic.[10]

John Wesley, George Whitefield, and Jonathan Edwards certainly were not democrats, but whatever concessions they failed to make to a broader public were swept away by the tidal wave of democracy that engulfed America in the first decades of the nineteenth century. While staid graduates of Harvard, Yale, and Princeton continued to serve solidly respectable congregations, they watched as bystanders to the real winning of America's soul—by relentless Methodist circuit riders, roughhewn Baptist preachers, and no-nonsense elders from the Disciples of Christ. The utterly unpretentious message of these groups, like that of Joseph Smith, founder of the Latter-day Saints, or William Miller, the Adventist, stripped away the power of creed and confession, the authority of staid institutional forms, and the inherent power of the clergy. What they promised in return was that people could make their own religious commitments rather than obeying those handed down to them.[11]

Charles G. Finney and Dwight L. Moody stand as the finest exemplars of this "proclamation theology."[12] Both did espouse coherent theologies, but both despised the formal study of divinity. This was precisely because it produced such dull and ineffective communication. Attuned to the needs and concerns of average people, both discarded hidebound forms for new methods that would awaken the unconcerned and re-awaken the complacent. "What do the politicians do?" queried Finney.

> They get up meetings, circulate handbills and pamphlets, blaze away in the newspapers, send their ships about the streets on wheels with flags and sailors, send coaches all over town, with handbills, to bring people up to the polls, all to gain attention to their cause and elect their candidate.... The object of our measures is to gain attention and you *must have* something new.[13]

Finney despised sermons that were read because the preacher remained content oriented rather than sensitive to the audience's reaction.

> The preacher preaches right along just as he has it written down and cannot observe whether he is understood or not. . . . If a minister has his eye on the people he is preaching to, he can commonly tell by their looks whether they understand him. And if he sees they do not understand any particular point, let him stop and illustrate it. If they do not understand one illustration, let him give another.

Finney noted elsewhere that the gospel had to be preached *to* men, not *about* them.[14]

Dwight L. Moody shared the same instincts about communication. For him, nothing was gained by mere allegiance to creed, church, or churchmen; the goal of preaching was to expose men and women to God, not merely to talk about him. Recalling his experience with Moody as a college student, Henry Sloane Coffin, then president of Union Theological Seminary, commented on Moody's personal style: "The gospel was never to him something to be discussed . . . but to be tried and passed on." Coffin remembered Moody as a peerless storyteller, but what stood out was his effectiveness in driving home the story's main point: "There was nothing bizarre, nothing spectacular, nothing theatrical, nothing irreverent," Coffin said of Moody telling the story of Daniel. "This was the Word of God, but it was so vivid to him that he made us feel that we were right on the spot."[15]

A FREE MARKET OF IDEAS

Such audience orientation had profound effects on the way American evangelicals came to organize and carry out religious thinking. As the common man rose in power in the early republic, the inevitable consequence was the displacement from power of the uncommon man, the man of ideas.[16] Democratic America would never produce another theologian to rank with Edwards, just as it would never elect statesmen of the caliber of Adams, Jefferson, and Madison. In the main, evangelicals did not simply become anti-intellectual; what they did was destroy the monopoly that classically educated and university trained clergymen had enjoyed. They threw theology open to any serious student of Scripture, and they considered the "common sense" intuition of people at large more reliable, even in the realm of theology, than the musing of an educated few.[17]

This shift involved new faith in public opinion as an arbiter of truth. Common folk were no longer mistrusted as irresponsible and willful; they now came to be seen as ready to embrace truth if only it was unclouded from the visionary speculations of the academic and uncoupled from the heavy hand of the past.[18] Arguing against the Standing Order in the 1790s, the Massachusetts reformer Benjamin Austin insisted that common people had always possessed an instinct for truth and virtue: "The multitude had received Christ with great acclaim," he suggested, while "the monarchical, aristocratical and priestly authorities cried crucify him."[19] By thus admitting the sovereignty of the audience, evangelicals, knowingly or not, undercut the structure that could support critical theological thinking on the level of a Jonathan Edwards or a John Wesley. Not only did theology proper recede in importance before the task of proclaiming the gospel; the new ground rules for theology, opening it to all, meant that the measure of theology would be its acceptability in the marketplace of ideas. This meant that uncomfortable complexity would be flattened out, that issues would be resolved by a simple choice of alternatives, and that, in many cases, the fine distinctions from which truth alone can emerge were lost in the din of ideological battle. In this process, few evangelicals would admit that further reduction to popularity could at times involve downright falsification.

In such a free market of ideas, Tocqueville feared a "tyranny of the majority,"[20] that serious thinking would be hooted down in the marketplace before it could mature. He objected to the American penchant for trusting the people to judge issues of awesome moment—as when Alexander Campbell debated Robert Owen for five days on the truth of Christianity, and then wanted to settle the issue by popular vote. One should not underestimate the high degree of theological literacy and self-education fostered in this culture. But neither can one dismiss the reality that Tocqueville found: expecting that great freedom of thought would generate great ideas, he found instead that Americans easily became "slaves of slogans."[21]

RADICAL PLURALISM

Orienting Christianity so profoundly around the free will of the individual also had implications for religious organizations. "Protestants in general," said H. Richard Niebuhr, "but American Protestants in particular, seem to have developed its institutions and orders not as ends in view or as representative of its purposes but as the necessary instruments and pragmatic devices of a movement that could not come to rest in any structure."[22] Whatever common spirit bound evangelicals together in the nineteenth century, it assumed few institutional manifestations. Recurrent dissentings blasted any semblance of organizational coherence. The array of denominations, mission boards, reform agencies, newspapers and journals, revivalists, and colleges is at best an amorphous collectivity, an organizational smorgasbord. Power, influence, and authority were radically dispersed, and most came by way of democratic means: popular appeals to the good will of the audience. "No minister can be forced upon his people without their suffrage and voluntary support," said Lyman Beecher. "Each pastor stands upon his own character and deeds, without anything to break the force of his responsibility to his people."[23] In this climate, Tocqueville said, where he expected to find priests, he found politicians.[24]

The democratic winnowing of the church produced not just pluralism but also striking diversity. The flexibility and innovation involved in American religious organizations meant that, within certain broad limits, an American could find an amenable group no matter what his or her preference in belief, practice, or institutional structure. Churches ranged from the most egalitarian to the most autocratic and included all degrees of organizational complexity.[25] One could be a Presbyterian who favored or opposed the freedom of the will, a Methodist who promoted or denounced democracy in the church, a Baptist who advocated or condemned foreign missions, and a member of virtually any denomination who upheld or opposed slavery. One could revel in Christian history with John W. Nevin or wipe the slate clean with Alexander Campbell. The range of options within evangelical communions seemed virtually unlimited: one could choose to worship on Saturday, practice foot washing, ordain women, advocate pacifism, prohibit alcohol, or practice health reform. Or, like Abraham Lincoln, one could simply choose a biblical form of Christianity without the slightest ecclesiastical encumbrance.[26]

The English sociologist David Martin, writing about secularization, comments that in America dissent has become universalized. While this theme has certainly not escaped church historians in the twentieth century, the implications Martin draws are strikingly different. Historians generally treat the atomistic structure of American Christianity as a maladaptive characteristic, a weakness, a sign of deficiency. The general impression given is that Christianity has somehow remained vital *despite* its fragmentation. Turning such thinking on its head, Martin argues in *A General Theory of Secularization* that the vitality of American Christianity can be correlated precisely with the degree of pluralism and dissent present here.

> Disassociate religion from social authority and high culture, let religion adapt to every status group through every variety of pulsating sectarianism. The result is that nobody feels ill at ease with his religion, that faith is distributed along the political spectrum, that church is never *the* axis of dispute.[27]

Luther P. Gerlach and Virginia H. Hine have made a similar argument, namely, that the success of a religious movement can actually spring from organizational fission and lack of cohesion. They argue for the inherent dynamism of certain reticulate religious movements—those that are weblike, with parts tied together not through a central point but through intersecting sets of personal relations and intergroup linkages. Splitting, combining, and proliferating can be seen as clear signs of health. Such movements are superb at recruiting new members and offering the individual a keen sense of personal access to knowledge, truth, and power.[28]

From these vantage points, the democratic structure of evangelicalism—audience centered, intellectually open to all, organizationally fragmented—takes on new import. One can more easily understand how popular culture in nineteenth-century America became thoroughly Christianized while the English laboring classes were becoming alienated from the church.[29] Tocqueville understood well the difference between Christianity here, firmly linked to democracy, and that of Europe, which after the French Revolution dismissed any taint of liberty, equality, and fraternity. "By allying itself with political power," he said of Europe,

> religion increases its strength over some but forfeits the hope of reigning over all. . . . Unbelievers in Europe attack Christians more as a political than as religious enemies; they hate the faith as the opinion of a party much more than as a mistaken belief, and they

reject the clergy less because they are representatives of God than because they are the friends of authority.[30]

Twentieth-century evangelicals have not relinquished their grip on democracy, and they have certainly not withered away, despite being largely alienated from the culture's intellectual centers, losing control of the mainline denominations, and experiencing recurrent fragmentation. Whatever their foibles, evangelicals have not lost the common touch. While Harry Emerson Fosdick or Shailer Mathews could rejoice that good theological education was solidly in the liberal camp by the time of the Depression, evangelicals were busy building Bible colleges by the score— 250 in the course of this century. The magna charta of the Bible school movement was to make Christian education possible for the widest possible audience.[31] Liberal prophets like Walter Rauschenbusch or neo-orthodox ones like Reinhold Niebuhr could bemoan the plight of urban America, but who was it that actually brought Christianity to Detroit's autoworkers, Gary's steelworkers, and migrant blacks in Chicago? It was black revivalists, black and white Pentecostals, and fundamentalists like Jack Hyles. Mainline Protestants in the twentieth century have been hardly more effective in deepening the layers of their audience than were old lights like Charles Chauncy and Jonathan Mayhew in the eighteenth century. For all its intellectual sophistication, liberal theology has always been a bit like deism of an earlier day in forgetting that God is a person who communicates, and that he delights to do so with the meek and the lowly.[32]

Evangelicals in this century, on the other hand, have virtually organized their faith around the issue of communicating the gospel. Evangelism and missions were the principal burden of leaders such as A. B. Simpson, A. J. Gordon, R. A. Torrey, Charles E. Fuller, V. Raymond Edman, Harold Ockenga, and Billy Graham;[33] and it is no accident that when evangelicals have gathered for major concerted purpose it is the subject of world evangelization that has preoccupied their attention.[34]

Evangelical thinking over the last fifty years reflects this audience orientation in at least four respects. In the first place, evangelicals have sustained the conviction that religious knowledge is not an arcane science to be mediated by an educated elite. "This is a layman's age," declared C. I. Scofield, whose notes to the King James Bible became a best seller for Oxford University Press.[35] They offered to tens of thousands the hope of understanding the Bible for themselves. A recent advertisement for another study Bible offered the same promise: "study notes that they [everyday people] can understand without having to be theologians."[36] Where but in America could a converted seaman named Hal Lindsey make bold to undertake the same kind of rational study of biblical prophecy that had taxed the mind of a Jonathan Edwards or an Isaac Newton? The popularity of *The Late Great Planet Earth*—the best-selling paperback book in America during the 1970s—is testimony to the confidence American evangelicals still have that truth is simple and open to all.

A second tendency is that evangelical scholars are far more likely to speak and write to a popular evangelical audience than to pursue serious scholarship. This pattern is quite evident in the extraordinary contingent of evangelicals who first did graduate work in theology at Harvard in the 1940s and 1950s. The collective experience of Merrill Tenney, Samuel Schultz, Roger Nicole, Kenneth Kantzer, John Gerstner, Harold Kuhn, Paul Jewett, Glenn Barker, and E. J. Carnell demonstrates a much greater concern with instructing the evangelical rank and file than in engaging in serious theological scholarship.[37] The career choices of these men were, no doubt, shaped partly by pastoral concern for the church and partly by pressing responsibilities of leadership. But that is just the point. Evangelicals characteristically subordinate the task of first-order thinking to tasks that seem to affect more tangibly the lives of people at large.

Even when facing the most serious and complex intellectual issues, the instinct of evangelicals is to play them out before a popular audience. Professor William Hutchison has made the fascinating point that *The Fundamentals,* published between 1910 and 1915, were more a warning to the general Christian public than they were a scholarly grappling with the roots of modernism. It seemed far more important to those backing the project to distribute 300,000 of *The Fundamentals* free of charge than to enter into serious doctrinal discussion with liberals. The effect was that the work was virtually ignored in those sectors of the theological community that might have been expected to respond.[38] Similarly, issues such as evolution, inerrancy, and "secular humanism" are much more likely to be treated in ways that rally a large constituency than in ways that admit of the genuine complexities involved and that allow scholars to retreat from ideological battle to carefully weigh and clarify the issues at hand. In this sense, it is the people who are the custodians of orthodoxy; and persons who tamper with these issues, as they are popularly understood, might well receive the same fate as would a greenhorn politician seeking to revamp the entire Social Security system.[39] The public simply will not stand for it.

Because of its democratic coloring, evangelical thinking also manifests a third tendency: it measures the importance of an issue by its popular reception. By this logic, any position worth its salt will command a significant following. A best seller by definition becomes a "classic"; to be read is to deserve to be read. A good case in point is the recent revamping of the magazine *Christianity Today* to become less an evangelical voice within the larger theological world and more a popular medium catering to a solidly evangelical audience. Such an appeal to a mass readership may well reflect financial necessity, but that has always been the dilemma of evangelical concerns.[40] Radically dependent on popular support, they easily drift into merely reinforcing rather than improving popular taste. Flushed with tangible success, they allow the issue of quality to become a moot point. Evangelicals take pride that they are the defenders of orthodoxy in the twentieth century. Yet they have now abandoned their one real attempt to represent evangelical thinking in broader arenas of the modern world, among those who do not find evangelical convictions self-evident. It is a telling commentary on evangelical priorities.

The keen sensitivity of evangelicals to public opinion also has a fourth implication: a tendency for the values of the audience to color the substance of thinking. If mainline Protestants in this century have taken their cues from secular and academic culture, evangelicals have remained in tune with popular mores. And if leadership in the former is a function either of academic renown or bureaucratic skill, leadership in the latter has been bestowed on those who best embody the hopes of mass audiences—the Charles E. Fullers, Billy Grahams, Jerry Falwells, and Robert Schullers. Evangelicals spoke the language of peace of mind in the 1950s, developed a theology of "body-life" and community in the wake of the 1960s, and are currently infatuated with a gospel of self-esteem that correlates precisely with the contemporary passion for self-fulfillment.[41]

But it is not only charismatic leaders like Robert Schuller and Jerry Falwell who seem to embody widely shared values. This talent is a much broader phenomenon among evangelicals. More progressive figures, such as Ron Sider, Jim Wallis, John Alexander, and Donald Dayton, are equally given to proclaiming an evangelical message premised on other self-evident values—in this case a progressive agenda of social action. I have often thought that the Moral Majority and the Sojourners Community, for all their differences, are in many ways birds of a feather: both are equally adept at offering moral solutions to an agenda drawn up by someone else. If this penchant for adaptation gives evangelical thinking a derivative quality, it is a problem not likely to go away: influential voices within the church growth movement on the right and among evangelical anthropologists on the left are both making forceful arguments that, if it is to survive, the church must develop theologies that are even *more* "receptor oriented."[42]

To say that evangelicals have certain widely shared assumptions about communications and certain common approaches to religious thinking is not to suggest that uniformity is the hallmark of the movement. Pluralism among evangelicals over the last fifty years has grown more intense, even as the burgeoning number of organizations manifest more of a cooperative spirit. But in the final analysis, power, authority, and influence are more widely dispersed than ever. There are many denominations that range from Orthodox Presbyterian to the Assemblies of God, organizations—generally lay controlled—within mainline denominations, a hundred or so liberal arts colleges, twice that many Bible colleges, scores of seminaries, foreign mission boards, evangelistic organizations, campus ministries, magazines, publishing firms, hundreds of radio and television stations and independent programs (with a combined weekly audience of some 129 million),[43] professional groups for doctors, lawyers, business men, the military, Bible study organizations, Bible conferences and camps. The evangelical world also includes powerful, magnetic personalities with driving visions: Pat Robertson, Robert Schuller, Bill Gothard, Francis Schaeffer, Jimmy Swaggart, Oral Roberts, Charles Colson, Chuck Swindoll, John Perkins, James Kennedy, James Dobson. The range of evangelical belief and practice is so broad that few conceivable interest groups are left unattended. One can join an evangelical church of thousands or a house church; enjoy music that ranges from Andre Crouch to Bob Dylan to Bill Gaither to J. S. Bach; take social ethics from John Howard Yoder or Harold Criswell; learn psychology from Robert Schuller, Jay Adams, or Paul Vitz; learn about the role of women from Phyllis Schlafly, Elisabeth Elliot, or Virginia Mollenkott; imitate the lifestyle of the Fellowship of Christian Athletes or the Sojourners Community; vote with the politics of Jesse Helms, Mark Hatfield, or Jesse Jackson. Such radical pluralism involves a healthy measure of entrepreneurial activity and is especially adapted to the task of spreading a movement across class and cultural boundaries. This enables evangelicals to meet a broad range of ideological, psychological, and social needs and to draw adherents from the widest possible backgrounds.

Yet for all this success at a popular level, evangelicals have failed notably in sustaining serious intellectual life. They have nourished millions of believers in the simple verities of the gospel, but have abandoned the universities, the arts, and other realms of "high" culture. Even in its more progressive wing, evangelicalism has little intellectual muscle. Feeding the hungry, living simply, and banning the bomb are tasks not inherently more intellectual than winning souls. Evangelicals have only begun to span the yawning chasm between modern modes of thinking and the safe and comfortable world view of evangelical congregations— mores that have changed little in the last century.

Part of the reason is institutional. Evangelicals spend enormous sums of money on higher education. But the diffusion of resources among hundreds of colleges and seminaries means that almost none can begin to afford a research faculty, theological or otherwise. The problem is compounded by the syndrome of the reinvented wheel. Democratic authority figures such as Bill Bright, Oral Roberts, Jerry Falwell, and Jim Bakker all assume that no education that has gone before is capable of meeting the demands of the hour. Despite the absence of any formal educational credentials, each man presumes to establish a genuinely Christian university. Small wonder that evangelical thinking, which once was razor-sharp and genuinely profound, now seems dull, rusty, even banal.

The net effect is that evangelical experience over the last fifty years has been schizophrenic, knowing extremes of strength and weakness. Within their own walls evangelicals have never seemed stronger; yet outside those walls the juggernaut of secularism rolls on, conquering position after strategic position—outposts abandoned by evangelicals years ago. When aroused by these reverses, evangelicals can only react by rallying the troops already within the walls. Those who most vigorously protest the danger of "secular humanism" are often least capable of winning the right to be heard by twentieth-century intellectuals. By continuing to exploit what they do best, reaching people at large, and continuing to abdicate what they pursue awkwardly, the life of the mind, evangelicals must sooner or later face the spector of Pyrrhic victory. The vitality of evangelical life does little to reverse the pervasive secularization of American thought—a current that undercuts the foundation while evangelicals are admiring the fine job of decorating being done on the third floor. "The problem is not only to win souls but to save minds," Charles Malik said prophetically to evangelicals at the dedication of the Billy Graham Center. "If you win the whole world and lose the mind of the world, you will soon discover you have not won the world. Indeed it may turn out that you have actually lost the world."[44]

Chapter 7

AN AMERICAN EVANGELICAL THEOLOGY: THE PAINFUL TRANSITION FROM *THEORIA* TO *PRAXIS*

DAVID F. WELLS

AN AMERICAN EVANGELICAL THEOLOGY? This is not a proposition to which evangelicals give willing consent very easily. Evangelicals have largely assumed that their theology has a timeless quality to it, that it is applicable to all people, ages, and cultures in the same way. To qualify such a theology by the word *American* implies a limitation to that theology. It appears as if there might be a multitude of evangelical theologies, each with only a limited geographical significance. The absolute, universal character of evangelical theology appears to have been betrayed. Such a betrayal repeats the very mistake the Protestant liberals made. In the end, it was not merely a universal theology that they surrendered through their infatuation with the "Christ of culture," but it was Christianity itself, and that is one thing that evangelicals are intent on avoiding.[1]

It is ironic, however, that some of those who are most fiercely resistant to the thought of contextualization are nevertheless unwitting exponents of their own form of "cultural-Protestantism."[2] Their faith is sometimes an unconscious amalgam of biblical teaching and cultural norms; their teaching resonates all too comfortably with the secular society of which they are also most critical.

The issue, therefore, is not whether our theology is going to be related to its own context and culture. The issue, rather, is whether we will or will not be self-critical about our theology, whether its contextualization will be deliberate and controlled or whether it will be haphazard and unconscious. It is a choice between paying the initial price which careful reflection exacts or paying the cost which a later bastardized faith will certainly demand.

CONTEXTUALIZATION: THE UNWELCOME TASK

In the twentieth century, evangelical theology has been largely unwilling, and at times unable, to deal with the question of contextualization. There are three main reasons for this: these are to be found, first, in its immediate history, second, in its theological form, and third, in its hermeneutics.

First, the immediate history that frames the question of contextualization is, of course, that of Protestant liberalism. There were, to be sure, different forms of liberalism, as Kenneth Cauthen[3] has suggested, but they were united under a common name because of the relationship they forged between Christ and culture.[4] It was not a relationship favored in any way by the fundamentalists. Harry Emerson Fosdick might claim that it was possible simultaneously to be "seriously modern" and "seriously Christian," but his claim was immediately jeopardized by his persistent habit of criticizing biblical faith in the light of modernity. It was, as a matter of fact, what evacuated liberalism in general of any serious claim to being Christian. Its oscillation between the poles of Christ and culture and its constant harping upon relevance are what, from a fundamentalist viewpoint, invalidated it permanently. To talk about contextualization seems, therefore, to ask for a return to this discredited interest.

Second, evangelical theology is constitutionally disinclined to deal with the issues raised by contextualization. This is so because as a theology it is, for soteriological reasons, constructed to reinforce the *discontinuity* between God and human nature. The *sola gratia, sola fide* motifs are structurally central because there is an epistemological disjunction between God and human nature which is the outgrowth of the disjunction between nature and grace. This in turn becomes part of a world sharply distinguished into natural and supernatural. It is a world view that easily accommodates a high Christology—perhaps even an Alexandrian Word-flesh model—and articulates it in terms of an intrusion of an other-worldly reality into the space-time world. For the same reasons, it believes easily in miracles and argues insistently for the necessity of divinely initiated special revelation, for if God does not disclose himself supernaturally he will not be found at all in a saving way within nature. This, in turn, lends itself to the idea that human nature itself is dualistically oriented, part relating to that divine reality which is absolute and the other part relating to that created reality which is relative, although evangelical theology does not require this. It nevertheless sees its object as knowing the absolute, transcendent God, and this is often pursued in defiance of the world that is shifting, changing, and relative. Consequently, Christ is often divorced from culture. Theology is seen to yield a kind of universal, transcendent knowledge that encompasses all cultures but is localized in none in particular.

This is, to be sure, only a rough sketch of the generic structure of evangelical theology. Different evangelical theologies articulate these themes with different degrees of conviction and stringency. Contextualization, however, remains a problem to all of them because in the translation of divine revelation into the language of a particular social structure and culture, the relative always threatens to consume the absolute, the God who is transcendent always begins to appear merely immanent, the supernatural always appears to be no different from the natural. And thus evangelical theology appears to be no different from liberal theology.

The third difficulty is a hermeneutical one. Historically, it emerged with the demise of the New England theology and the development of those theological systems that took its place. In 1880 advocates of the New England theology held forth at most of the major seminaries: at Andover, there was Edwards A. Park; at Yale, Samuel Harris; at Oberlin, James Fairchild; and at Chicago, George Boardman. By the turn of the century they were all gone, all replaced by men of liberal persuasion. The New England theology died with unkind abruptness. "In the night," said Frank Foster, "it perished from off the face of the earth."[5] Its demise also represented the end of the last indigenous theology that could be called, even loosely, evangelical. As such, the New England theology was also a model of the perils potential in such an understanding. It died because it had become too modern, too American. Its advocates rendered their own Calvinism so harmless that it was no longer worth believing. Predestination was simply a divine eccentricity that could be tolerated as a form of odd but benign knowledge in God; original sin was treated patronizingly; regeneration disappeared beneath the heavy psychological and moral apparatus designed to explain it; and grace yielded before American democratic impulses that to each is given an inherent capacity to vote for or against God. In its old age the New England theology was a clear case, as Joseph Haroutunian put it, of "the faith of the fathers [being] ruined by the faith of the children."[6]

The responsibility for articulating an evangelical orthodoxy now passed to the Princeton theologians and, in time, to the confessional theologians and the proponents of fundamentalism. In retrospect, what is extraordinary is that as different as these theologies were in their details, they were as one in their conception of what theology was. They assumed that theology was concerned solely with explicating the substance of biblical revelation, and as such the results would be timeless and culture-free. The new direction insisted on emancipating theology from its cultural context rather than anchoring that theology in it.

It is perhaps an exaggeration to claim that Scottish common sense realism was, single-handedly, responsible for this situation. Indeed, it would be extraordinary if it were, since this philosophy was already struggling for survival on university campuses even before the turn of the century. Nevertheless, its assumptions have continued to be believed and refined within evangelicalism.[7] They have been handed down from one generation of theologians to another without challenge or interruption. This means that evangelical theology in the twentieth century has been remarkably uniform in its conception. And what has this conception been like?

First, Scripture is the normative source for theology and, as such, it must determine both the form and substance of one's theology. This is, of course, precisely what one would expect of any theology that is evangelical. What is unusual is the way in which this assumption has worked. For evangelical theologians have often assumed that the teaching of Scripture is as amenable to objective understanding as the natural world is to the scientist's knowledge of it. Not only so, but the truth so grasped is as endurable and as unchanging as the laws that rule nature and that the scientist uncovers. It therefore follows that just as the laws of gravity will always mean the same thing and function in the same way throughout the world, so theology can be crystallized into a set of propositions that will be universally applicable in all situations in the same way.

It is this assumption, of course, that led the Princetonians to develop their conception of theology along lines that paralleled work in the natural sciences. The theologian has "facts" to discover and explain just as the scientist does. Theology, said Charles Hodge, is "the science of the facts of divine revelation so far as those facts concern the nature of God and our relation to him. . . ."[8] But Hodge was not alone in this. Dispensationalist Lewis Sperry Chafer defined theology as the "collecting, scientifically arranging, comparing, exhibiting, and defending of all facts from any and every source concerning God and his works."[9] Within Wesleyanism E. H. Bancroft spoke of it as "the science of God and of the relations between God and the universe."[10] H. O. Wiley, writing from an Arminian perspective, declared that the biblical revelation is "the source of the facts out of which systematic theology is constructed,"[11] the church being called upon to order those facts for the good of Christian life.

It follows from this that the proper audience for theology is the church and the form in which theology should present itself is doctrinal. Theology is thus the crystallization of divine truth into systematic form. Because it is *divine,* as Lutheran Theodore Mueller put it, "every possibility of doctrinal progress or development is therefore excluded."[12] Because it is *truth,* it is "held with certainty,"[13] Chafer asserted. F. Pieper, a traditional Lutheran, said that it cannot become confused with the theologian's ego or, one might also add, with the theologian's culture.[14] It has its own laws, said Presbyterian J. Oliver Buswell, and the theologian merely observes these, confident that their observation will yield doctrinal fidelity to God's truth.[15]

The second assumption common to most twentieth-century evangelical theologies concerns cognition. It has been widely assumed that reason is the factor that is largely dominant in cognition, that perhaps it is the exclusive factor, and that reason applied to the analysis of Scripture yields absolute results. As it turned out, this assumption coincided with that made in common sense realism. This philosophy argued the point that the mind was not, as Kant had proposed, an obfuscating filter interposed between the sensory world and our knowledge of it. If that were the case, then all we would know would be the yield of our own minds. This was seen—not without cause—as the first step into skepticism. The reply, therefore, was that the sensory world resonates with the perceiving mind such that what is known is not the mind but the world itself. When applied to the theological task, this assumption meant that a theology might be conceived within a specific culture but that it could be no more bounded by that culture than was God himself. Because reason is an absolute medium of communication, when it is in union with God's Word, its results are not time-bound. A theology so conceived addresses no culture in particular; it is theology for all seasons, for all times, for all people.

Theology is the "science of God," William Shedd declared, and it therefore aims at a knowledge that, quite unlike our knowledge of life, is "free from contradictions."[16] How can this be? The answer, according to E. H. Bancroft, is that "God is brought into actual contact with the mind" so that Scripture "reproduces in our minds the ideas with which the minds of the writers were at first divinely filled."[17] Alternatively, as Buswell argued, revelation confirms the laws of reason such that their essential compatibility is manifested in the process of knowing. Revelation, he says, explicitly conveys and verifies the laws of reason.[18] Revelation and reason, therefore, relate to one another, in his view, as the proverbial hand does to the glove.

A. H. Strong, a leader among Northern Baptists at the turn of the century, was an exception to this kind of understanding, at least in part. He was willing to affirm that "the laws of our thought are laws of God's thought and that the results of normally conducted thinking with regard to God correspond to the objective reality."[19] At the same time he did concede that "all knowledge is relative to the knowing agent; that is, what we know, we know not as it is objectively but only as it is related to our senses and faculties."[20] This was not, however, a concession that changed the shape of his theology. He still believed that reason could, in fact, arrive at a full and accurate understanding of God's truth.

These assumptions were regarded as self-evident truths. To most evangelical theologians in this century, the proposal that a person might be socially conditioned against "seeing" God's truth the way it is had seemed as unpromising a line of thought as to suggest that scientists with a predisposition not to find gravity in nature may in fact be able not to find it!

It is important to identify clearly what is at issue. The issue is not whether Hodge, Warfield, and Shedd were correct in their view of the nature of Scripture as inspired. The use of the word *evangelical* is meaningless if it can be used to encompass theological approaches that are at odds with the general outlook represented by these theologians. What is at stake is the *hermeneutics*. It is not a literary hermeneutics; it is philosophical. Is our knowledge of God as absolute, as culture-free as these theologians sometimes supposed? And should theology conceive of its task as finding cognitive emancipation from the world, or should it seek apologetic involvement in it even at the risk of violating its epistemological trust constituted by the truth of God's Word?

CONTEXTUALIZATION: THE INESCAPABLE RESPONSIBILITY

The theme of contextualization was first given visibility in 1972 in the World Council of Churches publication *Ministry in Context*. Shortly after that, in 1974, the Lausanne Congress on World Evangelization gave some attention to the relationship of gospel and culture. The Lausanne Congress was largely interested in missionary work in non-Christian countries, but four years later a conference held under the auspices of the Lausanne Committee for World Evangelization took up the issue more broadly and not least as it is encountered in the "sending" countries of the West.[21] Despite this interest, contextualization still inhabits the nether regions of evangelical discussion. It has been left to flit from footnote to footnote like some kind of disowned and disembodied ghost. The time to secure for it solid lodging in our discussion is more than ripe.

DEFINING CONTEXTUALIZATION

What is meant by *contextualization?* The answer, of course, is that it means entirely different things depending on whether the theological structure in which it is conceived sees the biblical Word of God as functionally authoritative or not. The attitude taken on how Scripture should function[22] leads to different understandings of what contextualization should mean. These approaches have been designated "accommodational-prophetism" and "accommodational-apostolicity" or, more simply, "existential" and "dogmatic."[23]

In the one case, the socio-political context is allowed to set the parameters for what Christian faith can mean.[24] The interpreter's pre-understanding, resulting from his or her experience within a particular social order, is allowed to prescribe the cognitive horizon beyond which the affirmations of the biblical revelation are not allowed to venture.[25] This approach, it seems clear, allows each situation to bring the biblical revelation into captivity to the obedience of its own sociological norms. Examples of this are not difficult to find in the variety of ethnic and liberation theologies that are sprouting in Asia, South America, and North America. Examples can also be found, however, in the utterances of the Christian New Right, despite the strong anticultural bias of its fundamentalism.[26]

This new "Babylonian captivity"—political in nature now rather than ecclesiastical, as it was in Luther's day—is obviously an outgrowth of the direction contemporary Western theology has taken, especially in its assumption that the interpreter is in some way emancipated from the controls of the biblical text.[27] This supposition, present in Dilthey and Kähler, was reshaped by Bultmann and Gadamer and was the common assumption in the New Hermeneutic.[28] In whatever form it is employed, it leads to a situational limitation on what truth may mean. It assumes that truth is necessarily the by-product of the existential dialogue between text and context. In the process, all too often, revelation is collapsed into reason, the particularity of Jesus Christ into general history, theology into culture, and faith into ethics. Carl Becker's dictum "everyone his own historian" is now paralleled within the sociological verities of each particular situation.

Where the normative function of Scripture is recognized, however, *contextualization* takes on an entirely different meaning, because the cognitive horizon of the interpreter must, in the nature of the case, be prescribed for him or her by the meaning of the biblical revelation. Thus it is that the modern world, rather than the biblical text, is what is unmasked and demythologized. The interpreter is emancipated not from the objective text but from the cognitive and psychological determinants of modernity. The biblical Word limits what the modern world can say; the modern world does not limit what God can say.

In this conception, then, contextualization is the process whereby what Scripture is discovered to mean through historical-grammatical exegesis is reaffirmed in ways that are native and germane to a particular culture. What Scripture says must be so translated that it is clear what it now means[29] in relation to behavioral patterns (such as social structures and organizations, family life, the exigencies of urban dwelling, the legal system, government, and industry) and to presuppositions (including the question of world views, the derivation of ethical values, the functioning of the cognitive process, linguistic forms, and motivational factors). What is required is not merely a practical application of biblical doctrine but a translation of that doctrine into a conceptuality that meshes with the reality of our social structures and the patterns of life dominant in contemporary life.

THE NECESSITY OF CONTEXTUALIZATION

Why, we need to ask, has the need for contextualization become more evident in recent years? In reply to this question, I should note immediately that the secularization of American life and the massive reorganization that industrialization has produced have together put severe strains on the country's Judaeo-Christian values. In what sense America ever was a "Christian country" can be debated, but it is certainly true that the Judaeo-Christian world view that has significantly determined the shape the culture has taken is now often a stranger in the culture it helped form. There are undoubtedly differences among evangelicals concerning the depth and extent of the secularizing phenomenon, but it is now inescapable that there is often as little understanding of the Christian *kerygma* in contemporary American society as there is in lands formally designated as part of the mission field. Evangelical theology, therefore, now finds itself as much in a cross-cultural situation as do many missionaries in other parts of the world.

Not only is this true, but it needs to be noted, secondly, that the formal functioning of evangelical theology is undergoing changes. One notes, for example, that the traditional alliance between philosophy and theology is breaking down sufficiently to allow for sociological insight to be incorporated in theological understanding. It was, of course, Karl Marx who pioneered the idea that culture determines individual perception, that social relationships create consciousness.[30] This approach to human understanding need not be allied, as it was in Marx's case, to atheism and an historical determinism. Without these encumbrances, it has yielded valuable insights, for example, in the work of Emile Durkheim, Peter Berger, and Jacques Ellul. From a theological point of view, it requires the recognition that reason is not an antiseptic tool that functions simply in terms of itself, that social structures implant in the members of society needs and functional norms that are often unexamined. These structures demand of contemporary people secular modes of behavior that almost become the *sine qua non* for being recognized as normal, functioning beings in society. These conditions of "belonging" bring with them a preunderstanding of reality, the cognitive horizon of which is substantially different from that of the biblical revelation. Theology, therefore, cannot address itself to people as if they were aliens in their own society.[31]

The clearer picture that is emerging of the shaping potential on the individual of each receptor-culture coincides, as it turns out, with comparable findings that have emerged within the field of biblical studies. By evangelical consensus, biblical revelation is transcultural in its content and intent; but it was, nevertheless, written within specific contexts and within their language, conceptuality, and social customs. Therefore, there is indeed a "revelatory trajectory" that requires the interpreter to discover the substance of that revelation in the original culture and to deliver it to the receptor-culture in which it is to be located. God's revelation therefore has to be decontextualized with respect to its *terminus a quo* and recontextualized for arrival in its *terminus a quem*.

On both ends of this trajectory there are questions to be addressed that earlier evangelical theology either failed to see or to which it gave insufficient attention. What biblical revelation meant in its original context is not so simple a matter as stumbling on the facts of nature.[32] What it now means is not self-evident in a culture whose cognitive horizon is quite different from that in which the revelation was originally given. For these reasons the task of contextualizing is a responsibility which is inescapable.

This call for a contextualized theology fits closely with the whole enterprise implicit in this volume. Cultural history ought to be a major component of an evangelical theological outlook. Not only must evangelicals be trained to understand the content of God's revelation, but they also should expend some comparable effort to understand the culture they propose to address. For foreign missions, an understanding of the cultural context in which one is to work is a *sine qua non* for effective work. The same should be true for evangelical Christianity at home, for the theologian, pastor, and layperson alike. An evangelical theology, then, must involve a serious study of one's culture and its history. In the American case, it should involve especially a consideration of how evangelicalism has fit into the culture and the ways the culture may have already reshaped the gospel. Moreover, the theological needs of a people may be illuminated by an appreciation of the cultural forces that shape their lives.

It is, of course, true that evangelical theology, because of its soteriological concern, is disinclined to engage in this kind of cultural analysis. It is more inclined to speak of the antitheses of nature and grace, Christ and culture, and to focus its attention upon what is divine, absolute, and unchanging. It is important to remember, however, that a biblical view of creation and natural revelation also inclines theology toward an engagement with culture. Psychologically, evangelicalism is drawn toward an other-worldly dimension, but some of the theological elements it affirms require of it a this-worldly involvement. For evangelicalism has seldom shown any interest in that kind of Barthian radicalism that denies natural revelation, rendering creation mute and meaningless prior to divinely given insight. Rather, it has always insisted that there is a common revelatory thread that binds together all people in all times, whose presence allows for the possibility of Christian discourse in all places and in the midst of vastly different cultural situations. This revelation, which is epistemological and moral in nature, is the foundation on which the contextualization of special revelation occurs.

There is an odd paradox that surfaces at this point, one that reveals itself intermittently throughout evangelical thought, experience, and practice. By its very structure, evangelicalism finds itself both affirming and denying culture, stressing both its continuity with and discontinuity from the world. It expresses its guardianship over creation and affirms its own expulsion from the course of life in a fallen world. It is disenchanted with society, and yet it is fiercely committed to preserving society from that moral dissolution which is the inevitable consequence of being fallen. It recognizes the intrinsic value of human life, but it recoils from the perversion of nature it finds in each person. The pendulum has tended to swing from side to side, touching first one set of antitheses and then the other. The design of churches, for example, has tended to oscillate between affirming the church's compatibility with nature and society and denying it, in which case the buildings become jarring (and oftentimes ugly) reminders that they have nothing in common with the world around them. A period of intense involvement in evangelism at the price of social involvement may be followed by a period of energetic involvement in society at the cost of a matching interest in evangelism. Church life itself goes through these cycles. A phase that is dominated by a proliferation of taboos against contact with the world may be followed by one in which even the most dubious joys of the world are readily sanctioned in the name of a biblical doctrine of creation!

These oscillations are far easier to understand than they are to endure. They have the power to wrench apart the fabric of Christian life as well as the garment of Christian doctrine. They sow disorder, confusion, and disillusionment. They should not occur. But the paradox should not be resolved. And it certainly should not be resolved in favor of one set of antitheses over the other. For God's own relationship to the world is steadily and unchangingly bipolar, in part characterized by his continuity with it and in part by his discontinuity from it.

In the fundamentalism of the early twentieth century, the pendulum swung far to the side of antithesis. It was fundamentalism *contra mundum.*

As we have seen, most evangelical theology that followed emphasized this same element and saw itself as being, in both a good and bad sense, other-worldly. The corrective to this rather strident expression of antithesis is not, however, so violent a form of compensation that all discontinuity is lost in continuity and a new form of liberalism is born in the process. The answer is an honest, careful, and self-critical process of evaluation in which the proper relationship between these elements is restored under the controls of Scripture.

This is nowhere more necessary than in the powerful shaping forces that have been created by our technology, our urbanization, and our mass media. Technology, as Jacques Ellul has cogently argued, is the metaphysic of the twentieth century; to be part of its life is to be encompassed by a view of reality that is secular and humanistic. Cities participate in this and have additionally demanded of us massive shifts in family life and daily routine. And the mass media blare forth these changes, transforming them into "transcendent" values and creating for them an aura of normality and acceptability. But these values are neither normal nor acceptable. They raise the question for us, sharply and insistently, of what it means to be Christian in our modern industrialized, urbanized, and secularized society. Where is the line between involvement and disengagement, acceptance and denial, continuity and discontinuity, being "in" the world and not being "of" the world?

Contextualization is the process through which we find answers to these questions. The Word of God must be related to our own context in such a way that its identity as divine revelation is authentically preserved while its relation to contemporary life is fully worked out. The preservation of its identity is necessary for Christian belief; its contemporary relevance is required if Christians are to be believable. God's Word has this bipolarity in it. It is at the same time other-worldly and this-worldly. And we should be, too.

Chapter 8

EVANGELICALS, HISTORY, AND MODERNITY

GEORGE MARSDEN

FACING EACH OTHER ACROSS THE CAMPUS of Wheaton College in Illinois stand two of the architectural wonders of the American evangelical world—Blanchard Hall and the Billy Graham Center. Dominating the landscape from the top of the ridge is Blanchard Hall, the "old main" of the campus, named for Wheaton's crusading founder, Jonathan Blanchard. Blanchard Hall appears to be a Victorian conception of a medieval fort. Towers and parapets abound. The statement this structure makes architecturally bears on the topic of evangelicals and modernity: one of the major themes in the American evangelical stance toward modern culture has been militancy. From Jonathan Blanchard's antislavery, anti-Masonic, anti-Sabbath-breaking crusades to the forays of fundamentalists against modernist theology and selected modern social trends, one attitude of evangelicals toward modernity has been to make war on it. As Timothy Smith has often reminded us, not all evangelicals were fundamentalists—not even all were Wheaton graduates. But whether we are talking about holiness groups, black Bible-believers, Southern Baptists, Lutherans, or Anabaptists, the same theme recurs, though with differing expressions: believers must be on guard because they are at war with modernity.

If we look to the base of the ridge, however, to the Billy Graham Center, we get a very different architectural message. The architectural style of the Billy Graham Center may be best described as "colossal colonial." The colonial motif suggests peacefulness, harmony, and tranquillity toward the culture. These themes suggest nonmilitant stances toward culture, at least toward early modern culture. Such nonmilitancy is also found flourishing throughout most of the spectrum of evangelical-ism, except among many blacks and some Anabaptists (I guess there are few black churches with colonial architecture). This theme, suggested by the colonial architecture of so many evangelical (and for that matter, liberal) churches is that Christianity ought properly to be at harmony with American life. For many evangelicals, it also represents a lost ideal—or, more accurately for them, an ideal that is slipping. This ideal, like much of the architecture, is bigger than life. America is the outgrowth of a golden age when her institutions were founded on the Bible. Colonial America embodied Christianity in its pristine condition before the Fall. Never mind the Enlightenment. Never mind the secularism and the materialism of the eighteenth century. Just as the classical motifs of Jefferson's architecture—writ large—are appropriated as the ideal for many conservative churches, so the American way of life as conceived by the Founding Fathers is viewed as drawn from Holy Scripture. This response to modernity, then, posits a lost golden age—usually lost only recently, in the past twenty or thirty years—whose harmonies of Christi-anity and the American way of life evangelicalism still represents.[1]

Occasionally, as in the past few years, this colonial model has been offered as a basis for a political agenda, as opposed to simply a peacefully harmonious alternative to the disharmonies of modernity. In this political guise the classical themes are combined with the militant; some secular-ists who take the rhetoric seriously even seem ready to believe that the basements of the colonial churches will be—like the Catholic churches reputedly were in earlier times—filled with guns. That the two themes suggested by our architectural examples tend to merge should not be surprising. After all, these architectural prototypes (these evangelical coun-terparts to the Platonic ideal forms) are on the same campus. The fortifications of Blanchard Hall are, after all, nonfunctional; and one can also see in that building, especially on a football afternoon, the quaint harmonies of the "old main" in a college town—in perfect peace with its surroundings. So evangelicals waver between the two poles rather than consistently embracing one or the other. Sometimes they state that to be Christian means to be at war with modernity; at other times it is the only key to living at peace with the American way of life.[2]

Central to each of these contrasting evangelical stances toward modernity is a view of history. Most people do not think that they think about history, and thus they are seldom aware of the degree to which their perceptions—and hence their practical actions—are shaped by historical theories. We can perceive the force of historical theories if we look again at the two views of culture introduced through our architec-tural examples. The stance of being at war with modernity has been shaped typically in American evangelicalism by millennial views of history. On this point, it makes little difference whether one was a fighting postmillennialist (as was Jonathan Blanchard) or a fighting premillennialist (as were his fundamentalist progeny). In either case, the view of history said that the approach of the millennium would be accompanied by convulsions, upheavals, and warfares that would demand taking sides and taking up arms, at least spiritually. Moreover, the dispensational view of the millennium that won the day in most of fundamentalism and Pentecostalism posited a more definite view of historical interpretation. Taking a stance almost exactly opposite to what prevailed among nineteenth- and twentieth-century academics, dispensationalists denied that history was best understood as gradually evolving natural cultural forces. Rather, said the dispensationalists, all that is significant about history can be found in the Bible. There the pattern of history of all the coming ages was written in advance. Modern cultural history is of almost no help in understanding ourselves, the church, or our spiritual mission. Modern history is of interest only as it produces some facts that document the cultural decline predicted in the Bible. God is entirely in control of history, and we can do little more than believe, preach the gospel, shun evil, and wait for God to act. The present is the church age when, as in the New Testament, we should regard the surrounding culture as Babylon.[3]

But another view of history, as we have already seen from our colonial architectural examples, has been an even more powerful force throughout the experience of most of white evangelicalism in America. In this view, America is God's chosen nation—the covenanted people, as the Puritans suggested. This view is drawn from the Old Testament and is directed toward culture-building rather than culture-avoiding. America, says this covenantal view, has been blessed with prosperity because she has been an essentially Christian nation.

In this latter, covenantal, or Christian-America view, some knowledge of cultural history is far more important than it is in the dispensationalist view, which wants to skip the past two thousand years and get back to the New Testament. In the covenantal or Christian-America view, it is important to be constantly measuring the spiritual health of the nation, especially by comparing the alarming present to the idyllic past. Sermons and treatises in this tradition hence are sometimes filled with history—facts from the American past. History, in this instance, provides examples or precedents to document the Christian character of the tradition. So we hear repeatedly, for instance, of how Benjamin Franklin, George Washington, or Thomas Jefferson made this or that positive statement about God, prayer, or the Bible.

The view of history here reflected is probably the most common one found in human cultures. History is a collection of useful myths—

that is, selected truths and half-truths—that define the identity of a people, establish a model that they ought emulate, and hence legitimate present action.

Recently the character of this widespread view of history was brought home to me by a visiting colleague, John Ngusha Orkar, who was presenting his research on the history of his own Tiv tribe in Nigeria. The Tiv have well-kept oral traditions concerning their ancestry. Each Tiv subgroup can trace its ancestry back to the same individual, who lived about A.D. 1500. In reality, Doctor Orkar's research shows, almost all these groups actually were assimilated into the Tiv and have adopted a version of the Tiv ancestral mythology as a way of establishing their identity and legitimacy.[4]

The case of the evangelical Christian-America use of history is strikingly parallel. Evangelicalism, although made up of many subgroups, is an essentially assimilative tribe in America. Distinguished from most religious groups in history in that it lacks the cohesion of a single ethnic identity (although it tends to be Northern European), it uses history to establish a religious-national identity. These historical myths also present a model for present action. So it has even been suggested that evangelical historians should not expose the historical fallacies of the mythology of the movement, when these beliefs are so important to present concerns. One editor recently went so far as to suggest that if it is not true that America's heritage is substantially Christian, then Christians might just as well turn the solutions of the nation's problems over to the secular humanists.[5]

*   *   *   *

Most people with contemporary historical sensibilities find either of the two evangelical views we have discussed—the dispensationalist and the Christian-America view—unsatisfactory and even implausible. In fact, many such people have seen these strange views of history as evidences of a deeper problem with evangelicalism: that it demands some essentially premodern beliefs, beliefs that people should get past when they get a proper education. Pivotal in the outlooks that would relieve people of their naive evangelicalism, says this view, is a *contemporary* sense of history. This issue of the nature of history is so central to understanding the relationship of evangelicals to twentieth-century modernity that we should briefly consider this contemporary view of history and contrast it to the evangelical views we have seen.

In the contemporary view, for the past hundred years, a strong tendency has been to reduce everything to history. Human life is best understood, says the standard wisdom of our academies, by looking at the natural-cultural and psychological processes that have shaped it. Human experience, including religious experience, is a process. The only pattern in history is that it is like a flowing stream, but no one can predict its direction or fathom its ultimate meaning. "Truth," then, is not a fixed entity that could be inscribed in granite; rather, truth is part of the stream itself, a matter determined by social convention.

In this contemporary view of history, moreover, historical knowledge itself is regarded not as the accumulation of fixed documented "facts" but rather as a dialogue between the *evidence* for an event and the present-day interpreters. Twentieth-century moderns accordingly consider themselves twice removed from the event itself. *Their* common sense tells them not to stake one's life on something so tenuous as the authenticity of ancient events, let alone on events that claim supernatural authentication.

Such contemporary views of history have conflicted most sharply, of course, with evangelical views of the Bible. The late nineteenth- and twentieth-century battle for the Bible has been a battle over history.

Probably because of this conflict over applying contemporary historical assumptions to Scripture, twentieth-century evangelicals have developed little sensitivity to contemporary standards of history in general. At least they have hardly applied such contemporary standards to their own traditions any more than they have to the Bible itself. But the fact that evangelicals have usually rejected contemporary standards for understanding the Bible, history, and culture does not mean that their outlook on these subjects has been premodern or lacking in the scientific standards of the modern age. Instead of being premodern, evangelicals have been distinctly early modern. This point is central to any consideration of evangelicals and modernity. Evangelicals are in many respects very modern people. They are among the masters, for instance, of the use of technique—for promotion, advertising, and so forth—in modern culture. But the structures of their thought, aside from biblical influences, are distinctly early modern as opposed to late modern (that is, twentieth-century modern). Evangelicalism as a distinct phenomenon was early modern in its origins and hence early modern in its assumptions. A recent study of John Wesley, for instance, illustrates how one of the central figures in pietistic evangelicalism drank deeply from the waters of Enlightenment intellectual assumptions.[6] Evangelicals have been, on the whole, champions of common sense, empiricism, and scientific thinking. In America even the "folk epistemology"[7] of popular culture involves the simple empiricism of a tradition established in the age of science.

So evangelicals' views of history, like their intellectual assumptions generally, are early modern as opposed to contemporary modern. Specifically, they view history as more or less a Baconian scientific enterprise of gathering and classifying fixed facts. They assume, as early moderns almost always did, that these facts will fit into a larger pattern established by the deity. Furthermore, our examination of the particular facts will confirm our knowledge of the larger pattern. Thus, in the two evangelical views of history with which we began, we find first of all established patterns of modern history derived from a scientific study of Scripture.[8] These overall patterns are the dispensational scheme or the covenantal scheme of observable national blessings or curses resulting from virtue or the lack thereof. Doing recent history, to the extent it is done at all, is basically a matter of collecting and classifying facts that fit the biblically derived pattern. The same mentality is evident in those evangelical histories that deal with current doctrinal disputes by collecting as many instances as possible of revered figures in church history who support one's own position. History is, like early-modern views of law, largely a matter of gathering precedents. It is not, as in contemporary modern history and in academic contemporary thought generally, a matter of tracing the cause and effect relationships in a cultural flow.

These contrasts bring us to our central question. Does evangelicalism somehow commit us to early-modern views of history? The answer in a volume such as this—to avoid building up too much suspense—is clearly no. As David Wells argues forcefully in his essay, we are saying here that evangelicals should engage seriously in cultural history. They should employ the best canons of twentieth-century cultural-historical inquiry to explore the flow of human cultural relationships especially in looking at their own tradition.

But how, then, do these commitments relate to the early-modern thought forms that are such a major part of our evangelical heritage?[9] Does our commitment to contemporary cultural-historical modes of analysis ultimately commit us to thought forms that, when consistently applied, will dissolve the evangelical heritage itself? Clearly those of us who are evangelicals think not. We need, however, to state clearly a principle that will allow us to discriminate between the good and bad features of both contemporary modernity and of early-modern outlooks. Certainly we can appropriate parts of either thought pattern without endorsing the whole. But on what principle do we select?

First of all, we should make a concerted effort to find our principle for discriminating among early-modern and contemporary thought patterns in a standard not drawn directly from either of those recent intellectual heritages. Of course, we will never entirely escape the influences of the thought of our times, even in finding the starting point for our thought. Nonetheless, if we attempt to gain a reference point or framework not drawn directly from the current fashion but from what we understand as God's Word, we have better possibilities for gaining a critical perspective on our age.

The starting point, frame of reference, paradigm, model, or whatever you want to call it, for our view of history should be the Incarnation. This is the point on which Scripture and the whole of Christian tradition centers. The model of God's revelation that we find here should be the model for understanding the rest of history.

What does the Incarnation reveal about history? It reveals that God—as the Bible asserts and the church has always affirmed—can and has entered real human history and can be known through ordinary human events. What does the Incarnation tell us, then, about how to sort out the strengths and weaknesses of early-modern and of contemporary-modern views of history? I see three main points. First, it posits as a fundamental starting point of our thought that the supernatural and the natural are not realms closed off to each other. The transcendent God, the wholly Other, the Creator of heaven and earth, can appear and be known in our ordinary history. With this starting point for our thought, it appears arbitrary and mistaken to accept the intellectual fashion of the past one hundred years or so that our real knowledge is confined to empirical and self-evident data, and that metaphysical data, if we consider it at all, must be placed in a category detached from ordinary historical knowing. Except for some theologians, most contemporary thinkers have simply ignored the metaphysical as inaccessible and started with the premise that nature is all there is. As Carl Sagan starts out, "The cosmos is all that is or was or ever was or ever will be."[10] In this view, because humans are inhabitants of nature and history, the Creator and the supernatural are excluded with such assumptions.

The second point, closely related, is that the early moderns were right on the epistemological point that we can know something of the actual events of the past and that this knowledge is of some eternal significance. These epistemological points, it seems to me, are presupposed by the ordinary understandings of the Incarnation that have prevailed through most of the history of the church. The modern conceit that we are twice removed from the past—that is, we only have interpretations of evidence from the past, but no access to the events themselves—is, it seems to me, too divorced from the commonsense experience of humanity. People in every race and culture, I suppose, except some philosophers and many academics today, have believed that we are equipped with abilities to know about past events. Matters of life and death in courts of law have always been settled on the basis of such belief. Faith in the Incarnation is premised on this basis also—on history, that historical facts can be important. The pre-Kantian early moderns were right on this score, and we evangelicals insist on it: "If Christ be not raised . . . we are of all people most miserable."

Let me add that, although this incarnational model may presuppose something like early-modern commonsense confidence in our abilities really to know something of past events, it does not entail everything else in that epistemology. For instance, it does not entail that we can know the past, even the biblical past, with the precision of an early-modern scientist. On this point Abraham Kuyper has a helpful view. Kuyper's view is helpful especially because he was a transitional figure who also was selecting between early-modern and more contemporary thought forms. Kuyper used an incarnational model for understanding Scripture and insisted that, because of the divine element in producing every word of Scripture, it did not err, even though it might be limited by human thought forms. Kuyper insisted, however, that the divine standards for error, that is, those indicated in Scripture itself, were different from modern human standards. Modern standards, especially early-modern standards, would suggest that errorless reporting would produce accounts that were accurate in the way a photograph is accurate. However, the biblical standard, Kuyper suggests, is more akin to the standard of an impressionistic painter than to that of a photographer. Real events are depicted errorlessly, but in richer tones than those of the unimaginative standards of modern scientific history.[11]

Moreover, we can add, the correctness of the early-modern view that we can know something of real historical events does not entail that we should be able to discern, except in the most general way, the overall patterns of history into which these events fit. Early moderns, having great intellectual confidence, assumed that they could discover complete intellectual systems. Even Isaac Newton spent years trying to reduce biblical prophecy to a system. The evangelical views of history with which we started both had this feature of providing a system into which current events could be fit. Nothing in the incarnational or the biblical model for history, however, entails that we should be able to discover such a neat overview for history. Rather, God's ways in history are often past our knowing, even though we know that God has his ways.

We come now to our third and final implication of the incarnational starting point for understanding history. The first point, that the supernatural need not be excluded from our views of ordinary history, and our second point, that we have access to past events, favored the early moderns—with some qualifications. This last point invites ready use of contemporary tools for historical-cultural understanding. This third point is that the incarnational model suggests that Christians should take ordinary human history with complete seriousness. The Incarnation, as we should understand it, is not docetic. Christ did not just *appear* to be human; so God does not just *appear* to reveal himself in ordinary human cultural and psychological circumstances, languages, and thought forms. Christ is not simply a deity disguised as a human. Neither is the Bible a set of golden tablets dropped from heaven but disguised as human writings. Nor is church history just a work of the Holy Spirit disguised as human cultural activity. History, in all these cases, is really human and, despite its incarnated qualities, ordinary.

Since we are dealing, then, with the ordinary, we should deal with it by using the best tools for ordinary understanding in our times—in this case the tools of contemporary historical-cultural scholarship (minus their naturalistic and skeptical premises). With such scholarship we can find in the Christian past not just a collection of precedents for our current beliefs and programs, but rather we can learn from the marvelously rich complexity of human experience in relation to God. We can find some triumphs and useful precedents, but we can learn much from failures as well. Perhaps more than anything else, if we do ordinary history honestly, we will discover the ironies, paradoxes, and contradictions in the experiences of even the best of God's people. Such examples should remind us all that our only hope is dependence on God's mercy.

Chapter 9

EVANGELICALS AND THE STUDY OF THE BIBLE

MARK A. NOLL

THEOLOGICALLY CONSERVATIVE AMERICAN PROTESTANTS have always nurtured a deep attachment to the Bible, even if it has not always been a particularly academic attachment. Since World War II, however, evangelicals have also acquired widely recognized academic credentials in biblical studies and have taken their place among the sophisticated students of Scripture at large. Much illuminating scholarship has flowed from this recent academic pursuit of Scripture. Yet the emergence of a new day in the study of the Bible among evangelicals has not been without problems—some caused by the engagement with modern scholarship itself and some more deeply rooted in the heritage of evangelical Americans and their traditional attitudes toward Scripture.

To put these more general problems into perspective, I need to sketch the emergence of the academic study of Scripture among evangelicals and to outline briefly the magnitude of the achievement during the last generation.[1]

HISTORY

During the first part of the nineteenth century, with but a very few exceptions like Moses Stuart of Andover Seminary, most of America's handful of academic Bible scholars were Unitarians and transcendentalists who usually lacked evangelical devotion to Scripture.[2] Later in that century, serious academic study of the Bible gained a firmer footing in America as a whole. The Society for Biblical Literature, for example, was founded in 1880. Significantly, however, the rise of a more professional study of the Bible coincided with a critical shift in American higher education. A traditional semi-Christian framework was being replaced by instruction grounded in largely naturalistic assumptions at precisely the time when scholarly study of Scripture began on a large scale.[3] It was thus only exceptional conservatives, like John Broadus, B. B. Warfield, or A. T. Robertson, who moved with ease amidst the new professional study of Scripture.[4] Then in the early years of the twentieth century, controversy between fundamentalists and modernists drove an even larger wedge between pious and academic study of the Bible, especially since fundamentalist leaders attacked the universities and seminaries that had adopted critical approaches to the Bible for hastening both apostasy and the decline of Western civilization.[5] While study of Scripture that was both current in its scholarship and fervent in its piety never entirely ceased, especially among groups that had avoided the fundamentalist-modernist disruption, it was still a rare commodity between the two world wars.

During and after World War II, the rise of a more visible "evangelicalism" encouraged also a quickened biblical scholarship. Dissatisfaction with separatistic fundamentalism led a healthy number of evangelicals to seek graduate education in America's finest universities, especially Harvard, where such well-known leaders as E. J. Carnell, Kenneth Kantzer, Merrill Tenney, Paul Jewett, George Ladd, Glenn Barker, and Samuel Schultz pursued doctoral studies in the 1940s.[6] Two significant books in biblical studies also stood out in this period as heralds of a new day, Ned B. Stonehouse's *The Witness of Matthew and Mark to Christ* (1944) and George E. Ladd's *Crucial Questions About the Kingdom of God* (1952). Stonehouse, the successor of J. Gresham Machen as professor of New Testament at Westminster Theological Seminary in Philadelphia, eschewed forced harmonizations of the synoptic evangelists, set about to wrestle seriously with "the most important questions which have been thrust forward in the modern discussion of the gospels," and argued forcefully for the use of all critical means available to understand the nature, intent, and historical setting of the Gospels.[7] Ladd, who taught at Fuller Seminary and was a graduate of Gordon College as well as Harvard, challenged the dispensational understanding of the kingdom of God and, by implication, the entire uncritical approach in Scripture that had characterized evangelical Protestantism for the preceding two generations.[8]

Even more important than the works of individuals was the emergence of institutions to support biblical scholarship. One of the most significant of these was the confessional Dutch-American publishing network in Grand Rapids, Michigan.[9] Especially crucial was the work of the William B. Eerdmans Publishing Company, which during the 1940s sponsored several competitions with major cash awards in an effort to elicit serious biblical scholarship from conservative Protestants.[10] In 1951 Eerdmans also began to publish a *New International Commentary on the New Testament.* This project, under the editorship first of Ned Stonehouse and then of F. F. Bruce, became a showcase for evangelicals from England, Scotland, Holland, South Africa, Australia, and eventually the United States, to publish critical yet orthodox commentaries in America.[11]

Mention of F. F. Bruce draws attention to perhaps the most momentous institutional developments. In 1936 supporters of Great Britain's Inter-Varsity Christian Fellowship founded the British Theological Students Fellowship in order to encourage evangelical students preparing for academic and clerical careers. Shortly thereafter, the Tyndale Fellowship for Biblical Research came into existence to promote these same goals among professional academics. The Tyndale Fellowship, with its network of scholars united in both technical qualifications and in broadly evangelical convictions, ushered in a new day for conservative Bible scholarship in Britain and greatly influenced the shape of similar scholarship in North America. F. F. Bruce, who eventually became the Rylands Professor of Biblical Criticism and Exegesis at the University of Manchester, was in the forefront of these institutional developments.[12] His first book, a brief examination of the reliability of the New Testament documents prepared for Inter-Varsity groups, appeared in 1943 and was quickly distributed also in the United States.[13] It was the first fruits of a great harvest which once again introduced the kind of reverent critical scholarship to Americans which they had earlier received from Lightfoot, Westcott, and Hort during the second half of the nineteenth century.

THE RECENT ACHIEVEMENT

A reinvigorated evangelical Bible scholarship has been continuing now in North America for more than a generation. Signs of intellectual vigor abound on every hand. Four of these are especially noteworthy.

(1) Evangelicals now are distinguished by superb academic qualifications. Recent catalogues from four of the largest interdenominational evangelical seminaries (Asbury, Fuller, Gordon-Conwell, Trinity) reveal that thirty-four of their thirty-six professors of Bible hold earned university doctorates, many from the great universities of the world (see Table I). Statistical tabulations for many of the evangelical colleges or for other evangelical seminaries are nearly as impressive (see Tables II and III). This rise in professional certification, moreover, has been as recent as it has been rapid. To cite just one instance from the college level, Wheaton did not have a Bible professor with a university doctorate until 1935. By 1952, seven of Wheaton's fifteen Bible professors held university-level doctorates

TABLE I

DISTRIBUTION OF UNIVERSITY DOCTORATES
FROM SELECTED EVANGELICAL SEMINARIES:
ASBURY, FULLER, GORDON–CONWELL, TRINITY

University	New Testament	Old Testament	Other*	Total
Harvard	5	3	1	9
Dropsie		5		5
Brandeis		2	1	3
St. Andrews	2	1		3
Aberdeen	2			2
Cambridge	2			2
Drew		1	1	2
Basel	1			1
Columbia	1			1
Duke			1	1
Emory	1			1
Johns Hopkins			1	1
London	1			1
Manchester	1			1
USC	1			1
Total doctorates	17	12	5	34
Total U.S.	8	11	5	24
Total United Kingdom	8	1	0	9
Total Europe	1	0	0	1
Total faculty	17	13	6	36

*Faculty listed in general biblical studies, without designation of New or Old Testament.

[This information comes from the following catalogues: Asbury 1982–83, Fuller ca. 1980–81, Gordon-Conwell 1982–83, and Trinity 1981–83.]

(three Harvard, one each Dropsie, Johns Hopkins, Chicago, and Princeton Seminary).[14]

The *Word Biblical Commentary*, which began to appear in early 1983, illustrates the kind of professional qualifications that Protestant conservatives can now bring to their work. This series, hailed in its prospectus as "a harvest of biblical scholarship from the evangelical renaissance," has enlisted forty-six scholars from the United States, Canada, the United Kingdom, and Australia. Of these authors, seven hold doctorates from Harvard, nine received their final academic degrees from Cambridge University, and six from the University of London. Others were trained at Oxford, Manchester, the universities of Scotland, and at some of the best American graduate schools. They teach both in North America's foremost evangelical schools and in a wide range of British institutions.[15]

TABLE II
DOCTORATES FOR BIBLE FACULTY[a]
AT COLLEGES OF THE CHRISTIAN COLLEGE CONSORTIUM (1983)[b]

College	Total Faculty	University Doctorates	Seminary Doctorates	Total
Asbury	7	5		5
Bethel	8	4	1	5
George Fox	3	3		3
Gordon	5	4	1	5
Greenville	3	2		2
Houghton	6	1	1	2
Malone	4	2	1	3
Messiah	4	1	1	2
Seattle Pacific	9	7	2	9
Taylor	5	3	1	4
Trinity	4	4		4
Westmont	6	3		3
Wheaton	13	10	3	13
Total	77	49	11	60

[a]Assistant professors or above, listed as teaching Bible, religion, theology, or similar subjects.

[b]Catalogues consulted: Asbury 1980–82, Bethel 1982–83, George Fox 1982–84, Gordon 1982–83, Greenville ca. 1980–81, Houghton 1981–83, Malone 1982–83, Messiah 1982–84, Seattle Pacific 1981–82, Taylor 1981–83, Trinity 1982–83, Westmont 1981–82, Wheaton 1982–83.

(2) Well-trained evangelical Bible scholars have also become increasingly active in the professional activities of their discipline. In recent years something like 10 percent of the participants at the annual meetings of the Society for Biblical Literature can be identified as evangelicals, confessional Protestants, fundamentalists, or Southern Baptists.[16] A similar percentage of the articles appearing in the major journals of the field, like *The Journal of Biblical Literature* and *New Testament Studies*, have come from these same groupings.[17]

(3) Besides this professional activity in the academic world at large, evangelicals have also formed vigorous societies of their own in which to discuss biblical research and related theological issues. The Evangelical Theological Society (founded in 1949) is the oldest of these, but in more recent years it has been joined by the Wesleyan Theological Society, the Institute for Biblical Research (limited to doctoral-level practitioners of biblical study), and the North American Theological Students Fellowship (with connections to American Inter-Varsity).[18]

(4) Evangelical Bible scholars in the last forty years have also produced a tremendously diverse literature on Scripture. In keeping with evangelical traditions, the bulk of this writing has been pastoral, sermonic,

TABLE III
SEMINARY AND UNIVERSITY TRAINING FOR BIBLE PROFESSORS
AT VARIOUS SEMINARIES[a]

Type	Total Faculty	University Doctorates (%)	Foreign (%)	Attended this seminary or sister institution[b] (%)
Evangelical (Asbury, Fuller, Gordon-Conwell, Trinity)	36	34 (94)	10 (29)	14 (39)
Conservative Evangelical (Dallas, Talbot, Grace)	35	7 (20)	4 (57)	30 (86)
Southern Baptist (Southwestern, Southern, New Orleans)	40	7 (18)	2 (29)	36 (90)
Northern Baptist (Eastern, Northern)	6	5 (83)	2 (40)	3 (50)
Conservative Baptist[c] (Denver, Western)	15	4 (27)	2 (50)	4 (27)
Reformed (Westminster, Calvin, Reformed)	15	11 (73)	6 (55)	13 (87)
Adventist (Berrien Springs)	6	5 (83)	0 (00)	6 (100)
Nazarene (Kansas City)	4	4 (100)	1 (25)	2 (50)
Missouri-Synod (St. Louis, Fort Worth)	16	9 (56)	2 (22)	12 (75)
Control (Harvard, Union)	10	10 (100)	3 (30)	0 (00)

[a]Information on the faculties comes from the following catalogues: Asbury 1982–83, Fuller ca. 1980–81, Gordon-Conwell 1982–83, Trinity 1981–83, Dallas 1982–83, Talbot 1980–81, Grace 1982–84, Southwestern 1980–81, Southern 1982–84, New Orleans 1982–83, Eastern 1981–83, Northern 1980–81, Denver 1983–85, Western 1980–81, Westminster 1982–84, Calvin 1981–83, Reformed 1981–82, Adventist 1982–83, Nazarene 1982–83, St. Louis 1980–81, Fort Worth 1980–81, Harvard 1982–83, Union 1982–83.

[b]That is, a member of the same denomination, or for fundamentalists, a closely related school.

[c]Denver (3 of 5 faculty with university doctorates); Western (1 of 10).

and devotional, but from individuals like James Boice, J. I. Packer, and John Stott, such popular exposition carries scholarly value as well. Evangelicals have brought out path-breaking studies on philosophical issues involved in interpreting Scripture, like Anthony Thiselton's *The Two Horizons* (1980). Following in the footsteps of Geerhardus Vos and, more recently, George Ladd, they have produced serious studies in biblical theology, even though this area is not a forte of evangelical study.[19] They have also done widely respected work on the text of Scripture, with the recent work of Gordon-Conwell's Gordon Fee especially worthy of mention. And beginning with the publication in 1951 of F. F. Bruce's *The Acts of the Apostles: The Greek Text with Introduction and Commentary,* evangelicals have produced a distinguished group of academic commentaries to stand alongside the more popular series. Scholars from the British commonwealth like Bruce, I. Howard Marshall, Leon Morris, and Gordon Wenham continue to supply the best such work to American evangelicals, but a growing number, including E. Earle Ellis, William Lane, Richard Longenecker, and Robert Mounce, have made signal contributions from this side of the Atlantic.[20]

YET NOT ALL IS WELL

Evangelicals would be fooling themselves, however, if they assumed that all is well with the study of the Bible today. Serious problems and manifest uncertainties concerning Scripture beset the restricted world of evangelical scholarship.[21] And they are even more obvious in the wider evangelical circles that provide the important contexts for that scholarship.

Evangelical Bible scholars live in Christian communities where fidelity to Scripture is both a badge of honor and an excuse for recrimination. This wider world is one in which dogmatic "separatists" lambaste the inconsistencies of other self-confessed "fundamentalists," who in turn decry the wishy-washiness of "conservative evangelicals," who in their turn snipe at the innovations of "progressive evangelicals," who look down their noses at all of the benighted brethren to their right. And each segment assumes its posture because of the others' purported mistakes in understanding and interpreting the Bible. Evangelicals inhabit a subculture where the Bible is brought to bear with telling force but also with great confusion on issues like divorce and remarriage, economic theory, the Christian character of the United States, the role of women in the church, and interracial marriage. Robert K. Johnston has put the perplexity well: "That evangelicals, all claiming a common Biblical norm, are reaching contradictory theological formulations on many of the major issues they are addressing suggests the problematic nature of their present understanding of theological interpretation. To argue that the Bible is authoritative, but to be unable to come to anything like agreement on what it says (even with those who share an evangelical commitment), is self-defeating."[22] This difficulty is not a new one, as Catholic critics of Protestantism pointed out well before the end of the sixteenth century. But it has been a special problem among American theological conservatives since World War II now that norms of the broader culture no longer reinforce more distinctly biblical ideals in morality or religious conviction.

The general tenor of evangelical appropriation of Scripture also deserves attention. American evangelicals are heir to many good things— dedication in missions and evangelism, forthright social service, sacrificial commitment to their churches. But they are also heir to a long tradition of religious extremism that stretches back to the eschatological conspiracy theories of the American Revolution and also includes substantial evangelical participation in racist, exclusionary, anti-Catholic, and anticommunist hysteria during the nineteenth and twentieth centuries.[23] This tendency to extremism has never been far from the recent history of evangelicals. It appears in the viciousness with which Billy Graham has been assaulted for consorting both with supposed liberals and with Richard Nixon. It is very much a part of the religious right's attack on evolution and secular humanism, and it is present in some progressive evangelical attacks on the far right. It has also affected evangelical approaches to Scripture.

Most obvious is what F. F. Bruce once called the "Maginot-line mentality where the doctrine of Scripture is concerned."[24] That is, American evangelicals have often regarded not only the general truthfulness of Scripture but also particular traditions of its interpretation—whether of Genesis 1–11, the authorship of Isaiah and Daniel, the historicity of the Chronicler, the harmonization of the synoptic Gospels, the authorship of the Pastoral and Petrine Epistles, or the meaning of Revelation 20—with such a heightened seriousness that it becomes psychologically, if not intellectually, impossible to examine alternatives. This spirit, which at its worst shades over into demagoguery, has not been limited to the uneducated or the uninformed. Nor is it the exclusive preserve of either the "evangelical left" or the "evangelical right." It exists wherever blanket condemnations take the place of respectful attention and careful study. Conservative evangelicals testify to its unfortunate effects when they dismiss modern approaches to biblical study out of hand. Progressive evangelicals do the same by heaping scorn on interpretations of Scripture which end by defending capitalism or traditional views of male-female relationships.

Evangelical experiences with Bible translations over the last generation offer sharp examples of the way in which general uncertainties about Scripture affect evangelicals both inside the academy and out. It is easy to write off the most virulent reactions to the publication of the Revised Standard Version in the early 1950s as the manic delusions of a lunatic fringe. To be sure, the preacher who reportedly ignited a copy of the RSV with a blowtorch in his pulpit while declaring that it was just as hard to burn as the devil, as well as those who wrote pamphlets against the RSV with titles like "The Bible of Antichrist" or "The New Blasphemous Bible," were not representative of evangelicals at large.[25] Yet the reactions of more sober-minded, scholarly evangelicals are also open to question. Dissatisfaction with the RSV, particularly for breaking with the King James Version in the translation of Old Testament passages like Isaiah 7:14 and Zechariah 12:10, and for providing new translations of terms referring to the atonement, was widespread among evangelical intellectuals. This dissatisfaction may have had something to do with the revived interest in the New American Standard Bible. It certainly had much to do with the efforts, first of the Christian Reformed Church and then of the National Association of Evangelicals and the New York Bible Society, to develop an entirely new translation, a labor which involved the efforts of 118 evangelical Bible scholars over several years and culminated in the publication of the New International Version.[26] The academic point here is whether the relatively small handful of passages in the RSV to which conservatives objected—and for all of which sound scholarly arguments exist on both sides—justified the launching of translation projects which preoccupied the academic energies of many evangelical scholars for many years.

The piquancy of the situation is sharpened by the fact that the NIV turned out to resemble very closely the RSV, whose malefactions it had come into existence to overcome. As one critic has recently written: "The NIV is closer in style and form to the RSV than to any other English version. It is an irony worth pondering: this Bible came into being as the result of the repudiation of the RSV by the majority of conservative Protestants in this country, and now that it has appeared it closely resembles the RSV. The principles that guided it in textual, exegetical, linguistic and stylistic matters are hardly distinguishable from those which guided the RSV."[27]

An additional paradox is that while evangelical scholars were laboring to prepare a translation correcting the relatively few problems in the RSV, the evangelical world at large took to its heart a translation, *The Living Bible,* that by academic standards is seriously flawed. The difficulty with this version is not the primary responsibility of its paraphraser, Kenneth Taylor; for Taylor has often urged those who read *The Living Bible* to go on to more scholarly translations for their serious study. The problem is rather that evangelicals, who protested so vigorously the transgressions of the RSV as an assault on biblical infallibility, should make a runaway best seller out of a nonscholarly paraphrase rife with eisegesis and marked by considerable disregard for the underlying Hebrew and Greek texts of Scripture.[28]

The positive gains from a renewed evangelical Bible scholarship have been compromised to a certain extent by the kind of instability manifest in responses to modern translations.[29] To put the problem in general terms, the depth of evangelical commitment to the truth-telling and life-giving character of Scripture has not been matched by an equally firm understanding of the relationship between the Bible and modern learning.

Contemporary uncertainties focus on questions of biblical criticism. They can be illustrated by the significant number of scholars who, while defending their right to the name "evangelical," are advocating positions which for decades had been regarded as trademarks of modernism. Five examples from the very recent past suggest the dimensions of the situation.

(1) In 1982, Robert Gundry, a graduate of Los Angeles Baptist College and Seminary and of the University of Manchester, published a literary and theological commentary on the Gospel of Matthew which argues that large sections of this book are the evangelist's own divinely inspired reflections on the meaning of Jesus' ministry, rather than a representation of the actual words and deeds of Jesus.[30] The book has received praise for its industry and ingenuity, but it has also had a curious critical reception. Secular students of the Bible have attacked it for conceding too much to inspiration, evangelicals for using too uncritically the tools of redaction criticism. (Redaction criticism focuses on the work of the biblical authors as editors, or redactors, of their work; some who practice this form of literary reconstruction assume that biblical redactors created stories or sayings to insert in their narratives when it suited their overall editorial purposes.)

(2) Also in 1982, James D. G. Dunn, a prolific British biblical theologian who is a member of the Tyndale Fellowship and who has long associated with British evangelicals, published a learned essay in the *Churchman*, a periodical sponsored by Anglican evangelicals, on "The Authority of Scripture According to Scripture." In this paper Dunn concluded that the commonly accepted evangelical concept of biblical inerrancy is "exegetically improbable, hermeneutically defective, theologically dangerous, and educationally disastrous."[31]

(3) Then in 1983, Bernard Ramm, who with E. J. Carnell and Carl Henry had sparked the postwar renewal in evangelical theology, urged theological conservatives to learn from Karl Barth how to make progress, in the words of his title, *After Fundamentalism*. Ramm especially recommended Barth's full acceptance of the "humanity" of Scripture, a humanity not untouched by foolishness and error, as a means of overcoming the "obscurantism" which, according to Ramm, has plagued evangelicals since the Enlightenment.[32]

(4) In late spring 1983, Gordon-Conwell Seminary accepted the resignation of Professor J. Ramsey Michaels as a result of an inquiry arising from his study of the life of Christ, *Servant and Son* (John Knox, 1981). Among its other conclusions, this book suggested that some of the

actions and words ascribed to Jesus and John the Baptist by the Gospel writers did not occur. In response, a committee of the faculty determined that the way in which the book employed modern theories of biblical interpretation stood in violation of Gordon-Conwell's statement of faith on the errorlessness of the Bible and the divinity of Christ, even though Michaels himself insisted on his loyalty to that statement. Michaels's case is even more poignant because he had taught at Gordon-Conwell for twenty-five years and had propounded in his classes ideas similar to those in *Servant and Son* for much of that time. The situation gives cause to ponder both why a self-professing evangelical would sit so lightly to the historicity of the Gospel narratives and why it took so long for the seminary to be able to interpret its own statement of faith for itself.[33]

(5) Finally, the *Word Biblical Commentary*, the latest and fullest demonstration of maturity in the study of the Bible from an evangelical source, appears ready to employ at least some of the academic resources which evangelicals have long associated with the destructive presuppositions and methods of unbelieving criticism. The early volumes in this series indicate that it may be a perplexing venture to many evangelicals. These first commentaries do include forthright assertions concerning the supernatural character of the teaching and the events of the biblical narratives, but they also accept some conclusions concerning the authorship and the historicity of these same books that evangelicals have usually regarded as dangerously modernistic.

The situation illustrated by these examples has at least two positive and two negative dimensions. Positively, it is gratifying to see evangelicals wrestling so vigorously with the results of modern scholarship. To the extent that this scholarship reflects creative or persistent study of natural and historical phenomena, it should find ready accommodation within traditional conservative theology. Evangelicals have long professed belief in common grace, the principle that God communicates some truth to all humankind, Christian or not, through study of the natural world and of history. In the past, however, a docetic approach to Scripture, which views the Bible as a magical book unrelated to the normal workings of the natural world, has exerted a widespread influence on the evangelical public and has not been entirely absent among evangelical scholars. Such docetism has often made it difficult for evangelicals to see how academic studies of the Bible and its world could contribute to a better comprehension of this intensely spiritual book. Now, however, a greater willingness to appropriate new proposals concerning literary form in the ancient world, to examine recent conclusions by historians and anthropologists about the setting of the Bible, and to countenance modern theories of science, psychology, and sociology as an aid to research suggests that evangelical Bible scholars are translating a formal belief in common grace into productive means for studying Scripture.

This willingness to exploit modern learning points to a second encouraging aspect of recent work on Scripture. It shows that evangelicals may once again be in a position to exercise a proper creativity in their work as the great lights of the church have done throughout the ages. Perceptive evangelical leaders have clearly seen the need for this kind of creativity, as illustrated by Geoffrey Bromiley, who recently called for a less restrictive attitude toward theology:

> The real problem does not lie . . . in the relation of Evangelicalism as such to theological work but rather in a defensive mentality, a fixation on Liberal extravaganzas of speculation, which inhibits the freedom of action in the field. . . . The moment has arrived for a shift of the main enterprise to positive and constructive work . . . which will consider but not let itself be dominated by what others are doing.[34]

John Stott has made a similar appeal:

> We need to encourage Christian scholars to go to the frontiers and engage in the debate, while at the same time retaining their active participation in the community of faith. . . . As part of their own integrity Christian scholars need both to preserve the tension between openness and commitment, and to accept some measure of accountability to one another and responsibility for one another in the Body of Christ. In such a caring fellowship I think we might witness fewer casualties on the one hand and more theological creativity on the other.[35]

Yet if recent evangelical innovations in the study of Scripture can be praised for creativity and a more open response to general revelation, they also reveal a darker side. One of the negative possibilities is the evacuation of meaning from the term "evangelical." If anything goes in the study of the Bible, if there is no practical way to discriminate between believing and unbelieving criticism, then the evangelical reliance on Scripture is itself in doubt. Not all tools of biblical research are used in a neutral manner.[36] Some uses presuppose a universe in which the historic Christian God who speaks, acts, and saves is excluded. As an example, while some evangelicals have been relatively successful in showing how redaction criticism can be used in consort with orthodox views of biblical inspiration, other redaction critics write as if it is a foregone conclusion that incidents in the Gospels sprang exclusively from the minds of the Evangelists. When self-professed evangelicals accept naturalistic presuppositions in biblical research, they subvert their own tradition. The desire to renew the evangelical study of Scripture by paying closer heed to the conclusions of the academic world is a worthy one, especially in light of the disregard for scholarship which has frequently characterized the American evangelical heritage. But to exploit this scholarship without careful discrimination is to darken rather than brighten the future of evangelical Christianity.

The second problem is more general. Evangelicals seem to have few settled coordinates by which to take a fix on modern biblical criticism. The well-articulated theologies of the Reformation age, the orthodoxies of the seventeenth century, and the stately dogmatics of Lutherans, Presbyterians, and Wesleyans in the nineteenth century all provided previous generations of theologically conservative Protestants with a certain measure of ballast, with a relatively secure position from which to deliberate on newer work concerning the Bible. Evangelicals, however, have lacked this kind of theological anchorage for nearly a century. As a result, voices on both sides of the Atlantic have increasingly drawn attention to the striking absence of anything like a secure evangelical standpoint for the modern study of Scripture, and especially for modern criticism. So, according to the Scotsman David Wright, "One of our most urgent unfinished tasks is the elaboration of a satisfactory doctrine of Scripture for an era of biblical criticism. . . . In particular, we have to work out what it means to be faithful *at one and the same time both* to the doctrinal approach to Scripture as the Word of God *and* to the historical treatment of Scripture as the words of men."[37] And for Americans, complete with an unflattering comparison to Karl Barth, are these words of Bernard Ramm:

> [Here is] the primary problem: *there is no genuine, valid working hypothesis for most evangelicals to interact with the humanity of Scripture in general and biblical criticism in particular.* There are only ad hoc or desultory attempts to resolve particular problems. Barth's method of coming to terms with the humanity of the Scripture and biblical criticism is at least a clearly stated program. . . . To date, evangelicals have not announced such a clear working program. If Barth's paradigm does not please them, they are still under obligation to propose a program that does enable an evangelical to live creatively with evangelical theology and biblical criticism.[38]

A further sign of the uncertainty concerning the character and meaning of Scripture is the massive and massively diverse literature of the last decade on the inspiration, inerrancy, infallibility, and authority of Scripture.[39] For every one effort to derive a theology from Scripture for life or thought in the late twentieth century, it seems as if there are several devoted to formal questions of biblical authority. However much at least some of the books and articles in this great outpouring may be necessary to meet a critical need of our time, the suspicion lingers that the net result is an addition of heat rather than light. Only rarely do such works carefully discriminate among the historical, literary, theological, cultural, and hermeneutical dimensions of the issue of biblical authority. A few evangelicals do write on this subject with humility, perspective, creativity, and orthodoxy. Yet tendentiousness, short-sightedness, anti-intellectualism, and a propensity to play to the galleries descend upon the evangelical world in nearly limitless quantities as well. The tragic result is that on this most fundamental issue we often communicate the impression of being wise as doves and innocent as serpents.

EXPLANATIONS

It is not possible here to offer more than tentative explanations for both the signal accomplishments and the manifest uncertainties in the recent study of Scripture by evangelicals. But a few circumstances, both historical and contemporary, may shed light on why we evangelicals deal with the Bible as we do.

These circumstances would include the fact that the separation between the pew and the academy is a broad one for evangelicals. The recent *Christianity Today*-Gallup Poll revealed that more evangelicals believe in biblical inerrancy than actually read the Bible regularly or possess even rudimentary Bible knowledge (e.g., 50 percent of the evangelicals could not name even five of the Ten Commandments).[40] Yet given the democratic dynamics of American church life, it is often the evangelical community at large that is called upon to adjudicate complex debates over the nature of Scripture, especially by bestowing or withholding funds.

Patterns in American education also contribute to the strengths and weaknesses of the evangelical study of Scripture. By comparison to European training in biblical studies, American training is fragmented and diffuse. Aspiring Bible scholars must pursue their studies at different colleges, seminaries, and universities, and under radically shifting sets of critical assumptions.[41] This situation does act as protection against a monopoly by unbelieving instruction. But it also means that evangelicals are always dependent on other institutions for crucial elements in the educational process. The sharpest example of this exists for doctoral studies. Theologically conservative American Protestants have harvested the fruits of liberal scholarship at Harvard and Chicago, of Jewish scholarship at Brandeis and Dropsie, of British scholarship at Manchester and Cambridge; but they have not provided institutions of their own at which to study the Bible at the highest level.

Most important, however, for the evangelical study of Scripture has been the historical shape of religious culture in the United States. That culture has long been characterized by strong strands of individualism and egalitarianism. It has been at once intensely ideological and determinedly antitraditional. And it has been generally antitheological.[42]

From several perspectives American individualism and egalitarianism deserve praise. These traits account in part for the continuing vitality of fundamentalist and evangelical movements. These groups continue to take seriously the reformers' profound conception of the priesthood of believers. Conservative bodies continually press home the necessity for the common people to "be in the Word." These constant injunctions sustain the vast numbers of serious Bible readers among evangelicals from whose number emerge the scholars. Whatever else may be said about these cultural traits, the emphasis on individual responsibility has created a fruitful setting for a religion of the Book.

On the other hand, the extremes of American democracy make it very difficult for scholarship to receive its due. American evangelicals have largely lost the Reformation's sense of the corporate solidarity of the church.[43] The American myth that one man's testimony is as good as another's destroys the proper respect which, all things being equal, sophisticated scholarly investigation deserves to receive in its character as a facet of common grace. This unwillingness to accede to scholarly authority, especially concerning the Bible, which is so widely available that even he who runs may read, is sharpened among evangelicals by the undeniable fact that biblical scholars have often led the faithful astray. General American individualism and the specific memory of scholarly defalcation constitute, in a native metaphor, two strikes against the evangelical scholar who would communicate a new interpretation of Scripture to the faithful.

American attitudes toward tradition exacerbate this situation. The founding fathers praised the United States as the world's "first new nation" where "we have it in our power to begin the world anew."[44] This bright-eyed self-assurance prevails widely in American churches, and it has been especially characteristic of evangelicals whose banners so often and so naively read "No Creed But the Bible."[45] Nowhere else in the world have independent churches, parachurch organizations, and ad hoc voluntary agencies flourished as in America. These structures have done great good for evangelical structures in general—but not for biblical scholarship in particular.

The antitraditional attitude creates a number of problems for the evangelical study of Scripture. It is one of the things that robs evangelicals of an historical sense. And this is a debilitating handicap when one is attempting to understand an ancient text. Commonsense traditions in both academic and popular forms have encouraged Christians to appropriate without delay the whole of Scripture for themselves.[46] Meanings that appear to lie on the surface are the ones that count. This conviction has served a beneficial purpose in keeping Scripture in the minds, as well as in the hands, of the people. But it also short-circuits what John Higham has called "that crucial act of human sympathy by which the historian identifies himself with another time and place, reenacting the thoughts and reliving the experiences of people remote from himself."[47] For Bible scholars the danger is twofold. It is all too easy to allow forms of thought which appear to be only common sense in our century, but which are largely foreign to the world of Scripture, to dictate interpretations of what the biblical writers must have intended. But it is also a temptation for scholars to let the valid fruits of their empathetic research languish for fear of upsetting the dearly held commonsensical opinions of the wider evangelical community.

The latter circumstance brings us to another difficulty created by evangelical antitraditionalism. It is a problem arising from the universal human need for traditions that exists even among those who profess to be without traditions.[48] The problem is analogous to Chesterton's dictum that where God has died, the demons prevail. American evangelicals who profess to live without ecclesiastical, denominational, and theological traditions do in fact sustain a virile ideological traditionalism in its place. That is, they have oriented their thinking around a set of principles, ideas, and assumptions that serve evangelicals much as institutions, creeds, or denominations have served the church in the past.[49]

Evangelicals cannot stand together on the meaning of free will, baptism, the Lord's Supper, church order, or eschatology. We do not agree on creeds, confessions, doctrinal statements, or even if we should have them. Many of our most powerful institutions are but the lengthened shadows of living men. And so we are left with a few ideas, mostly concerning the sacredness of Scripture, around which to unite. When these then become our tradition, we hold to them with dogged commitment. The result is an ideological traditionalism as powerful as the institutional or creedal traditionalism of other Christian groups. Thus to substitute "maiden" for "virgin" in Isaiah 7:14 becomes not primarily a matter for scholarly discussion or reasoned theological argumentation, but for great alarm;[50] to postulate a certain ahistorical character for Genesis or a rabbinical exegesis for Paul produces not the usually careful counterargument, but fearful counterattack. To be sure, there are exceptions. Especially among evangelicals who gladly own the value of traditional confessions and venerable institutions, there is less ideological excess. It is not surprising to observe that often even the most determined arguments of those with a British or continental background, where strong

Christian institutions exist alongside vigorous theological convictions, appeal to reason and a deeper penetration into Scripture rather than to emotion and a flight from serious wrestling with the text.[51]

The evangelical study of the Bible has also been affected by a weakness in theological construction. The first problem here is the absence of theology itself. The naive empiricism of the American intellectual heritage leads not to depth but to superficiality.[52] Ironically, it leads also to a perverse kind of authoritarianism, in which a leader claiming to have no guide but the Bible rigidly imposes his form of scriptural interpretation on followers who likewise profess to be heeding no guide but the Bible.[53]

The main theological problem, however, takes us back to the absence of well-rooted foundations from which we may examine new proposals concerning Scripture and its interpretation. Evangelicals in general lack theology that is constructive and self-confident rather than reflexive and fearful. They often seem unable to discriminate between those aspects of biblical criticism that enhance an understanding of Scripture as it is and those that bend the messages of the Bible to the secularism of our century.

Examples from other periods reveal more promising patterns. B. B. Warfield (1851–1921), who taught systematic theology at Princeton Seminary for thirty-four years, provides just such an example.[54] At the risk of offending progressive evangelicals (who dislike Warfield's formulation of biblical inerrancy), conservative evangelicals and fundamentalists (who may disagree with his exegetical conclusions on scientific matters), and Arminians (who find his unbending Calvinism distasteful)—I nonetheless think it possible to hold up Warfield's work as the kind that achieved a mature perspective on questions concerning Scripture.

Warfield may be recommended, first, for his careful scholarship. The scores of different publications that he devoted to the question of Scripture are marked by an almost excruciating attention to the details of biblical exegesis and to the arguments of opponents.[55] As is well known, Warfield concluded that the Bible itself testifies to its own inerrancy and that arguments to the contrary are not persuasive. This was an important conclusion. Perhaps just as important, however, was the method by which Warfield arrived at this conclusion: cautious step by cautious step, with full critical scrutiny at each point along the way, and with a painstaking evaluation of the merits as well as the weaknesses of other positions.

Warfield, next, was catholic in his learning. He was open to general revelation, he pursued the modern approaches which held out promise for enhancing our understanding of Scripture, and he drank deeply from the well of historical theology.[56] Warfield greatly valued linguistic, literary, and historical study as means of illuminating the human dimensions of

Scripture. And he pursued these studies, which sought to discern what the words of the biblical authors meant in the terms of their own day, even if they called into question traditional evangelical beliefs about the Bible's meanings. As an avocation Warfield also read scientific literature appreciatively throughout his life. And he was an avid learner from the classic theologians of the past.

It was precisely the combination of his commitments to these various fields of study that enabled Warfield to bring newer scientific developments into his overarching allegiance to Scripture. On the basis of both exegetical and historical study, for example, Warfield concluded that "the question of the antiquity of man has of itself no theological significance."[57] And through his study of Calvin's treatment of creation, he reached conclusions on cosmic and human origins that harmonized aspects of the then-current theories of evolution, a high view of God's providence, and a faithfulness to Scripture.[58]

The reason Warfield could move with such relative freedom in drawing upon both general revelation and modern biblical studies points to his most important legacy for modern evangelicals—the example of a well-articulated theology from which to assess questions in biblical criticism. The crucial element in this theology was Warfield's conception of *concursus,* a word that expressed his belief that God had made it possible to examine the same phenomenon from very different but coherent perspectives.[59] The concept of *concursus* enabled Warfield to study without fear the humanity of Scripture while retaining belief in its divine origin and character. It was this concept that allowed him to focus on authorial intent when discussing the doctrine of Scripture, and it allowed him to approve a providential form of evolution.[60] To Warfield, *concursus* was grounded in general considerations of both God's immanence and his transcendence, and it was a conception that Warfield linked to doctrines of both providence and grace. It was, in other words, an interpretive device growing out of mature theological reflection. There may be difficulties in Warfield's conception of *concursus,* but it cannot be denied that evangelical theology after Warfield has produced very few interpretive concepts of comparable theological depth or exegetical usefulness.

It would be foolishness to conclude that Warfield was free from the limiting assumptions of his own day, that evangelicals should slavishly follow him in every particular, or that he is even the most valuable figure from the church's past to show us how to construct a theology for biblical criticism in the present. In particular, Warfield's laudatory attention to the Bible's linguistic and theological contexts was not matched by a similarly astute attention to questions of cultural context in either the biblical or the modern worlds. Yet his methods and his mentality offer a better way of solving problems relating to the study of Scripture than evangelicals have often followed. Warfield did not fear modern learning, he mined the biblical text with many different tools, and he valued the testimony of the historic Christian traditions. Perhaps most importantly, his balance was extraordinary. He embraced the living reality of the church, but he was not blown about by ideological catchphrases; he valued the vigorous give and take of the academy, but he did not fall prey to unbelieving naturalism.

Evangelicals today may be pleased with the renewal of biblical scholarship in their midst. It would be in accord with traditional evangelical practice to pray that the faith not be subverted by either sterile attachment to received conventions or indiscriminate devotion to critical fashion. And it would comport well with traditional evangelical belief to look forward confidently to further illuminating instruction from Scripture, not because of evangelicalism's own abilities to resolve current difficulties, but because of the faithfulness of God, who first brought Scripture into being and who through it continues to shine the light of his grace into a dark and sinful world.

Chapter 10

THE SEARCH FOR "WOMEN'S ROLE" IN AMERICAN EVANGELICALISM, 1930–1980

MARGARET L. BENDROTH

THE CHURCH IS PERHAPS THE ONLY SOCIAL INSTITUTION other than the home in which the two sexes are not simply obliged but divinely commanded to relate harmoniously. Thus it is that, especially in recent years, the issue of "women's role" has absorbed a large share of the energy and interest of American evangelicals. Though part of a broader secular debate, the "woman question" within the church has aroused unusually intense controversy. The emotional tenor of the discussion among evangelicals, however, reflects not so much lagging conservatism as a fundamental level of historical confusion. George Tavard has pointed out, for example, that historic Protestantism has never developed a clear, consistent theological model of "Christian womanhood."[1] Further, for the last two hundred years American evangelicals have embraced a variety of conflicting practices regarding women's public role, some with a strong tradition of female ministry and others with equally firm strictures against it. In the last half century, moreover, the pervasive ambiguity surrounding the question has intensified.

Without a unified past or a present theological consensus, evangelicals have often merely reacted to changing social practices instead of influencing their direction. Thus, in the first half of the twentieth century, the typical evangelical response to shifting sexual mores and an increasingly public role for women was to perpetuate a traditional, Victorian model of femininity. After World War II, in a period of rapid social and economic change, evangelicals reacted in two fundamentally conflicting ways. Some reasserted the traditional notions of male and female roles with even greater insistence, while others began to question the very

122

existence of seemingly arbitrary sexual roles. As a result, therefore the context of most present-day debate regarding women's "place" has become a forced choice between two extremes. Though the range of opinion has varied widely, traditionalism and feminism have become the ideological poles which, to a large degree, have set the limits of creative discussion.

Part of the problem is intrinsic to evangelicalism itself. Disparaging but not rejecting an earlier fundamentalist pattern of retreat from "worldliness," evangelicals have vacillated between nostalgia for a less secular past and a yearning for social relevance in the present.[2] Thus, in maintaining their separation from the world, they have clung to ideas about women rooted in nineteenth-century Victorianism; however, in their desire for social leadership, they have also embraced, often uncritically, the philosophy and goals of modern feminism. Consequently, conservative Protestants have often appeared to endorse two opposite convictions, and they have seemed unsure whether women and men are inherently equal or at opposite ends of the human spectrum.

One result of this confusion has been, except for some Pentecostal evangelists, a consistent absence of evangelical female leadership, particularly in the past fifty years. On the surface it would appear that both the personnel and basic orientation of conservative Protestantism have become overwhelmingly masculine. In 1929, for example, a Presbyterian writer opposed women's ordination because it was "unmanly." The genius of orthodoxy, he argued, "has lain in a certain robustness which in its active aspect is essentially masculine." Similarly, a contributor to *Moody Monthly* declared that "the very fact that preaching the gospel is tough, trying work . . . ought to challenge us to tackle it. Since when," he demanded, "are we such panty-waists that we must run from a responsibility because it is hard?"[3]

Numerically, however, women have dominated both the liberal and conservative wings of American Protestantism for the last two centuries. In the nineteenth century, observers estimated that women comprised two-thirds to three-fourths of the members of Protestant denominations. Though the proportion declined throughout the twentieth century, a perception of religious "feminization" persisted. In 1929 a Presbyterian observer warned of an "alarming tendency to throw the whole burden and the responsibility of church work upon women. What we need is not more activity among the women," he urged, "but a shaking of the dry bones among the men."[4] But similar fears of female dominance also prevailed among women. A major study published in 1949 found that many "were concerned lest women take over so much that the men would feel no need to be active." Another investigation reported that some women had "refused official positions in order that they might be filled by men.""[5] Only in recent years, when the proportion of men and women has reached 45 percent and 55 percent respectively, have women felt relatively free to participate more widely in church leadership.[6]

Beyond this generalized ambivalence, however, is a legacy of drift, both in theology and in practice. Though this fact is most easily illustrated by events within the "mainline" Protestant denominations, it also holds true for evangelicals. In both traditions, women's organizations have exhibited a loss of spirit and purpose. Maintaining the form but not the ideology of their original design, they no longer voice their particular interests or concerns of the majority of churchwomen. Thus, though not restricted to separate activities simply on the basis of sex, women have not yet achieved full and equal participation in church life. For most of the twentieth century they have been at once both inside and outside the Protestant mainstream.

Here a short digression into the nineteenth-century background is necessary. After the Civil War, in nearly all the major denominations women formed a variety of exclusively female organizations for evangelism, social welfare, and moral reform. This parallel array of associations compensated in a sense for their near total exclusion from the church hierarchy. Preferring "to keep the dimes and distinctions to themselves," Frances Willard charged, the denominations had instead classified their women members as mere "hewers of wood and drawers of water." Only in their own separate organizations, she argued, could women develop their own latent gifts for leadership.[7]

Denominational leaders generally responded to the growth of women's societies with pragmatic approval. Recognizing the potential financial benefits of their work, they deferred exacting theological questions concerning women's place for the sake of practicality. Pragmatic concerns thus governed the prevailing approach to those biblical passages that appeared to restrict women's role in church assemblies. Though most defenders of women's work admitted that the Bible offered few proof texts, they argued, like one Methodist spokesman, that "the book is pervaded by principles which . . . sanction [their] most advanced ideas." Many thus rejected a literal interpretation of Pauline pronouncements, "as if what he said to a few dancing Greek and Asiatic women could be meant for all coming time, in all countries of the world." A single "dyspeptic utterance," one woman argued, should not be allowed to prevent Protestantism's most able and committed members from taking active leadership.[8]

Though this pragmatic approach brought some immediate benefits, it left a legacy of confusion. Nineteenth-century women's organizations arose from a popular conviction that the two sexes possessed unique social responsibilities. Separate associations were therefore a necessary means for women to pursue their special feminine calling in evangelism and relief work. Though this idealism declined in the twentieth century, however, the pattern of segregated women's work had already become institutionalized. Within a modern context, the arrangement thus begged the enormous question of women's true status as church members. Were they fully responsible in all aspects of church life, or answerable in only a few specialized areas? Largely unaddressed in the early decades of the twentieth century, the answer to this question was to become all the more perplexing in years ahead.

Within the large, theologically liberal Northern denominations, women's organizations encountered a particularly complex set of problems. In a sense, they were victims of their own success. Missionary work enabled many women to develop their skills in administration, teaching, and evangelism; in time, however, large numbers of them began to move into full-time church-related occupations. Thus by 1932, for example, the Methodist church reported more than 9,000 full-time female employees in a variety of educational and support positions. Most of these jobs, however, were low-paying and lacking in prestige.[9] Once incorporated into the larger church structure, moreover, laywomen also lost their previous status as "outsiders." Though at times a disadvantage, women's position outside of the ecclesiastical mainstream had also cultivated an optimistic, reformist spirit in their organized endeavors. As part of an enlarging bureaucracy, however, women began to see themselves less as a solution and more as part of the problem.

This declining sense of mission was particularly significant within mainstream Protestant women's organizations, for by virtue of their numbers and visibility they set a pattern for women in other denominations. Therefore, at least partly because the idea of "woman's mission" originated within these groups, their subsequent loss of momentum was all the more significant. In this sense, their struggles provide valuable insight into the nature of the confusion that dogged Protestants of all kinds as they tried to retrace the boundaries of women's place.

Identity problems in women's organizations first became apparent in the 1920s, when many of them began to merge with their denominational mission boards. In the process of reorganization, women gained some representation but in many cases lost control over their separate educational facilities, budgets, and programs. Their sudden entry into the ecclesiastical mainstream thus necessitated psychological as well as institutional readjustment. As Lucy Peabody, a Baptist leader, observed in 1927, "Our place and contribution seem to be at this moment in question."[10] Many women were particularly apprehensive about sharing their organizational responsibilities with men. "While they can hold their own fairly well with individual man on most questions," Peabody wrote, "collective man on a Board is another and a modern problem."[11] Thus, as denominational reorganization presented churchwomen with new opportunities for leadership, many faced the prospect with mixed emotions. Years of activity in distinctly feminine interests and concerns had convinced them that "women's work" was an indispensable contribution to the church. In the end, they gave it up only with difficulty.

Attitudes among Presbyterian women provide a good example of this process. Although they were genuinely disturbed over the loss of their separate organizational status, they moved hesitantly toward equal participation within the denomination. When the church dismantled their independent home and foreign mission boards in the early 1920s, they became increasingly restless about their status within the church. In 1929, as a conciliatory gesture, the General Assembly proposed three overtures, acknowledging women's right to become ministers, elders, or evangelists. A selected committee of 100 women met to discuss the measures and offered its support, but with some significant reservations. According to one report, they approved the innovation only as a means of attracting younger women. Almost every committee member, moreover, admitted that "she personally did not want to be a pastor or an elder, and would doubtless vote against a woman pastor in her local church."[12] Their hesitation apparently did not arise from theological concerns, for after a single presentation on the subject, the women readily agreed that all of the "alleged" scriptural arguments against women's ordination had been "convincingly answered."[13] It would appear that the women themselves wanted neither full equality nor their old independent status; in the end, therefore, they received neither. Largely because of their own indecision, Presbyterian women remained "in but still out" of the denominational mainstream for the next half century.[14]

Because of their ambivalent attitude, women's organizations failed to achieve broad and consistent influence within their various denominations. In some cases they drifted toward generalism and goals so large as to be meaningless. A group of women attending an ecumenical luncheon in 1938, for example, discussed such mutual interests as "developing a world government and world police department," "good sportsmanship in race relations," and "maintaining a spiritual interpretation of the universe."[15] This is not, of course, to downplay the goals and effectiveness of these organizations. The United Council of Church Women, formed in 1941 as a union of several women's boards, vigorously promoted various ecumenical causes and led in efforts toward racial unity and world peace. Its approach to social problems, however, tended to be pragmatic rather than ideological. Describing women's work in the 1920s, for example, one woman noted proudly that though "the battle of Fundamentalism versus Liberalism might rage in the pulpits, and the

Scopes trial make headlines in the newspapers . . . these would not throw the women off course. There was too much that needed to be done."[16] Consequently, as one recent critic has contended, their work has often been characterized by a "certain naivete" toward social evils. "I have also known groups of Christian women," she writes, "who seemed lost in an uncritical humanism."[17] According to a survey conducted in 1949, many local groups participated in church projects in much the same way as they did in secular organizations like the Red Cross and Community Chest.[18] Because of this lack of direction, many women's organizations were unable to exert a consistent influence within their parent denominations. A conviction of feminine mission first gave rise to their separate status; but as they lost this idealism, they maintained only a muted sense of purpose.

True, during this period many of the liberal denominations relaxed or removed restrictions against women's ordination. By itself, however, this step was not necessarily an advance. As one recent study has concluded, "Equal access to the ordained ministry has not resulted in equal access to positions of leadership traditionally available to the clergy." By the 1960s, moreover, the number of women ministers, always small, was actually in decline.[19] Thus, Sara Maitland has observed, "the recent history of women in institutional Christianity proves only that ordination itself does not solve any problems." Though it has perhaps brought more recognition of women's gifts for leadership, it has also made it "*harder* for other women to lay claim to their own vocation, because the most obvious charge of discrimination is eliminated."[20]

During the 1930s and 1940s developments within the evangelical denominations mirrored the growing confusion within the mainline churches. Among conservatives, however, the result was not organizational diffusion but a narrowing perception of women's role in church life. Many conservative Protestants simply relied on the inherited, traditional model of femininity, which stressed the necessity of male leadership. This silence, however, was not without long-term effect: in the absence of thoughtful discussion, women's ecclesiastical role became increasingly brittle and constrictive.

This development relates in part to the nature of fundamentalism after World War I. During this time, the movement was in the midst of its most reactive phase. Thus, in denouncing the rapid decay in American morals, fundamentalist leaders took special outrage at the national sin of sexual permissiveness. They also began to equate female leadership with feminine sensuality, for both, they believed, originated in rebellion against a divinely ordained social order. Thus James M. Gray, a leading dispensationalist, interpreted women's growing social prominence as a literal sign of the Last Days. Most often, however, fundamentalist writers attacked current fashions of dress as an ultimate symbol of worldliness. They never tired of contrasting true Christian womanhood with the modern "bobbed haired, painted faced, varnish lipped, step-ladder-heeled, knicker-clad, cigarette-smoking, card-playing jazz flapper." As one writer warned, "A Christian woman may be absolutely *fundamental in her doctrine*, yet defeat the power of the Word by the *modernism of her appearance.*" Godly women were thus urged to maintain a careful, quiet deference to male headship. Rebellion against God's standard was doomed to failure, fundamentalist writers emphasized, for the divine order fitted women "for so distinct and individual a service that transgression is ridiculous."[21]

This narrow perception of women's role was perpetuated by the exclusive nature of women's missionary organizations. In conservative denominations, like the Southern Baptist and the Lutheran Church—Missouri Synod, for example, women's work consisted almost entirely of fund-raising for missions. This limited focus perpetuated the pattern of separation set by nineteenth-century women's associations, but without its overarching sense of purpose. In fact, much of women's missionary work served to underscore their peripheral relationship to the ongoing theological and social concerns of the larger church.

The Lutheran Women's Missionary League (LWML) of the Lutheran Church—Missouri Synod first organized in St. Louis in 1930, and evolved primarily as a fundraising auxiliary to the denomination's home and foreign mission board. The organization grew slowly and with only the barest administrative structure, hampered by denominational policy against extracongregational activities.[22] When the LWML became a recognized church auxiliary, it gradually acquired a degree of organizational and financial independence, but continued to specialize in mission work. Consequently, as critic Alan Graebner has maintained, it "did not even recognize the existence, let alone the viability, of a new life pattern for women. Even for 'woman's sphere,' the home and family," he argues, "the Lutheran associations were largely irrelevant."[23] A study published in 1961, moreover, suggested that the LWML's purpose was primarily social, since its members were demonstrably less active in neighborhood evangelism than were nonmembers.[24] In fact, the LWML did not develop a distinct indentity as a women's organization. Restricting its energies to a single specialized purpose, it became in time unable—or perhaps unwilling—to address the larger issue of women's role within the Missouri Synod.

Even a large and expansive women's society such as the Southern Baptist Women's Missionary Union (WMU) remained relatively isolated from its denominational mainstream. The WMU was formed in 1888 as an auxiliary of the denomination's mission boards. Organized state by state, it did not commission or support its own female missionaries but instead raised money for Southern Baptist projects. Moreover, unlike some of its Northern counterparts, the WMU also maintained a careful distance from any taint of women's rights sentiment: until the 1960s it regularly appointed a male representative to read its annual report to the General Convention. Though it pursued a broader missionary program than did the LWML, the WMU remained similarly insulated from issues of Southern Baptist policy. As recent statistics suggest, its exclusive concern with missionary work did not translate into a larger role of church leadership. In 1969 only six of the sixty-six-member Foreign Mission Board and seven of the sixty-five-member Home Missions Board were women. By 1975 women filled only 7 percent of all Southern Baptist leadership positions, though the WMU virtually subsidized its missionary program.[25]

The strength of this pattern is evident in the difficulties encountered by those who diverged from it. When laywomen in the National Baptist Church, the largest black denomination, organized a separate Women's Convention in 1900, they drew immediate opposition from church leaders. Denominational officials had hoped that they would simply support existing missionary projects; instead, the Women's Convention, led by Nannie Helen Burroughs, established a diverse, independent educational and evangelistic program. In an effort to assert more control over the women's work, National Baptist leaders tried to remove their right to incorporate and hold property. In 1938 they advised church boards, auxiliaries, and local congregations to withdraw support from the women's National Training School in Washington, D.C. In spite of this, Nannie Burroughs remained adamant on the importance of a separate arm of "women's work." As she argued, "The National Baptist Convention is distinctly and as it should be, a 'man's organization.' Negro Baptist women should have a parallel organization just as distinct and powerful."[26] This independent stance, however, made the Women's Convention a continual focus of irritation for the denomination's leaders. As a women's organization, they believed, it exercised undue independence and power.

Nannie Helen Burroughs and the Women's Convention are thus important as an exception proving a general rule. The opposition they encountered from denominational leaders is first an indication of their divergence from the popular ideal of women's associations. National Baptist leaders were hard-pressed financially and troubled by divisive disagreements; the Women's Convention, though never affluent, was still debt-free and constantly expanding its activities. As an auxiliary, it would have given the struggling denomination a valuable amount of financial stability and control; as an independent body, however, it was a constant source of controversy. The experience of National Baptist women also illustrates, by way of contrast, the peculiar theological forces that contributed to women's narrow role in the other evangelical denominations. Black churches remained largely unaffected by the cultural paralysis that gripped many conservative Protestants in the twentieth century. The wide-ranging social goals of the Women's Convention, moreover, witness a degree of idealism and hope largely absent in women's missionary organizations in the white denominations. This fact suggests that, to a large degree, in conservative white denominations women's role became wooden and restrictive as it lost its social dimension. Thus, as conservative Protestants retreated from their commitments to moral and social renewal, they also began to draw in the boundaries of women's place.

In general, women's groups from both ends of the theological spectrum suffered from a similar problem of definition. Whether highly specialized or overly diffuse, they became increasingly irrelevant to the task of representing women's interests in ecclesiastical affairs. This pattern had perhaps its most serious consequences in evangelical churches where women's groups were the most removed from issues of doctrine or polity. There they could offer little in the way of insight or encouragement as the church adjusted to the rapid social changes of the post–World War II era. Unable to construct a positive response, evangelicals faced those years with perplexed and divided minds.

This confusion was amplified by larger uncertainties within conservative Protestantism. Though the 1950s and early 1960s marked gains in church attendance and institutional growth, they also heralded some rapid and disconcerting social shifts. Thus, in spite of their unparalleled prosperity, many evangelicals felt a growing social anxiety, particularly in regard to the family. The stories of juvenile delinquency, desertion, and divorce that filled denominational magazines during this period all pointed to a mysterious ailment affecting the American home. Though rarely articulated at first, at the root of much of this discomfort was the age-old question of "woman's place."

During the postwar period a growing number of observers pointed with some alarm to the increasing formlessness of American society. Rapid suburbanization had brought increasing social and geographic mobility, and also a significant effect on family structure. One study concluded that the suburbanized family of the 1950s was "a little like a country which, having operated under an authoritarian form of government, has suddenly switched to a democratic form, without too much preparation for the change."[27] As David Mace noted, family patterns of the 1950s "brought equality and cooperation, but [also] the complete disintegration of the old-fashioned, fixed, interchangeable roles." "Our ideals of what is 'manly' and what is 'womanly' seem confused," another observer agreed.[28]

Furthermore, accelerating geographic and social mobility had removed some of the traditional protections of the institution of marriage. "The increase in urban and suburban living has broken down . . . some of the . . . external, societal forces acting to hold marriages structurally intact," one scholar contended. In short, "there is much less emphasis upon the institutional aspects and much more upon the personality aspects of marriage and family life."[29] In such a fluid, individualistic context, seemingly arbitrary roles based on sex began to appear quaint and even meaningless. Early feminist books like Betty Friedan's *The Feminine Mystique* were thus in many ways a product of this confusion rather than a simple call for justice. Women's restlessness and discontent mounted as their role in the home appeared to lose much of its moral and social significance.

Some evangelicals responded to this growing formlessness by trying to reassert traditional notions of social order. But here they faced a problem: the traditional family ideal, with its distinct marital roles, would no longer fit into a twentieth-century context. The older pattern was a product of the Victorian era: it emphasized the social rather than the strictly personal dimensions of the marriage contract. Nineteenth-century theorists argued that social morality depended on women's strict adherence to their maternal and domestic responsibilities. Divorce, in their view, was thus not an individual affair but an act with grave social implications. Such arguments, however, were much less persuasive a century later, when personal fulfillment had replaced social utility as the primary purpose of marriage.

Consequently, evangelical theorists shifted their line of argument. Instead of basing marital roles on their social value, they turned to metaphysics, invoking a divine "order of creation" as the rationale for male dominance and female submission in the church and family. The theory was, of course, not a new invention. To a degree, it was implicit in the traditional ideal of male dominance and female submission.[30] In the postwar era, however, various writers began to outline the sexual hierarchy in stricter terms—and with greater insistence. Noting the sudden appearance of the order-of-creation ideology in the Missouri Synod after World War II, Edward Schroeder has traced it to the English translation of an influential German work on *The Office of Woman in the Church* by the theologian Fritz Zerbst.[31] In the spate of marriage advice literature that emerged from evangelical publishing houses during this time, the concept began to enjoy wide popularity. In recent years, moreover, writers and lecturers such as Tim and Beverly LaHaye, Larry Christensen, and Bill Gothard have broadened its appeal to a wider evangelical audience.

The order of creation idea was clearly an intensification of the traditional notion of male and female spheres. Instead of basing women's status in the Fall and curse of Genesis 3:16, the newer theory rooted female subordination in creation itself. Thus, because they were created after men, women ranked below them in a divinely instituted hierarchy. Further, as a fundamental principle of creation, this order was not affected by the work of Christ. According to Charles Ryrie, "As long as the race continues, and men are men and women are women, then women are to be subject to their husbands as unto the head."[32]

Several factors contributed to the popularity of this ideology. The postwar resurgence of evangelical biblical scholarship brought new attention to problematic texts, including the difficult Pauline passages on women. No longer able to simply explain them as a single "dyspeptic utterance," a new generation of scholars turned to Paul's words with scientific care. The concept of a created order was also an important means of reducing the world to manageable proportions. In the words of Elisabeth Elliot, "A Christian home . . . is a world in itself, a microcosm, representing—as the Church also represents—the hierarchy of the cosmos itself."[33] Such a comforting view of the universe had wide appeal. As one woman confessed, "I agree with the principle of 'headship.' It gives a definite sense of identity and a proud position in the home." And she added parenthetically, "This is very important in today's society."[34] Another author agreed. "Order is important to us as human beings," he wrote. "When we live in chaos we experience suffering. We tear ourselves to pieces like two gears that don't mesh. We need order."[35] As these statements illustrate, the notion of a strict hierarchy in marriage was more than a reaction to the growing influence of secular feminism; it was also a means of introducing order into the increasingly amorphous boundaries of parental roles within the family.

Instead of looking for a divine sanction for women's role, however, a growing number of evangelicals dispensed with the idea entirely. In the words of Virginia Mollenkott, "The hierarchical concept of dominance and submission, even when softened to male 'headship' and female 'supportive role,' [is] an unbiblical and anti-Christian concept."[36] As Nancy Hardesty declared, "Beneath all the rhetoric and controversy [of the women's liberation movement], women simply want to be recognized as *persons*."[37] In Christ, she and others argued, all are one: there is no male or female.

Evangelical feminism arose in part as a response to the women's liberation movement of the early 1970s. Various scholars have noted the connections between nineteenth-century evangelical Protestantism and the rise of the woman suffrage movement; however, it is clear that this new resurgence was in many ways a distinctly late twentieth-century phenomenon. Although books and articles on Christian egalitarianism appeared sporadically throughout the late 1950s and 1960s, the movement first became visible in 1973. That year, when a number of influential, socially concerned evangelicals gathered in Chicago, they issued a declaration that denounced the sin of ecclesiastical sexism. The following year, evangelical feminists began to organize in earnest and began publishing their own periodical, the *Daughters of Sarah*. The Evangelical Women's Caucus formed in 1975 and endorsed the Equal Rights Amendment as one of its first acts. The movement's popularity grew rapidly. *All We're Meant to Be*, the ground-breaking exposition of evangelical feminism by Nancy Hardesty and Letha Scanzoni, was *Eternity* magazine's Book of the Year for 1975. The following year, it took first place in a readers' poll of significant evangelical books.

Evangelical feminists rejected the traditional notion that men and women were fundamentally different in function as well as form. As one proponent argued, "women in society ought to be viewed and treated not as women *per se*, but as spiritual beings no different from men. . . . In the Father's perspective, there is no spiritual distinction between male and female (Gal. 3:28)." Emphasizing the importance of human individuality, another writer declared that "social distinctions are meant to be transcended—not perpetuated—in the body of Christ."[38] Evangelical feminist leaders also criticized the segregated pattern of women's church work. As Scanzoni and Hardesty wrote pointedly, "Most churches do permit women a variety of lay ministries—making pies for the church supper, doing macrame for the bazaar, redecorating the social hall, collecting clothes for the missionaries, teaching the toddlers, and even leading a housewives' Bible study. But these ministries are usually limited to the domestic sphere and seldom integral to the church's mission to the world."[39] Rejecting traditionalist theories as "warmed-over hash of what our culture teaches, cloaked in biblical languages," evangelical feminists proposed a new ethic of personhood, which they believed was fundamentally biblical. Instead of arbitrary roles, they emphasized "the humanity of women and God's desire that *all persons* be able to develop themselves to their fullest potential."[40]

In doing so, however, they fell into a central contradiction. As one observer pointed out, "The trick is to denounce others for letting traditional culture be their authority instead of the Bible, while I let contemporary culture be my authority." The largely unquestioning support evangelical feminists gave to the philosophy and goals of secular feminism, he argued, allowed them "to pronounce judgment on traditional culture without making them perform the embarrassing task of proclaiming God's judgment on the new *status quo*."[41] Other critics have been more direct. "Since the New Testament seems to . . . be the alleged rather than the real impetus for the movement," one has maintained, "traditionalists believe that they discern its actual genesis elsewhere. Put simply, they believe that the true impetus behind evangelical feminism is not the spirit of the New Testament, but rather the spirit of the present age."[42] Observer Richard Quebedeaux similarly has charged that "the emergence of evangelical feminism presents a clear example of the influence of trends in the wider culture on contemporary evangelical Christianity—a profound instance of the world setting the agenda for the church, rather than vice versa."[43]

These two fundamentally opposing ideas gradually came to form the context of evangelical debate on the subject of women's role in the church. While these two poles certainly do not encompass all views, they have in many ways set the limits of discussion. In the absence of any clear historical Protestant consensus on the subject, moreover, the debate has tended to become circumscribed and circular. Practical questions concerning the nature of women's contribution have often been deferred to detailed analyses of the pros and cons of women's ordination. While certainly an important issue, it is clearly not an ecclesiastical panacea, as is evident from the experience of women in the liberal denominations. Further, the ordination question has often become entangled in a debate over the nature of biblical authority. With equal sincerity, each side has charged its opponents with worshiping the Baals of American culture rather than the God of Scripture. But this theological stalemate, escalating into a full-fledged battle for the Bible, has obscured the larger issue of women's role within evangelical Protestantism. It is clear that the "woman question" has no solution outside of a renewed attention to the social dimensions of the Christian faith, for only then can the static concept of women's "role" be discarded in place of a more fluid, open-ended emphasis on Christian calling. The question of women's place thus remains an important part of the church's ongoing task of incorporating diversity into a larger unity. At present it is still waiting for an answer.

Chapter 11

OFFSPRING OF AN ODD UNION: EVANGELICAL ATTITUDES TOWARD THE ARTS*

ROGER LUNDIN

I

"THE NEW ADAM AND EVE," one of Nathaniel Hawthorne's lesser-known stories, first appeared in 1843, the same year that William Miller and his Millerites had predicted for the return of Christ to earth to claim his faithful. This intriguing tale holds more than casual relevance for the attitudes that many evangelicals have held toward the arts in the past fifty years. As the story opens, Hawthorne asks us to imagine "good Father Miller's interpretation of the prophecies to have proved true."[1] We are to conceive of all the earth's inhabitants as having been whisked away from the world of nineteenth-century America.

But though all living beings have disappeared, all the remnants of their lives—their tools, homes, clothes, food, and books—have been left behind them. Into this world Hawthorne introduces a New Adam and a New Eve, who, in his words, have "been created, in the full development of mind and heart, but with no knowledge of their predecessors, nor of the diseased circumstances that had become encrusted around them." This Adam and this Eve can easily distinguish between art and nature, recognizing the "wisdom and simplicity of the latter," while remaining baffled by the "elaborate perversities" and puzzling complexities of the human artifacts they find.

* This essay was prepared while I was a Visiting Fellow at the Calvin Center for Christian Scholarship in 1982–83. I wish to thank Calvin College for the generous support I received that year.

As they make their way through the deserted streets of Boston, they stumble upon a dry-goods store, a church, a courthouse, a statehouse, a mansion with its table set for dinner, a jeweler's shop, and the Bunker Hill monument. Repeatedly, as they gaze at these objects whose use and purpose they cannot fathom, Adam and Eve feel frustrated by their inability to interpret the artifacts placed before them. Adam seems to need to know the meaning of these things. "Eve, Eve! What can this thing be?" he cries out as they stand before a gallows. Eve's response—in this particular instance and in general—dismisses all such bedeviling complexities. What are the gallows? "I know not," answers Eve, "but, Adam, my heart is sick" (754). Adam is curious; Eve wishes to remain oblivious. Adam would decipher the mysterious "hieroglyphics"; Eve would leave them as they are, mute and uninterpreted.

But in one place, the Harvard University Library, Adam is overwhelmed by a mystery. He has taken up a large book whose meaning he must discover, and he "stands poring over the regular columns of mystic characters . . . ; for the unintelligible thought upon the page has a mysterious relation to his mind, and makes itself felt, as if it were a burden flung upon him" (760). Entranced, Adam tells Eve that "nothing is so desirable as to find out the mystery of this big and heavy object with its thousand thin divisions . . . " (760). Eve too has picked up a book, but unlike Adam she has no interest in such objects. And so she tosses "the volume upon the floor," calling upon Adam to do the same, to "fling down that stupid thing; for even if it should speak, it would not be worth attending to." Adam replies, "I cannot help thinking that the interpretation of the riddles amid which we have been wandering all day long might here be discovered." But Eve remains firm: "It may be better not to seek the interpretation. . . . If you love me, come away!" (761).

There follows a remarkable paragraph in which Hawthorne applauds, with hardly a trace of irony, Eve's promptings and Adam's capitulation. It merits quotation in full:

> She prevails, and rescues him from the mysterious perils of the library. Happy influence of woman! Had he lingered there long enough to obtain a clue to its treasures,—as was not impossible, his intellect being of human structure, indeed, but with an untransmitted vigor and acuteness,—had he then and there become a student, the annalist of our poor world would soon have recorded the downfall of a second Adam. The fatal apple of another Tree of Knowledge would have been eaten. All the perversions and sophistries, and false wisdom so aptly mimicking the true; all the narrow truth, so partial that it becomes more deceptive than falsehood; all the wrong principles and worse practice, the pernicious examples and mistaken rules of life; all the specious theo-

ries, which turn earth into cloud-land, and men into shadows; all the sad experience, which it took mankind so many ages to accumulate, and from which they never drew a moral for their future guidance—the whole heap of this disastrous lore would have tumbled at once upon Adam's head. There would have been nothing left for him, but to take up the already abortive experiment of life, where we had dropped it, and toil onward with it a little further.

But, blessed in his ignorance, he may still enjoy a new world in our worn-out one. (761)

"If you love me, come away!" Eve demands of Adam. And come away he does, away from the pain, the ambiguity, the sophistry, and the sin of history, away from all that might blight his unsullied innocence. "If you love me, come away!" It sounds familiar. In fact, one remembers the specific phrase from one of the early, highly romantic poems of William Butler Yeats:

> Come away, O human child!
> To the waters and the wild
> With a faery, hand in hand,
> For the world's more full of weeping than you can understand.[2]

Another passage, from a very different source, also echoes Hawthorne's description of Adam's discarding of the book. "For six thousand years," the prominent fundamentalist I. M. Haldeman wrote early in this century,

> [a] break in the faith relationship has been written in human history. For six thousand years man has continued to eat of the tree of knowledge. . . . For six thousand years he has battled with the problem of good and evil. For six thousand years, he has studied and thought, searched and investigated. He has attained to much knowledge. . . .
> [But] by wisdom he knows not God.
> He knows good and evil.[3]

And finally, an American evangelical novelist only recently depicted the Christian artist as one who, like Hawthorne's Adam, succeeds in escaping the particular culture deposited about him:

> The way of the Christian artist is to clothe the timeless in the timely, to express in contemporary forms the Eternal Word. He will not be swept by the sensate culture of his time, fractured into a thousand atoms. He will be in it, aware of his age, speaking to it, but also above and beyond it.[4]

The similarity we discover here is not simply a matter of coincidence, for many passages culled from the works of romantic artists and theorists, fundamentalist preachers, gospel songwriters, and evangelical aestheticians exhibit uncanny familial resemblances. They do so, moreover, because to a great extent modern evangelical aesthetics represents the product of a union of specifically American attitudes toward social tradition, romantic aesthetic notions, and fundamentalist views of culture. And—to complete my thesis—it is precisely the singularly evangelical blending of these elements that has made significant achievements in the arts so difficult for American evangelicals.

To better comprehend that difficulty, let us imagine Hawthorne's Adam becoming a writer of his own stories. He has given up his attempt to interpret the mystic characters in other books, in which clues are hidden to the enigmas that lie around him. He refuses to enter into the history—to belong to the tradition—that could make sense of his world, but turns instead to face the future armed only with his ignorance and the love of his blissful, innocent Eve. In so doing, Adam resembles countless other Americans, for as recent scholars have observed, the figure of Adam early became the archetype for man in America, the new-found land. In 1630, for example, John Winthrop told the group of English men and women sailing toward Massachusetts Bay that though all of them had been born as children of the Old Adam, earlier parentage reigns only " 'til Christ comes and takes possession of the soul, [and] so by little and little expels the former."[5]

Very early in the American experience, theological doubts about the potential of this new man slipped quietly away. By the mid-eighteenth century, what the Puritans had called man's crippling sins had become the amendable *errata* of Ben Franklin's *Autobiography;* Winthrop's New Adam growing in a covenantal relationship with God through Jesus Christ had become St. Jean de Crevecoeur's ideal American, actively "leaving behind him all his ancient prejudices and manners" in order to be "melted into a new race of men."[6] A century later Henry David Thoreau can argue in *Walden* that only our "tedium and ennui" and not our sins are as old as Adam. For Thoreau, the past becomes a record of timid failure and not a repository of profound truths about possibilities and limitations. He declares: "You may say the wisest thing you can, old man. . . . I hear an irresistible voice which invites me away from all that. One generation abandons the enterprises of another like stranded vessels."[7]

Such American attitudes toward the past have exerted a powerful influence on evangelical thinking about the arts. George Marsden has observed, for example, that traditional American convictions about the irrelevance of the past and the American tendency to make a radical separation of the present and future from the past were in part responsible for fundamentalism's eager embrace of dispensationalism and other non-developmental views of history.[8] This legacy in turn helped to make evangelicals receptive to aesthetic theories that celebrate the radical originality of the creative act. For instance, American evangelicals have shown a special fondness for an analogy, put forth in the works of Dorothy Sayers[9] and others, which likens man the artist to God the Creator.[9] Despite attempts to temper the analogy by distinguishing between God's creation *ex nihilo* and man's use of pre-existent material, evangelical theorists often portray the artist as a creative demiurge who shapes the unformed masses of nature and history. One evangelical novelist claims that

> all significant art is an attempt to give form to the chaotic, disorganized elements of experience, and to give a measure of permanence to the evanescent, the fleeting elements of experience. It is the God-like, creative energy of man, shaping a lump of clay and blowing the breath of life into it; turning water to wine.[10]

Or, as a Christian musician has argued,

> Culture is his [man's] handiwork, his fingerprint on the creation, and it is in the realm of his imagination that he comes closest to the godly prerogative of *ex nihilo*. He yearns for mastery over materials, to create shapes and articulate relationships. . . .
>
> If God senses faith at work, faith which makes us free of conditioned reflexes, he smiles, whatever the supposed level of achievement *at the time*. And the important words are *at the* time, because he ever expects us to be on the move. The question to us is not, "What have you achieved?" but, "What is your next move?" Only when we are in this restless attitude is the Spirit free to work a newness.[11]

The latter quotation is particularly informative and points to the way in which these three separate elements—an American disdain for tradition, romantic aesthetic assumptions, and fundamentalist ideas about culture—become all but indistinguishable in an evangelical approach to the arts. The definition of culture given here—"Man's handiwork, his fingerprint on the creation"—assumes that imaginative activity makes humanity resemble God. Culture is not the record of humankind's sustained, dynamic response to God, nature, history, and society, but rather the recorded legacy of intermittent bursts of human creativity, the saga of those creaturely deeds that rival without surpassing divine creative achievements.

This evangelical notion of culture fits equally well with typical American attitudes toward the past, with romantic thoughts on creative genius, and with fundamentalist doubts about the merits of culture. Like Adam in Hawthorne's tale, the artist envisioned here has little to learn from the past; indeed, the artist-as-Adam must struggle beneath the weight of those past achievements merely to preserve his health and claim his godlike prerogatives. Harold Bloom speaks of the anxiety of influence that has bedeviled poets since the Romantic age; such anxiety drove Hawthorne's Adam to drop that book of the past and causes evangelical theorists to celebrate cultural discontinuity as a liberating force which allows the artist to act like God.[12]

But evangelical ideas about the arts also owe a debt to sources far beyond America, especially to those romantic movements in England and on the Continent in which convictions about the divine nature of human creativity first gained significant acceptance. M. H. Abrams argues in *Natural Supernaturalism* that the Romantics felt they were involved in a giant and desperate effort to salvage traditional Christian belief.[13] Faced with a universe denuded of significance by empiricism and the science of Isaac Newton, a world in which the Christian story seemed to have been rendered trivial or pushed to the periphery, the Romantics attempted to reanimate nature and the human spirit by appropriating for that spirit the powers that once belonged to a now distant or nonexistent Christian God. William Blake wants us to reclaim our rightful prerogatives from that vacant Nobodaddy we have cast upon a blank heaven out of great fear; John Keats's Apollo proclaims that

> Knowledge enormous makes a God of me.
> Names, deeds, gray legends, dire events, rebellions,
> Majesties, sovran voices, agonies,
> Creations and destroyings, all at once
> Pour into the wide hollows of my brain
> And deify me. . . .[14]

Ralph Waldo Emerson tells us that he believes "man has been wronged; he has wronged himself. He has almost lost the light that can lead him back to his prerogatives."[15] But humanity can find that light when it realizes that "the doors of the temple stand open, night and day, before every man, and the oracles of the truth cease never, it is guarded by one stern condition; this namely; It is an intuition. It cannot be received at second hand. Truly speaking, it is not instruction, but provocation, that I can receive from another soul."[16] And once a person receives the jolt of that provocation, she can then possess what is hers by right of her nature and become a god—a god, moreover, who can begin to finish the work left undone by the theists' distant lord.

Three very different works illustrate how radical romantic ideas have become mixed into our evangelical tradition. Each exploits a favorite romantic metaphor of the human spirit as an Aeolian harp called into song by powerful spiritual forces. The first excerpt is from Shelley's famous "Ode to the West Wind":

Make me the lyre, even as the forest is:
What if my leaves are falling like its own!
The tumult of the mighty harmonies

Will take from both a deep, autumnal tone,
Sweet though in sadness. Be thou, Spirit fierce,
My spirit! Be thou me, impetuous one!

Drive my dead thoughts over the universe
Like withered leaves to quicken a new birth!
And, by the incantation of this verse,

Scatter, as from an unextinguished hearth
Ashes and sparks, my words among mankind!
Be through my lips to unawakened Earth

The trumpet of a prophecy! O Wind,
If Winter comes, can spring be far behind?[17]

The next passage is from Georgiana Taylor's well-known gospel song, "Oh, To Be Nothing":

Oh, to be nothing, nothing,
  Only as led by His hand;
A messenger at His gateway,
  Only waiting for His command,
Only an instrument ready
  His praises to sound at His will,
Willing, should He not require me,
  In silence to wait on Him still.[18]

And the final one appears in an early essay by Thomas Howard, one of evangelicalism's leading spokesmen on the arts:

Alas for the man for whom the vision of beauty . . . becomes . . . a searing agony that ravages him daily, hourly, in images too sweet to bear. . . .

[The artist] finds himself wounded with stabbing visions of some aching and elusive joy, some burning fever of desire; and he knows that in order to be true to his own being, he must *invite* the shafts and ask where in God's name they come from, while the rest of us must offset and quell these lance-like imaginings with practical considerations in order to make our way in the world and keep our sanity.[19]

In each of these three works we find a sensitive soul waiting passively to be filled with power by the spirit of God or the spirit that animates all life. Ravished, filled, and quickened by such power, that individual soul then becomes an agent of transformation in the world. In

Shelley's poem the artist played upon by the spirit becomes the source of moral, aesthetic, political, and spiritual regeneration in the larger world; in Taylor's hymn the broken and emptied vessel becomes, once filled, "for the Master's use made meet"; and in Howard's essay the ravaged artist commits himself to "the plastic immortalization of human beauty and the effort to shape visibly the chaotic phenomena of life." Though their goals differ, these three share a rhetorical vision, that of the isolated individual who appears powerless but actually has been called and filled to do a great work.

We can account for this similarity in part by noting the distinctly Protestant tone of a great deal of romanticism. As we have seen, many of the great romantic artists sought to resuscitate the battered body of Christian belief. Many of them—the early Wordsworth and Coleridge, Blake, Shelley, Emerson, Thoreau, and Walt Whitman—sought to breathe life into that tradition by claiming rights and responsibilities for the imaginative human spirit which theism traditionally had assigned to a transcendent God. "Nothing is at last sacred but the integrity of our own mind," Emerson wrote in "Self-Reliance";[20] and in the "Prospectus" to a verse epic he never completed, Wordsworth claimed that not "Jehovah" nor his "choir/Of shouting angels" nor the "empyreal thrones"

> can breed such fear and awe
> As fall upon us often when we look
> Into our Minds, into the Mind of Man,
> My haunt, and the main region of my Song.[21]

With romanticism, then, the stripping of sacramental significance from nature and ritual that had begun in the radical Reformation was now completed. Nature and history lay "without form and void" before the potent human spirit, perfect material to be molded by the activity of that shaping agent. The earth, Thoreau said, and "the institutions upon it, are plastic like clay in the hands of the potter."[22]

Both fundamentalists and evangelicals have been careful to avoid making precisely these kinds of Promethean claims about the power of the artist. Yet evangelicals have come very close to saying such things and have been ever so sympathetic to the substance and rhetoric of the romantic tradition. That sympathy grew out of perceptions of culture held alike by romantics and fundamentalists. Both tended to see themselves as the rightful proprietors of a world from which they had been displaced. In The Feminization of American Culture, Ann Douglas details the way in which liberal ministers, women, and serious artists experienced disestablishment in nineteenth-century America.[23] Shorn of real power in a culture ruled by men and the acquisitive principle, these groups found what solace they could by influencing those who exercised true power.

Douglas's conclusions pertain to the first sixty years of the nineteenth century, when, as Marsden claims, evangelical Protestants "thought of America as a Christian nation" and "considered their faith to be the normative American creed." That "old order of American Protestantism," however, built as it was "on the interrelationship of faith, science, the Bible, morality, and civilization, . . . was about to crumble."[24] Late in the century, faced with threats from higher criticism of the Bible, from Darwinian theory, and from the secular mores of an increasingly urban and industrial America, evangelicals suddenly found themselves on the outside looking in. As Marsden documents, the evangelicals' feeling of alienation was to lead, among other things, to the fundamentalist embrace of dispensational premillennialism and the definition of Christian life as an existence untainted by a short list of social vices.

In H. Richard Niebuhr's categories, evangelicals of the early nineteenth century embraced a "Christ of culture" position, because they saw America as a Christian nation, an antitype fulfilling the promise of biblical types. Their fundamentalist heirs, however, could hardly see the "Christ of culture" in the late nineteenth century as they witnessed what Grant Wacker has termed "the demise of biblical civilization."[25] So they came to adopt a "Christ against culture" position, which Niebuhr trenchantly describes:

> Practically the problem arises for radical Christians when, in their concentration on the Lordship of Christ, they seek to defend his authority, to define the content of his commandment, and to relate his law or reign to that power which governs nature and presides over the destinies of men in their secular societies. The extreme temptation the radicals meet when they deal with these questions is that of converting their ethical dualism into an ontological bifurcation of reality. Their rejection of culture is easily combined with a suspicion of nature and nature's God; their reliance on Christ is often converted into a reliance on the Spirit immanent in him and the believer; ultimately they are tempted to divide the world into the material realm governed by a principle opposed to Christ and a spiritual realm guided by the spiritual God. Such tendencies are evident in Tertullian's Montanism, in Spiritual Franciscanism, in the inner light doctrine of the Quakers, and in Tolstoy's spiritualism. At the edges of the radical movement the Manichean heresy is always developing. If on the one hand this tendency leads exclusive Christianity to obscure the relation of Jesus Christ to nature and to the Author of nature, it leads on the other to loss of contact with the historical Jesus Christ of history, for whom a spiritual principle is substituted.[26]

Niebuhr's description allows us to see a perfect confluence of aesthetics of the high romantic tradition and fundamentalism. The early fundamentalists, of course, would hardly have seen the parallel and would, no doubt, not have appreciated having it pointed out to them. Fundamentalists of the first half of our century wrote almost no essays of significance on the arts. When the arts are mentioned in fundamentalist works, either their value or their use is called into question. Some forms, like theater, dance, and film, seem by their very nature to belong to this "material realm governed by a principle opposed to Christ," while others, including fiction, appear to waste precious time better spent in pursuit of the goals of the Kingdom.[27]

Around 1950 a different attitude began to appear. We find articles extolling the virtues of the arts in the life of the Christian. Indeed, some celebrate their centrality and claim, as we have seen, that in his agony and inspiration the artist somehow comes closer to God than any of the rest of us do.[28] But what remains constant in this theory, what provides the continuity between fundamentalist opponents of the arts and evangelical advocates for them, is a tendency to divide the world into opposing camps—one controlled by God and one abandoned either to Satan, to chaos, or to the unshaped void. We contemporary evangelicals have been far more subtle than have our fundamentalist forebears in the exposition of this dualism. Yet we have largely accepted the bifurcation that pervades not only the fundamentalist tradition but also most aesthetic theory from the time of Immanuel Kant to the present day of Paul de Man and Roland Barthes.

In retrospect, it seems quite logical that when we as evangelical students of culture began to emerge from the dusky passageways of fundamentalism, our eyes would be dazzled by the enchanting romantic tradition. Because of its skepticism about the relevance of history and the historical process, because of its desire to assign to art a special separate status, and because of its sense of alienation about both unadorned nature and mass culture, romantic theory has offered an appealing sight to those of us whose aesthetic lenses have been ground, whether we appreciate it or not, in the shop of American fundamentalism.

II

It may be appropriate at the close of a historical survey to offer a prophecy of the way evangelical attitudes toward the arts may develop in the coming years. Though the subject is vast, several recent books suggest possible directions for the future.

But first a final word about Hawthorne. In a well-known review of a collection of Hawthorne's tales, Herman Melville made note of the "great power of blackness" he found in Hawthorne. Melville attributed this power to Hawthorne's intense awareness of "Innate Depravity and Original Sin, from whose visitations, in some shape or other, no deeply thinking mind is always and wholly free. For, in certain moods, no man can weigh this world, without throwing in something, somehow like Original Sin, to strike the uneven balance."[29] But that very knowledge of good and evil is something that the innocent Adam of "The New Adam and Eve" lacks. And because he does not have it, he cannot understand the fully human world through which he moves. As Hawthorne repeatedly documented in his life and art, the pose of innocence has been a constant temptation for Christians in America. It is a temptation to which fundamentalists and evangelicals have more than once succumbed, especially by depicting the battle against pride, lust, injustice, and oppression as having already been won convincingly. Oscar Cullmann presents a view closer to the biblical one when he suggests that for Christians the battle with evil is roughly at the point where the allied armies stood after D-Day, the invasion of Normandy in 1944. The beachhead has been established, the tide of the battle has turned, and victory appears assured. But the conflict goes on.[30] Evangelical attempts to claim premature victory, whether in our art or in theories about the redeemed imagination, run the danger of contradicting the truth of our experience in history. Such presumption neglects as well the profound understanding of sin that we find in the Sermon on the Mount and in Christian figures such as the Apostle Paul, Augustine, Luther, Calvin, Edwards, and Reinhold Niebuhr.

The historian C. Vann Woodward argues that the American myth of exemption from history was one the South could not readily share. "The South has had its full share of illusions, fantasies, and pretensions," Woodward writes,

> but the illusion that "history is something unpleasant that happens to other people" is certainly not one of them—not in the face of accumulated evidence and memory to the contrary. . . . For the South had undergone an experience that it could share with no other part of America—though it is shared by nearly all the people of Europe and Asia—the experience of military defeat, occupation and reconstruction. Nothing about this history was conducive to the theory that the South was the darling of divine providence.[31]

Perhaps because of this fact, Southern culture has produced a body of significant art—in the literary works of writers like William Faulkner, Robert Penn Warren, and Flannery O'Connor—that seems more profoundly Christian in its sympathies (and in the case of O'Connor, its commitments) than any comparable group of works in nineteenth- or twentieth-century America.

Perhaps these writers were able to produce work with deep Christian implications because they lived in, criticized, and sustained within their art a culture for which the Christian story, however strangely, was more than a tale of personal triumph and innocence. They wrote within a larger socio-historical order whose reality they took seriously and whose experience of brokenness, humiliation, and longing resonated with the biblical saga of Exodus, Crucifixion, Resurrection, and Return. In *The Eclipse of Biblical Narrative,* Hans Frei argues that the seventeenth and eighteenth centuries witnessed a dramatic loosening of the firm grip that the biblical narrative had once held on the Western mind.[32] As a result, artists and biblical exegetes, among others, no longer found themselves looking at the world and the scriptural text from within a narrative framework established by a biblical view of history and human destiny. Indeed, as we have seen, many Western artists attempted to salvage the rich resources of biblical tradition by appropriating them for a description of the inner drama of the individual creative spirit at war with a largely hostile world. In *Natural Supernaturalism,* M. H. Abrams charts this turn inward and shows how it left the English-speaking world with an aesthetic tradition replete with Christian imagery yet largely void of traditional Christian belief.

The Reformed philosopher Nicholas Wolterstorff has recently claimed that modern aesthetic theories have "in large measure been determined by the social realities of the role of art in a certain segment of our society. . . . [We participate in] our society's *institution of high art.*"[33] According to Wolterstorff, that institution exalts the act of perceptual contemplation when it speaks of the role of art. A work of art is valuable because it has no tangible value, useful because it has no practical use, and permanently beautiful because it is untouched by time and all its sordid complications. In effect, the work of art offers a surrogate redemption, a surrogate eternity. Wolterstorff calls for us to "break the spell which our participation in the institution of high art has cast over us."[34] He would have us break the spell because the range of actions for which works of art equip us should not be narrowly defined by the act of perceptual contemplation but "is very nearly as broad as the range of human action itself. The purposes of art are the purposes of life. To envisage human existence without art is not to envisage human existence. Art—so often thought of as a way of getting out of the world—is man's way of acting *in* the world. *Artistically man acts.*"[35] One of those actions is to envision other and better worlds than the one we now inhabit. But many other of those actions should involve responding to the order we find rather than imposing another one—responding, that is, to the order that Christians who believe in a sovereign God discover in nature, history, society, and Scripture.

"It is because we all live out narratives in our lives," the philosopher Alisdair MacIntyre writes in *After Virtue*, "and because we understand our own lives in terms of the narratives that we live out that the form of narrative is appropriate for understanding the actions of others."[36] It would help us as evangelicals, I believe, if we could see the role of the artist as one of service to the community of the Christian church, of service to a church which in turn is a servant to the world and which finds itself in the midst of a story being told and unfolded by God. "What the poet naturally and properly wants to do is simply to deepen and extend the fundamental sense of life underlying a culture, and so to preserve it," Henry Zylstra claims in *Testament of Vision*.[37] Zylstra does not mean that preserving the culture involves unthinkingly endorsing what has been received. No, the prophet and visionary belong within the church and within the artistic community that serves within that church. But when they challenge the church and offer visions of what it might become, they do not do so as divine visitants from the realm of the sovereign imagination. Instead, they speak as human creatures who have received the truth handed down through the ages and who hold the treasure of the gospel in earthen vessels. We understand ourselves most fully, as artists and as Christians, when we can see our individual dreams, whether spiritual or aesthetic, as parts of a much more comprehensive story that has already begun, the outline of whose ending is known but whose details have not yet been told in full.

"Fiction," Zylstra wrote, "does not spring out of the mind of man in isolation. Fiction which, as the critics say, touches on life at many points and touches on it powerfully, must shoot its roots deeply into a tradition and culture. If there is no Christian tradition, no Christian culture, can we . . . get a novel which is satisfyingly Christian at the same time that it is satisfyingly full and complete?"[38] No doubt many in our midst have fled to aesthetic isolation because they find in the kingdom of high art a richness and understanding too often lacking in our evangelical communities. But that is a subject for another essay. Let it suffice for us to agree with Zylstra that "for the rest we must get on with providing for the Christian writer or painter or musician or actor a Christian culture which he can, without conflict, love and explore."[39]

We can be grateful that some writers like Shirley Nelson have loved and explored with great skill an often unattractive Christian world. Nelson's novel *The Last Year of the War* chronicles the life of a young woman entering the fictional Calvary Bible Institute in Chicago for the 1944-45 school year. "Happiness was a kind of badge at Calvary; it was not only nice to be happy, it was right. It was a sign that things were as

147

they should be on the inside."[40] And for most of the men and women at Calvary, things appear to be as they should be, on the inside as well as the outside. In this world of the victorious life, hearts beat hard and true for Christ. Except, it appears, the heart of young Jo Fuller. A recent convert and the daughter of unbelieving parents, Jo cannot seem to stride with those steady steps that would lead her to and keep her within the kingdom of sanctified living. Recalling Hawthorne's story, we might say that Jo lives in a world of new Adams and new Eves at Calvary Bible Institute. Though they await the imminent return of their Lord, these well-scrubbed young men and women have already in one sense been raptured. In their theology, their practices, and their simple living they have come away from all the sad consternation that is the lot of men and women in history.

If we recall Cullmann's metaphor of D-Day, it is interesting to note that one character in Nelson's novel actually believes the fate of the Allied armies hangs on him in this last year of the war. Clyde McQuade has a pathetic love for Jo and tries to convince her that the outcome of the entire war depends on whether or not she responds to his spiritual love and joins him in expecting God to work a miracle of victory. A triumph of inwardness, of the solitary spirit working on itself, can supposedly alter the destiny of nations.

Burdened with guilt and confused desires, Jo struggles through most of the novel to come to self-understanding and resolution as a Christian. Only once does she seem able to accept the way to resolution promised to those who journey down Cal Bible's path of holiness. Rededicating herself at a special missionary meeting, Jo feels she understands for the first time what "it meant to be Christ-like."

> People noticed the change in her. Ruth said, "Jo, you've grown so much spiritually. It's a blessing to see it." It bothered Jo a little to win Ruth's approval, but what people thought was not serious anyway. In fact, she had begun to detect in others the shallowness and self-concern that she had just left behind. The girls on the floor annoyed her often. Qualities she had noticed in them earlier now seemed to predominate: Beverly was silly, Karen aloof, Soup coarse. She felt advanced and special. Then that shocked her, that it could be so easy to become judgmental, and that pride could be the by-product of an experience so good. One had to be on guard all the time.
>
> One thing she knew: She never, never wanted to come down off this mountaintop, back to the valley of her old defeated life. This plane of living, she was sure, was what God intended for His people, and she meant to stay there on it, whatever the cost.[41]

But the feeling does not last. Interestingly enough, Shirley Nelson gives only three pages (in a 255-page novel) to the section dealing with Jo's sanctified triumphs. This three-page section, which is set apart as one of the three main sections of the novel, falls in the middle of the book. Were this a traditional evangelical artistic depiction of the Christian life, this life on the mountaintop might have been given to us as the final word about victorious life in the age and realm of the spirit. But Nelson moves Jo off the mountaintop. The conclusion of the novel does provide a resolution but not one as triumphal as Jo's pause on the spiritual peak. Instead, it gives us a picture of life that rings true to our experience in the midst of the world in which God has placed us and to which he would have us respond with patience, love, and the best of our creative efforts.

Chapter 12

THE DILEMMA
OF EVANGELICAL SCIENTISTS*

RONALD L. NUMBERS

FOR MORE THAN A CENTURY scientists of evangelical persuasion have lived simultaneously, often uncomfortably, in two intellectual worlds: a religious world that insisted on the divine inspiration of the Genesis account of creation and a scientific world that overwhelmingly accepted the truth of organic evolution. From the beginning, evangelicals responded to this situation in a variety of ways. The most conservative rejected the testimony of biologists and geologists in favor of a recent special creation in six twenty-four-hour days, while the most liberal identified evolution as God's method of creating the world and interpreted Genesis figuratively. Still others took an intermediate position by postulating one or more acts of special creation in an otherwise evolutionary process, a view that came to be known as progressive creationism.

This paper explores the efforts of evangelical scientists to come to terms with the issue of origins during the period between the end of the fundamentalist controversies of the 1920s, which left conservative Christians united in their opposition to evolution but divided over the correct interpretation of Genesis, and the early 1980s, which found evangelicals less united in their opposition to evolution and even more polarized theologically. Throughout my discussion I use the term "evangelical" in an admittedly loose manner to designate that amorphous body of conservative Protestants who have believed, among other doctrines, that the Bible is "the inspired Word of God, the only unerring guide to faith and

---

* This paper is based in part on Ronald L. Numbers, "Creationism in 20th Century America," *Science* 218 (1982):538–44, which provides all documentation not cited below.

conduct."[1] Fundamentalists, according to my usage, are those who have occupied the militant right wing of the evangelical movement.

Although evangelical scientists all professed faith in the inerrancy of Scripture, they often disagreed over the meaning of the first chapters of Genesis. Some viewed the days of creation as representing great spans of time, each corresponding to successive epochs in the natural history of the world, and thus they allowed for considerable evolutionary development. This day-age theory enjoyed great popularity among the leading evangelical scientists of the late nineteenth century, such as John William Dawson, the Canadian geologist, and George Frederick Wright, who contributed an essay on evolution to *The Fundamentals* (1910–1915). Even such fundamentalist stalwarts as William Bell Riley and William Jennings Bryan found it attractive. In fact, on the eve of the Scopes trial, the latter confided that he had no objection to "evolution before man but for the fact that a concession as to the truth of evolution up to man furnishes our opponents with an argument which they are quick to use, namely, if evolution accounts for all the species up to man, does it not raise a presumption in behalf of evolution to include man?"

Other evangelical exegetes identified two separate creations in the first verses of Genesis: the first "in the beginning," perhaps millions of years ago, and the second, in six actual days, approximately 4,000 years before the birth of Christ. According to this so-called gap theory (also known as the ruin-and-restitution theory), most fossils were relics of the first creation, destroyed by God prior to the Adamic restoration. The *Scofield Reference Bible* (1909), a fundamentalist favorite, sanctioned this view, as did the Presbyterian minister and self-styled "research scientist" Harry Rimmer, who, despite limited scientific training obtained during one term at a small homeopathic medical school, for decades ranked among the evangelical community's leading interpreters of science and the Bible.

The most literal reading of Genesis—but a minority view even among fundamentalists during the 1920s—held that God created all terrestrial life, past and present, in six twenty-four-hour days about 6,000 years ago and that a universal Noachian flood accounted for most of the fossil record. The leading exponent of this position was George McCready Price, a Seventh-day Adventist educator and self-trained geologist, who regarded the day-age theory as "the devil's counterfeit" and the gap theory as only slightly less objectionable. During the 1920s he emerged, according to the editor of *Science,* as "the principal scientific authority of the Fundamentalists," and for decades his reputation continued to grow among the rank and file. By the mid-1950s his influence had, in the opinion of one observer, reached "staggering" proportions, with his flood geology forming "the backbone of much of fundamentalist thought about geology, creation, and the flood."[2]

This failure of evangelicals to agree on such a vital issue as the interpretation of Genesis prompted some scholars to attempt in the mid-1930s to create "a united front against the theory of evolution" by organizing a Religion and Science Association to which all parties would be invited. The driving force behind this undertaking seems to have been L. Allen Higley, a Wheaton College professor of chemistry and geology who had earned a Ph.D. in organic chemistry from the University of Chicago. A nondenominational evangelical, he subscribed to the ruin-and-restitution theory of Genesis and, according to one associate, headed "a large and enthusiastic group of non-sectarian creation religionists throughout the middle west."[3] Higley became the association's first president, while Price, representing flood geology, served as chairman of its board of directors.

The Religion and Science Association held its first —and perhaps only—meeting in the spring of 1936 in Chicago's Moody Memorial Church. The program reflected the association's irenic goals. Among the scheduled speakers were spokesmen for each of the three major creationist camps, including Price, Rimmer, and W. Bell Dawson, who, like his famous father, advocated the day-age theory of Genesis. Despite their laudable intentions, the leaders of the association soon discovered that their theological differences outweighed their common opposition to evolution. Higley's "pre-adamic theories are the most absurd which I have ever run across," wrote one of Price's disciples following a conversation with the society's president:

> [H]e told me that Lucifer was the first being created on this world and that he was put here several million years ago and that his fall was the cause of several million years of chaos in which the earth was without form and void. That was the time when the stratified rocks were laid down; and then in six 24-hour days, God recreated the earth and the habitations upon it.[4]

In the face of such revelations, the Price faction bolted the organization, leaving it in shambles.

Disillusioned about the prospects of ever working harmoniously with creationists like Higley, Price and some like-minded friends, many of them Adventist physicians, organized a Deluge Geology Society in 1938 in the Los Angeles area. As described by Price, the group consisted of "a very eminent set of men. . . . In no other part of this round globe could anything like the number of scientifically educated believers in Creation and opponents of evolution be assembled, as here in Southern California." But in spite of the group's religious homogeneity, it too soon foundered—on "the same rock," complained a disappointed member, that wrecked the Religion and Science Association, that is, *"pre-Genesis time for the earth."*

The third attempt to create a society of evangelical scientists in America proved more successful. In 1941 the president of the Moody Bible Institute invited five evangelical scientists to Chicago to discuss the need for such an enterprise. From this meeting grew the American Scientific Affiliation (ASA), originally headed by F. Alton Everest, a professor of engineering at Oregon State College. Although the society took no official stand on the evolution question, members were required to sign a doctrinal statement attesting to their belief in the inspiration of the Bible, and Everest allegedly assured at least one early recruit that the ASA would be "antievolutionary." Certainly the association's first book, *Modern Science and Christian Faith* (1948), reflected this orientation, containing as it did a strong antievolutionary chapter by two creationist biologists, Walter E. Lammerts and William J. Tinkle.[5] Within a decade of its founding, membership in the ASA had grown from five to 220, over half of whom belonged to the Mennonite, Baptist, or Presbyterian churches and resided in the middle Atlantic or midwestern states.

By the late 1940s the ASA was beginning to show signs of tension, brought on in part by the growing presence of some young, well-trained scientists who wanted to bring evangelical Christianity more into line with mainstream science. The most vocal of this group was J. Laurence Kulp, a geochemist, who took Price and his followers to task for their unscientific effort to squeeze earth history into less than 10,000 years. A Wheaton alumnus and member of the Plymouth Brethren, Kulp held a Ph.D. in physical chemistry from Princeton University and had completed all but a dissertation in geology before joining the faculty of Columbia University. Despite his fundamentalist upbringing, he had come to accept the testimony of geology regarding the history and antiquity of the earth; and as one of the first evangelicals professionally trained in the science, he felt a responsibility to warn his colleagues in the ASA about the scientific flaws in Price's work. He feared that Price's views had already "infiltrated the greater portion of fundamental Christianity in America primarily due to the absence of trained Christian geologists." Conservatives within the ASA—not unreasonably—suspected that Kulp's exposure to "the orthodox geological viewpoint" had eroded his faith in a literal interpretation of the Bible.

Similar suspicion greeted the announcement in the early 1950s by Cordelia Erdman, an instructor in geology at Wheaton College, that she also accepted the conclusions of geologists regarding "the over-all sequence in which organic forms have made their appearance," which she contrasted with the "pseudo-scientific" findings of the Price school. Although she stopped far short of embracing general organic evolution, critics immediately questioned her orthodoxy. Miss Erdman's paper "is a fair statement of the position of the standard geologist," noted Tinkle. "However," he went on, "the standard geologist is an evolutionist."[6]

Before long it became evident that a growing number of ASA members, like Kulp and Erdman, were drifting from strict to progressive creationism and sometimes on to theistic evolutionism. Indisputable evidence of this shift came to light at the annual meeting of 1957, when Russell L. Mixter, a zoologist on the faculty of Wheaton College, conceded the evolution not only of species but of whole orders of plants and animals. In essence, wrote one admirer, Mixter had declared:

> I, an evangelical Christian, can accept the basic concepts of evo-
> lution. Although not exclusively demanded by the data involved
> it is certainly allowed, and in fact I can see no better or more
> logical way to handle the data. I believe in Creation, and simply
> affirm that in the light of the evidence now available, I think some
> evolution—that is, development of present-day forms by differen-
> tiation of previously existing forms—the most likely way God
> accomplished much of His Creation.[7]

Mixter's candid remarks touched off a spirited debate over the relative merits of progressive creation and theistic evolution that continued for over a year. The upshot, reported one troubled member, "appeared to be a growing conviction that inexorable pressure of expanding knowledge is about to force us to accept some formulation of the theory of evolution, including the evolutionary origin of man, and that we must adjust our thinking in accordance with this eventuality."[8]

Additional evidence of the ASA's drift from strict creationism ap-peared in 1959, when the association published a collection of essays, *Evolution and Christian Thought Today*, marking the centennial of Darwin's *The Origin of Species*. Edited by Mixter, the volume made a clean break with what one contributor called the "hypertraditionalist" interpretation of Genesis, including such notions as a young earth, a universal flood, and the absolute fixity of species. A few authors openly espoused theistic evolution. For example, biochemists Walter R. Hearn and Richard A. Hendry, who described Genesis as a "beautifully poetic narrative," argued that Christians must be willing to accept "that life arose from inanimate matter through a series of physico-chemical processes no different from those we can observe today." Such thinking strained evangelical theology to its limits and prompted some conservative reviewers to question whether the book, and by implication the ASA, represented evangelical thinking at all.[9]

By 1960 it was clear to most observers that the ASA had experienced something of an intellectual revolution. "[I]n fifteen years," wrote one member sympathetic to the change, "we have seen develop within A.S.A. a spectrum of belief in evolution that would have shocked all of us at the inception of our organization."[10] This shift, it seems, resulted less from the discovery of new scientific evidence in favor of evolution than from a growing familiarity with evolutionary theory gained in part from advanced training. "Although knowledge is expanding," said Frank Cassel, "I would judge that it is not the new information as much as the better understanding through more honest consideration of the old that accounts for the shift of emphasis by the A.S.A. with respect to evolution."[11]

Heightened scientific consciousness, however, explains only part of the transition. For Bible-believing Christians, it was also important that any new position on evolution be scripturally as well as scientifically sound. Fortunately for them, evangelical scholars like Bernard Ramm offered just the theological validation they needed. In 1954, Ramm, a Baptist theologian and philosopher of science, published a path-breaking work entitled *The Christian View of Science and Scripture,* in which he castigated the Price school for its "narrow bibliolatry" and for its perversion of true Christianity, arguing that evangelicals need not believe in a young earth, a universal flood, or even in the recent appearance of humans. Although he personally favored a progressive-creation model, he allowed for considerable evolutionary development and granted the orthodoxy of theistic evolution.[12] His influential work offered restless ASA scientists the very theological freedom their scientific studies seemed to demand. And as one of the theistic evolutionists confessed, "Naturally when I see the need of more time, and some Biblical scholar says, 'Sure, you may have more time,' I tend to jump on his band wagon very quickly."[13] Ramm, who dedicated his book to Everest and acknowledged the assistance of Kulp, thus became the theological guru of the ASA, which published a special issue of its *Journal* in his honor on the occasion of the twenty-fifth anniversary of his book.[14]

For most evangelical scientists, giving up strict creationism involved immense personal stress. J. Frank Cassel, who went on from Wheaton College to become chairman of the Department of Zoology at North Dakota State University, captured some of the turmoil in the following autobiographical testimony:

> First to be overcome was the onus of dealing with a "verboten" term and in a "non-existent" area. Then, as each made an honest and objective consideration of the data, he was struck with the validity and undeniability of datum after datum. As he strove to incorporate each of these facts into his Biblico-scientific frame of reference, he found that —while the frame became more complete and satisfying—he began to question first the feasibility and then the desirability of an effort to refute the total evolutionary concept, and finally he became impressed by its impossibility on the basis of existing data. This has been a heart-rending, soul-searching experience for the committed Christian as he has seen what he

had long considered the *raison d'etre* of God's call for his life endeavor fade away, and as he has struggled to release strongly held convictions as to the close limitations of Creationism.

Cassel went on to note that the struggle was "made no easier by the lack of approbation (much less acceptance) of some of his less well-informed colleagues, some of whom seem to question motives or even to imply heresy."[15]

As these comments suggest, the pain suffered by Cassel and his friends elicited little sympathy from conservatives within the ASA, who thought the association had gone "soft" on evolution or, in the colorful phrase of one member, "had gone to the apes."[16] In their opinion, the drift toward evolution was motivated not by intellectual honesty but by "the malignant influence of 'that old serpent, called the Devil, and Satan, which deceiveth the whole world' (Revelation 12:9)."[17] The term "progressive creation" they regarded as merely a euphemism for heterodox theistic evolution, the acceptance of which, declared one critic, was tantamount to placing "a kiss of death on [the] Master."[18] Assurances that even theistic evolutionists believed in God as Creator, and efforts to distinguish between evolution as a biological theory and evolutionism as a quasi-religious world view, all failed to allay the suspicion of heresy.[19]

The ASA liberals, for their part, displayed equally little charity toward the plight of the conservatives. Often self-conscious about their own fundamentalist heritage and increasingly embarrassed by the anti-evolution rhetoric of their creationist colleagues, they damned strict creationism as "pseudo-science" and a menace to the Christian faith.[20] By the early 1960s a split between liberals and conservatives, mirroring the rift that had already divided the larger evangelical community into fundamentalist and neo-evangelical camps, appeared inevitable.

The intellectual leader of the creationist insurgents was a Southern Baptist engineer, Henry M. Morris, who as a young adult had embraced Price's flood geology as a means of harmonizing science and the Bible. In the late 1940s he joined the ASA—just in time to protest Kulp's attack on Price's views. But Morris's words fell on deaf ears. In 1953, when he presented some of his own opinions to the ASA, one of the few compliments came from a young theologian, John C. Whitcomb, Jr., who belonged to the Grace Brethren. The two creationists subsequently decided to collaborate on a major defense of the Noachian flood. By the time they finished their project, Morris had earned a Ph.D. in hydraulic engineering from the University of Minnesota and was chairing the Civil Engineering Department at Virginia Polytechnic Institute; Whitcomb was teaching Old Testament studies at Grace Theological Seminary in Indiana.

In 1961 they brought out *The Genesis Flood,* the most impressive contribution to strict creationism since the 1920s. In many respects, their book appeared to be simply "a reissue of G. M. Price's views, brought up to date," as one reader described it. Beginning with a testimony to their belief in "the verbal inerrancy of Scripture," Morris and Whitcomb went on to argue for a recent creation of the entire universe, a Fall that triggered the second law of thermodynamics, and a worldwide flood that in one year laid down most of the geological strata. Given this history, they argued, "the last refuge of the case for evolution immediately vanishes away, and the record of the rocks becomes a tremendous witness . . . to the holiness and justice and power of the living God of Creation!"

Despite the book's lack of conceptual novelty, it provoked an intense debate among evangelicals. Progressive creationists and theistic evolutionists denounced it as a travesty on geology that threatened to set back the cause of Christian science a generation, while strict creationists praised it for making biblical catastrophism intellectually respectable. Its appeal, suggested one critic, lay primarily in the fact that, unlike previous creationist works, it "looked *legitimate* as a scientific contribution," accompanied as it was by footnotes and other scholarly appurtenances. In responding to their detractors, Morris and Whitcomb repeatedly refused to be drawn into a scientific debate, arguing instead that "the real issue is not the correctness of the interpretation of various details of the geological data, but simply what God has revealed in His Word concerning these matters."

Whatever its merits, *The Genesis Flood* unquestionably "brought about a stunning renaissance of flood geology" and created an intellectual climate conducive to the establishment of a scientific society for strict creationists only. Shortly before the publication of his book, Morris had sent the manuscript to the Lutheran geneticist Walter E. Lammerts, a fellow ASA member who for a time had worked with Price in the Deluge Geology Society. Disgusted by the ASA's flirtation with evolution and encouraged by the Morris and Whitcomb manuscript, Lammerts in the early 1960s organized a correspondence network, dubbed the "team of ten," which included Morris and eight other strict creationists. In 1963 seven of the ten met with a few others of like mind in the home of a team member in Midland, Michigan, to form the Creation Research Society (CRS).

The society began with a carefully selected eighteen-man "inner-core steering committee" (including the original team of ten), the composition of which reflected, albeit imperfectly, the denominational, regional, and professional bases of the creationist revival. Of the seventeen members for whom information could be found, six were Missouri Synod Lutherans, five Baptists, two Seventh-day Adventists, and one each from the Reformed Presbyterian Church, the Christian Reformed Church, the Church of the Brethren, and an independent Bible church. Eleven lived in the Midwest, three in the South, and two in the Far West. The committee included six biologists, but only one geologist, an independent consultant with a master's degree. Seven members taught in church-related colleges, five in state institutions; the rest worked for industry or were self-employed.

To avoid the creeping evolutionism that had infected the ASA and to ensure that the society remained loyal to strict creationism, the CRS required members to sign a statement of belief accepting the inerrancy of the Bible, the special creation of "all basic types of living things," and a worldwide deluge. To legitimize its claim to being a scientific society, it published a quarterly journal and limited full membership to persons possessing a graduate degree in a scientific discipline.

At the end of its first decade, the society claimed 450 regular members, plus 1,600 sustaining members, who failed to meet scientific qualifications. Eschewing politics, the CRS devoted itself almost exclusively to education and research, funded "at very little expense, and . . . with no expenditure of public money." Its journal reported such projects as expeditions to search for Noah's ark, studies of fossil human footprints and pollen grains found out of the predicted evolutionary order, experiments on radiation-produced mutations in plants, and theoretical studies in physics demonstrating a recent origin of the earth. In addition, a number of members collaborated in preparing a biology textbook based on creationist principles. In view of the previous history of such organizations, it was an auspicious beginning.

During the seventies and early eighties strict creationists mounted a remarkably successful campaign to carry their message beyond societies like the CRS to the masses. In addition to persuading two state legislatures and various local school boards to require the teaching of their interpretation of Genesis, they stemmed—and perhaps even reversed—the drift of evangelical Christians toward theistic evolution. A survey in 1979 revealed that American evangelicals believed, "by almost an eight to one margin, that God created Adam and Eve to start human life."[21] Such a statement did not preclude the acceptance of progressive creationism, but it certainly ruled out theistic evolution.

In recent years various writers have noted a marked tendency among evangelicals to believe in a recent creation and universal flood. In fact, the advocates of a young earth so successfully identified their views with creationism that they co-opted the very term, forcing other creationists into reluctantly giving up the label. In the preface to his book entitled *Christianity and the Age of the Earth* (1982), the evangelical geologist Davis

A. Young explained why, despite believing in creation, he intended to argue against creationism:

> I regret the fact that in this book I must call those with whose views I disagree, "creationists," because I am a creationist, and I believe the biblical record of creation. Unfortunately, however, those who advocate the creation of the world in seven literal days only a few thousand years ago have come to be known generally as creationists.[22]

Similarly, in the late 1970s an ASA officer explained that while his association was "a creationist group in the biblical sense of the term," its members were "not generally considered to be true blue 'creationists' in the most restricted use of the term that has come into being in the last five to ten years."[23] Indeed, the language of creationism has evolved so much that, were he alive today, not even William Jennings Bryan, once the leader of American creationists, would qualify as a creationist.

Many factors contributed to the resurgence of strict creationism: its conformity to a commonsense reading of the Bible, its uncompromising attitude toward evolution, and the skill with which Morris and his associates presented it as a scientifically respectable option. Ironically, in recent years strict creationists, who derived their views from the Bible, have begun calling their teachings "creation science," just as many liberal evangelicals, who read Genesis through an evolutionary lens, once insisted on being regarded as "creationists." "If you call something a rose you expect it to smell like a rose," explained the sagacious Russell Mixter.[24]

In view of their many victories, it would be easy to overestimate the influence of the strict creationists. While it is true that they cultivated a large following in the evangelical churches of America, they nevertheless failed by and large to capture evangelical colleges, many of which continued to provide sanctuary for scientists of a more liberal inclination. A survey in the 1970s of faculty who taught science in the Christian College Consortium showed that "the majority of the science faculty members take either a progressive creationist or theistic evolutionist position."[25]

By the early 1980s the evangelical community was probably more deeply divided over the issue of evolution than at any time in its history. Compared with the 1920s, when antievolutionists papered over their theological differences, at least in public, recent years have found evangelical scientists split into two hostile camps, neither of which makes much of an effort to accommodate the other. But some things remain unchanged. Many evangelical scientists continue to find themselves, like their forebears, living uncomfortably in two separate cultures. "I feel something of a stranger in two quite different worlds, two worlds of which I—as one of God's creatures—am very much a part," revealed the Australian D. Gareth Jones in a poignant personal testimony. "It is this sense of alienation which is at the heart of my personal dilemma."[26]

Chapter 13

THE NEW RELIGIOUS RIGHT
IN AMERICAN POLITICS

RICHARD V. PIERARD

ALTHOUGH EVANGELICALS HAVE HAD A LONG HISTORY of involvement in public life, during the era of fundamentalist predominance they were much less visible. To be sure, they made a continuing effort to secure a Christian Amendment (insertion of a reference in the Constitution acknowledging the country's allegiance to Jesus Christ), they vigorously defended national Prohibition and bitterly lamented its repeal, and they mounted a fierce campaign to prevent the "wet," Catholic governor of New York, Alfred E. Smith, from being elected President in 1928. By and large, however, fundamentalist political expression was conservative and negative in character, and most pastors, evangelists, and journalists condemned the New Deal, socialism, racial integration, Jewish radicalism, trade unionism, and, of course, communism. A few people were elected to public office who openly identified themselves as evangelical Christians, but their visibility was low until the 1950s, and their political stance was generally conservative.

In the pages that follow I will examine the literature dealing with the political involvement of evangelicals and the eventual emergence of the New Christian Right. Since the problems inherent in defining evangelicals and fundamentalists have been discussed throughout the volume, I will pay no further attention to the matter. Also, space precludes a general bibliographical essay on modern evangelicalism, but James A. Hedstrom has quite thoroughly covered this enormous body of writing in a 1982 dissertation at Vanderbilt University, which is as yet unpublished.

THE HISTORICAL BACKGROUND

The conservatism that constitutes the wellspring of modern-day Christian rightism has deep roots in the evangelical past. To be sure, evangelicalism contributed a positive vision of social reform, as Donald W. Dayton, *Discovering an Evangelical Heritage,* Timothy L. Smith, *Revivalism and Social Reform,* Ronald G. Walters, *American Reformers, 1815-1860,* James B. Stewart, *Holy Warriors,* Bertram Wyatt-Brown, *Lewis Tappan and the Evangelical War Against Slavery,* and Norris Magnuson, *Salvation in the Slums,* have so clearly pointed out. Temperance, feminism, the peace movement, rescue missions and relief agencies, urban reform efforts, the abolition of slavery, and ultimately the social gospel all had evangelical sources.

But there was an unpleasant side to the evangelical experience. The nineteenth-century evangelicals bought heavily into the ideas of American "chosenness" and national mission, as demonstrated in Ernest L. Tuveson, *Redeemer Nation,* and Conrad Cherry, *God's New Israel;* and they were firmly committed to the civil religion, a point made forcefully in *Twilight of the Saints* by Robert D. Linder and Richard V. Pierard, the only comprehensive account of American evangelical civil religiosity. Their reform efforts were flawed by an inadequate social vision (Clifford S. Griffin, *Their Brothers' Keepers*), a pervasive racism (Robert Allen, *Reluctant Reformers*), and a condescending and hostile outlook toward native Americans (Henry W. Bowden, *American Indians and Christian Missions*). They were largely supportive of the nation's military endeavors, as Ray H. Abrams, *Preachers Present Arms,* and the contributors to Ronald A. Wells, *The Wars of America,* point out. In an important dissertation, John E. Smylie shows that they also were behind imperialism in the late nineteenth century.

Like most of their fellow countrymen, the evangelicals were intensely patriotic and suspicious of all "foreign" ideologies that might threaten genuine Americanism. This outlook was present from the very beginning of the republic and could be seen in the endeavor in the late 1790s to combat the Illuminati conspiracy, described in an older work by Vernon Stauffer, *New England and the Bavarian Illuminati,* and the anti-Masonic movement three decades later, dealt with in William P. Vaughn, *The Antimasonic Party in the United States, 1826-1843.* It is thus not surprising that evangelicals supported the nativist Know-Nothings in the antebellum era, the theme of Ray A. Billington's *Protestant Crusade,* and participated actively during the 1880s and 1890s in such movements as the American Protective Association, documented in Donald L. Kinzer's *An Episode in Anti-Catholicism.* In his classic account, *History of Bigotry in the United States,* Gustavus Myers brings out the point that religious intolerance and persecution directed at dissenters from the official consensus were deeply rooted in the American past. This was closely linked to the antiforeignism that dramatically increased in tempo as the twentieth century dawned, a facet of history analyzed by John Higham in *Strangers in the Land.* Thus evangelicals had become deeply involved in what today would be labeled "rightist extremism" long before fundamentalism emerged in the period after World War I.

George Marsden shows in *Fundamentalism and American Culture* that evangelicalism was reshaped by the movement to uphold doctrinal orthodoxy, and Timothy P. Weber's *Living in the Shadow of the Second Coming* points to the impact that eschatological ideas had on the evangelical world view; both elements contributed to a loss of interest in social action. Marsden in particular argues that the fundamentalists adopted an essentially negative stance to the liberal social gospel, and in social and political matters they were intensely conservative. Already in the 1920s the militantly right-wing Ku Klux Klan, ably described by David M. Chalmers in *Hooded Americanism,* was drawing much of its support from fundamentalists and people who had evangelical leanings. That the genuine Christian commitment of Klan members very often was less than their outward professions of religiosity is vividly brought out in the moving first-person account by Thomas Tarrants, *The Conversion of a Klansman.* The symposium edited by David E. Harrell, *Varieties of Southern Evangelicalism,* leads one to see how theological conservatism in that area helped to orient many Christians in the direction of the political right.

Evangelicals in significant numbers were attracted by an assortment of right-wing prophets in the 1930s—William Dudley Pelley, Gerald Winrod, Gerald L. K. Smith, and others—who railed against liberalism, communism, and Jewish influence. In his impressive volume *The Old Christian Right,* Leo P. Ribuffo deals with these relatively unknown figures and the attempt to squelch them during World War II. At the same time a Roman Catholic "radio priest," Father Charles Coughlin of suburban Detroit, gained national attention by attacking Franklin D. Roosevelt's policies; he amassed a large following among conservative Protestants and Catholics alike. Although he was permanently silenced by his superior in 1942, his rightist views, explicated in Charles J. Tull, *Father Coughlin and the New Deal,* and Sheldon Marcus, *Father Coughlin: The Tumultuous Life of the Priest of the Little Flower,* had a significant impact on public opinion at the time.

The emergence of the Cold War in the later 1940s fueled a new outburst of evangelical conservatism. Carl McIntire and his American Council of Christian Churches stood in the forefront of the conservative Protestant attack on liberalism and communism, but he found allies in such men as Verne P. Kaub, Edgar C. Bundy, and Billy James Hargis. The endeavors of these and others during the decade following World War II are reported in Erling Jorstad, *The Politics of Doomsday,* and Ralph Lord Roy, *Apostles of Discord.* Although not so hawkish as the ACCC, the National Association of Evangelicals was still quite conservative, as one can see in its first official history, *Cooperation Without Compromise* by James DeForest Murch.

In this period there were some elected officials who identified themselves openly as Christians. One was the Baptist Frank Carlson of Kansas who served in the U.S. House of Representatives from 1935 to 1947, as governor of Kansas from 1947 to 1950, and then as U.S. Senator until 1969. He was a regular advocate of Christian causes and a prime mover behind the prayer breakfast idea. (Abram Vereide, the founder of the prayer breakfast movement and International Christian Leadership, now called "The Fellowship," is the subject of an admiring biography by Norman P. Grubb.) Robert D. Linder is currently preparing a definitive study of Carlson that will shed much light on the person who some feel was the first of a new breed of evangelical politicians.

Another public figure and one who was very much in tune with the conservativism of the postwar years was Dr. Walter H. Judd, a former medical missionary who served ten terms in the U.S. House, from 1943 to 1963, and was an outspoken anticommunist and leader of the "China Lobby." His views are presented in a volume edited by Edward H. Rozek. On the other hand, Congressman Brooks Hays of Arkansas, a prominent Southern Baptist layperson who served eight terms in the House of Representatives in the 1940s and 1950s, was a person ahead of his times. He gained distinction for his efforts at reconciliation in racial and civil rights matters. His courageous stand during the Little Rock school crisis of 1957 finally cost him his seat, but, as he emphasized in two autobiographical works, this was for him a clear matter of Christian conviction.

The 1950s was an era of genteel conservatism under the benevolent leadership of Dwight D. Eisenhower. It was viewed as a time when the nation was returning to godliness because the new president, as his pastor Edward L. R. Elson put it, had "brought a new moral tone and spiritual vitality into American life" and was "the focal point of a moral resurgence and spiritual awakening of national proportion." However, I show in my essay in *Christian Social Ethics* that it was also marked by an intense civil religiosity in which the Judaeo-Christian religion-in-general functioned as the social glue binding Americans together. The phrase "under God" was added to the Pledge of Allegiance; "In God We Trust" was adopted as the national motto; and evangelicals became increasingly visible in Washington and the state houses of the land, as was shown by the proliferation of prayer breakfasts, the growing number of officeholders who identified with evangelical churches, and the friendship which evangelist Billy

Graham had established with President Eisenhower and especially Vice President Richard Nixon. Meanwhile, the National Association of Evangelicals' Office of Public Affairs in Washington faithfully represented the conservative viewpoint of its constituency by combating Catholic encroachment on religious liberty, opposing federal aid to education, working to obtain legislation restricting the liquor industry and outlawing pornography, and encouraging the investigation of subversive activities and enactment of laws protecting the nation from the menace of communism. *Christianity Today,* founded in 1956 and financed heavily by the staunchly conservative oil millionaire J. Howard Pew, served as the voice of the "new" or "neo" evangelicalism, and its editorial policy was not to call into question the political consensus among evangelicals.

THE CHANGING MOOD IN THE EVANGELICAL CAMP

Nevertheless, the easing of the Cold War, the McCarthy debacle, and the moderation that characterized many who called themselves neo-evangelicals contributed to an unease about the traditional conservatism. A bellwether of change was Carl F. H. Henry, whose books *The Uneasy Conscience of Modern Fundamentalism* (1947) and *Aspects of Christian Social Ethics* (1964) were important indicators of a mellowing attitude on social and political issues. The civil rights movement and growing unrest about the Vietnam conflict further sensitized some individuals to the need for change. *Inasmuch: Christian Social Responsibility in the Twentieth Century,* written by sociologist David O. Moberg in 1965, reflected just how far a few evangelicals had started to move from the conservatism of their peers. Billy Graham's associate Sherwood Wirt spoke out in behalf of a more moderate social stance in *The Social Conscience of the Evangelical* (1968), and in that same year Robert Clouse, Robert Linder, and Richard Pierard called into question the long-standing evangelical ties with political and social conservatism in a symposium entitled *Protest and Politics.*

Soon more books appeared urging broader social involvement by evangelicals: Foy Valentine, *The Cross in the Marketplace;* Vernon Grounds, *Evangelicalism and Social Responsibility;* Henry, *A Plea for Evangelical Demonstration;* Moberg, *The Great Reversal;* Charles Y. Furness, *The Christian and Social Action;* Clouse, Linder, and Pierard, *The Cross and the Flag;* Ronald J. Sider, *The Chicago Declaration;* Jim Wallis, *Agenda for a Biblical People* and *The Call to Conversion;* Robert E. Webber, *The Secular Saint;* Richard J. Mouw, *Called to Holy Worldliness;* John Perkins, *With Justice for All;* and Stephen Mott, *Biblical Ethics and Social Change*—just to mention a few of the more prominent works. Magazines like *The Reformed Journal, The Other Side, Sojourners,* and *Radix* articulated the concerns of the new activists.

Just as remarkably, evangelicals began to confront the matter of political involvement. Among the openly professed Christians elected to public office were two legislators who broke with knee-jerk conservatism: Republicans John B. Anderson of Illinois, a member of the House of Representatives, and Mark O. Hatfield, governor of Oregon and then U.S. Senator. As both men showed in widely read and discussed books, being a Christian required them to take positions on issues that would not always be understood or appreciated by fellow believers. Anderson's stand on racial and family issues and Hatfield's on the Vietnam War evoked intense criticism from many in the evangelical camp. Anderson's difficulty in rallying evangelical support was evident in his abortive presidential bid in 1980, chronicled in *Diary of a Dark Horse* by Mark Bisnow. A study of Hatfield by Robert Eels poignantly reveals the trials that he underwent at the hands of conservative evangelicals. Billy Graham himself became an intimate adviser of Presidents Johnson and Nixon, but as I show in an article in the *Journal of Church and State,* his uncritical support of presidential policies, the Vietnam imbroglio, and the fallout from the Watergate scandal dealt a crushing blow to the hope that he would provide evangelicals an effective voice at the center of power.

There was a spate of books from evangelical presses urging greater involvement by Christians in the political process: Foy Valentine, *Citizenship for Christians;* Daniel R. Grant, *The Christian and Politics;* James M. Dunn, *Politics: A Guidebook for Christians;* Linder and Pierard, *Politics: A Case for Christian Action;* Paul B. Henry, *Politics for Evangelicals;* Perry C. Cotham, *Politics, Americanism, and Christianity;* and James W. Skillen, *Christians Organizing for Political Service.* These are among the more noteworthy works that urged Christians to grapple with issues, vote, and seek public office, and at the same time sensitized evangelicals to social justice concerns. There were also important theoretical treatments of political matters from an evangelical perspective, for example, Richard J. Mouw, *Political Evangelism* and *Politics and the Biblical Drama;* Stephen V. Monsma, *The Unraveling of America;* Albert F. Gedraitis, *Worship and Politics;* John Howard Yoder, *The Politics of Jesus;* and James Skillen, *Christian Politics: False Hope or Biblical Demand.*

The growing number of Christians in high places generated a virtual cult of born-again politics. Three books in the 1970s heralded the faith of public officials: Wesley Pippert, *Faith at the Top;* Wallace A. Frazier, *Politics and Religion Can Mix!;* and James C. Hefley and Edward G. Plowman, *WASHINGTON: Christians in the Corridors of Power.* In 1976 an avowed born-again Christian, Southern Baptist Jimmy Carter, was nominated for the presidency, and the evangelical backers of President Gerald Ford were forced to portray their man as a born-again believer as well. There can be no question about the genuineness of Carter's faith, as

Wesley Pippert shows in his treatment of the Georgian's religious views; but many traditionalists in the evangelical camp still wanted a person closer to their political position, and so they backed Ronald Reagan in 1980.

In an objective but rather plodding fashion, Robert Booth Fowler, *A New Engagement: Evangelical Political Thought, 1966-1976*, surveys the development and diversity of evangelical political and social attitudes during the years 1966-1976, and he shows that it was a time of intellectual and activist ferment in which evangelicalism "engaged" the political and social issues of the day with a vigor it had not exhibited since the nineteenth century. He explicates the different groupings among evangelicals (mainstream, reformists, and radicals), the mechanisms for change, and the various concerns that occupied their attention during this crucial decade. An interesting contention he makes is that *Christianity Today* during the 1960s and early 1970s became a pole around which the conservatives in the fold rallied as the political consensus broke apart. Erling Jorstad in *Evangelicals in the White House*, a briefer account of the 1960-80 era, insists that there were two strains in the evangelical movement—the "holders fast," or conservatives, and the "pressers on," those who wanted increased social involvement.

Both writers see evangelicals as having come of age politically in the 1970s and as a force to be reckoned with in American politics, but know that whether they will line up on the side of social change and justice is quite another matter. Although intellectuals and social activists were arguing for a more just political order, evangelicalism still rested on a firm foundation of conservatism that was reluctant to countenance far-reaching changes in the social structure or any diminution of American power. This became patently clear with the emergence of the New Christian Right at the end of the decade and the intense concern with "social" issues that gripped conservative Protestantism in the ensuing years.

THE RESURGENCE OF THE CHRISTIAN RIGHT

Although evangelicalism was starting to moderate in its political outlook in the early 1960s, the Christian Right gained a new lease on life as the reaction set in against the unrest sweeping the country. Numerous preachers and evangelists exploited the civil rights demonstrations, urban riots, student violence, opposition to the Vietnam War, and declining moral standards to rally support and funds for their organizations. Groups like the Christian Anti-Communism Crusade (Fred Schwarz), Christian Crusade (Billy James Hargis), Christian Freedom Foundation (Howard E.

Kershner), Church League of America (Edgar C. Bundy), Circuit Riders (Myers G. Lowman), National Education Program (George S. Benson), American Council of Christian Laymen (Verne P. Kaub), and the Twentieth Century Reformation Hour (Carl McIntire) attracted funds and followers. Such religiously oriented organs as *Christian Economics* (Kershner), *Christian News* (Herman J. Otten of the Lutheran Church—Missouri Synod), *Western Voice* (Harvey Springer), *Dan Smoot Report, The Capital Voice* (Dale Crowley), *The Truth Crusader* (Ernest Miller, a combination of health faddism and right wing politics), and *Voice of Americanism* (a radio program mixing religion and politics run by Steuart McBirnie) reached people in all parts of the country with the political gospel.

The innumerable books and articles on the right that poured off the secular presses frequently commented on the various manifestations of Christian rightism, and by the end of the decade voices of concern were being raised within the Protestant community itself. Richard V. Pierard in *The Unequal Yoke*, Erling Jorstad in *The Politics of Doomsday*, and John H. Redekop in *The American Far Right* subjected the evangelical radical right to searching criticism. I went after their ideological principles, Jorstad provided a careful analysis of four leading Christian rightists, and Redekop zeroed in on Hargis and his Christian Crusade. In *Religion and the New Majority*, Lowell Streiker and Gerald Strober scrutinized the sociological base of Christian rightism, especially as it was reflected in the ministry of Billy Graham. Gary K. Clabaugh, in *Thunder on the Right: The Protestant Fundamentalists,* examined the leaders, methods, resources, and ideologies of the religious right, a movement he saw as a genuine threat to American democracy.

One thing about the Christian right of the 1960s that deserves mention is the limited role played by anti-Catholicism—in contrast to the situation in the 1920s. Although many fundamentalists were disturbed about the candidacy of John F. Kennedy, rightist hostility toward him really was due more to his liberalism than his religion. Evangelical Protestants welcomed the Roman Catholic Church as an ally in the struggle against international communism, while many Catholics resisted social reforms at home and backed rightist enterprises like the *Twin Circle* publication of Patrick Frawley and the Cardinal Mindszenty Foundation. Included among the ranks of Catholic activists by now were William F. Buckley, Clarence Manion, Phyllis Schlafly, and Daniel Lyons.

The religious right appealed to disaffected groups in society and used the same kinds of tactics that the secular right did. A symposium edited by Daniel Bell in 1955 entitled *The New American Right* (updated and reissued in 1963 under the title *The Radical Right*) argued that the social sources of the right are not in economic interest group conflict but in status concerns and status politics. Seymour Martin Lipset and Earl Raab applied the status concern hypothesis to extremism in American history in *The Politics of Unreason*, while Richard Hofstadter suggested in *Anti-Intellectualism in American Life* and *The Paranoid Style in American Politics* that the rightists demeaned critical thought processes and their actions were dictated by irrational beliefs.

The most useful treatises on the far right written in the 1960s are Harry and Bonaro Overstreet, *The Strange Tactics of Extremism*, Arnold Forster and Benjamin R. Epstein, *Danger on the Right*, Brooks R. Walker, *The Christian Fright Peddlers*, George Thayer, *The Farther Shores of Politics*, and Franklin H. Littell, *Wild Tongues*. The most complete account of the chief secular organization, the John Birch Society, is by German scholar Rüdiger Wersich, but unfortunately it remains untranslated. The latest work on this era, Jonathan Kolkey's published dissertation, *The New Right, 1960-1968*, is merely a content analysis of several periodicals and books and does not significantly advance our understanding of the topic.

FROM OLD TO NEW CHRISTIAN RIGHT

The evangelical Christian right was in a state of disarray in the early 1970s. The rapidly growing number of moderates challenged more and more people to rethink their traditional conservatism, and a document like the Chicago Declaration of 1973 was greeted favorably in many quarters. A substantial segment of the evangelical community had backed Richard M. Nixon in 1968 and regarded him as one of their own because of his public piety, White House religious services, and ties with Billy Graham; but the Watergate scandal made a shambles of his presidency. The leaders of the Christian right were aging and they lacked new ideas for the 1970s, especially as the Vietnam War ended, urban riots tapered off, and detente with the Communist bloc became official policy. One major figure, Billy James Hargis, was discredited in a sex scandal. Then in 1976 an attempt to form an evangelical political coalition to elect conservative candidates to public office spearheaded by Campus Crusade for Christ leader Bill Bright and Arizona congressman John Conlan was thwarted when *Sojourners* editors Jim Wallis and Wes Michaelson exposed the operation.

Nevertheless, conservative evangelical activists in 1976 had established contacts with those men who were putting together a "New Right" coalition. The latter group, described in Alan Crawford's cogent analysis *Thunder on the Right*, understood the importance of political power. Through the sophisticated, computerized fund-raising techniques of Richard Viguerie (his personal philosophy and program are detailed in *The New Right: We're Ready to Lead*) and the interlacing network of organizations set up by Paul Weyrich, Howard Phillips, John T. Dolan, Reed Larson, Morton Blackwell, and others, the New Right set out to conquer power. They drew first blood in 1978 by helping to elect three conservatives to the Senate. One of the losers, Thomas J. McIntyre of New Hampshire, recounted his experiences in a chilling book entitled *The Fear Brokers,* which intimated what lay ahead. In the following year the secular new rightists joined forces with evangelical conservatives to form the three organizations that would be the most visible part of the New Christian Right: Christian Voice (Gary Jarmin), the Moral Majority (Jerry Falwell and Robert Billings), and the [Religious] Roundtable (Ed McAteer).

With the enthusiastic involvement or at least backing of several television evangelists (their ministries are examined in Jeffrey Hadden and Charles Swann, *Prime-Time Preachers*), the New Christian Right groups threw themselves wholeheartedly into the 1980 election to secure the election of Ronald Reagan, who had identified with their cause at the Roundtable's National Affairs Briefing in Dallas in August. Reagan also was now affirming an evangelical faith, and this aided the Christian conservatives in the effort to persuade fellow believers to reject the other two "born-again" candidates, President Jimmy Carter and John Anderson. However, when it became clear that the New Christian Right had not been the decisive influence in his election, the new president placed their "social program" (antiabortion, school prayer, and tuition tax credits) on a back burner. Although he continued to view these favorably, his support for their passage became lackluster.

A vast body of literature has grown up around the New Christian Right, much of which I discussed in articles in *Choice* and *Foundations* in 1982. Ernie Lazar has prepared a definitive bibliography on conservative thought and activity in the United States, to be published in 1984, while the reproductions of the Data Center in Oakland, California have made the rich periodical literature on the right available to the general reader. The central figure in the drama, the suave and personable Rev. Jerry Falwell, sets forth his views in *Listen, America!* and *The Fundamentalist Phenomenon* (the latter actually written by two of his associates), and they are further explicated in an anthology compiled by William Goodman and James Price. Laudatory treatments of Falwell and his empire, comprised of Thomas Road Baptist Church in Lynchburg, Virginia, the Liberty Baptist College and Seminary, the *Old-Time Gospel Hour* TV program, and the Moral Majority, Inc., are contained in Gerald Strober and Ruth McClellan, *The Jerry Falwell Story,* and William Willoughby, *Do We Need the Moral Majority?*

On the other hand, all the works evaluating the religious right pay particular attention to Falwell, but some demonstrate a deficient understanding of the dynamics of the movement by casually throwing around the term "moral majority" as a collective term for it. The news media first picked up on the New Christian Right, and this was followed in 1981–82 by a deluge of books and articles, many of which were largely impressionistic and journalistic in nature. The majority of these were written by people who are active in the church. Erling Jorstad, *The Politics of Moralism,* delivers a capsule summary of the major conservative groups and their leaders. Peggy Shriver, *The Bible Vote,* makes good use of the statements by various religious bodies to provide an incisive analysis of the right. John Cooper, *Religious Pied Pipers,* sees the movement as an expression of political religion that is harmful both to Christianity and American values. Robert Webber, in a misnamed book, *The Moral Majority: Right or Wrong?,* sets up the Moral Majority as an ideal type of the religio-political right, contrasts it with the World Council of Churches, and critiques both.

Gabriel Fackre, *The Religious Right and Christian Faith,* is probably the best theological assessment, while Roman Catholic ethicist Daniel Maguire in *The New Subversives* condemns the Christian right for its bigotry, nonbiblical message, and threat to American pluralism. Martin E. Marty, *The Public Church,* gives a helpful discussion of the tensions Christians are facing as they draw closer to one another and of how they need the church's guidance to keep from being sidetracked by inadequate conceptions of Christianity such as those professed by the New Christian Right. John L. Kater, *Christians on the Right,* shows that the movement is in fact an ideological justification for preconceived beliefs about the world, and Samuel Hill and Dennis Owen, *The Religious-Political Right in America,* is a thoughtful assessment from a sociological standpoint. Their research included extensive interviewing and television watching. Evangelical political scientist Robert Zwier analyzes the New Christian Right as a political interest group in *Born-Again Politics: The New Christian Right in America,* while Anson Shupe and William Stacey maintain in *Born-Again Politics and the Moral Majority* that empirical studies show the religious right had less of an impact than commentators had believed.

Those unsympathetic to the religious concerns of the right have produced harsh and not particularly satisfactory accounts. Humanist Edward L. Ericson, *American Freedom and the Radical Right,* attempts to refute what he perceives to be a growing assault on the foundations of liberty in the United States. Robert Vetter, *Speak out Against the New Right,* is an assemblage of articles and essays attacking the right from numerous perspectives. Perry Deane Young, *God's Bullies,* and Flo Conway and Jim Siegelman, *Holy Terror,* are journalistic hatchet jobs unworthy of further comment. However, the volume prepared by David Bollier under the auspices of Norman Lear's People for the American Way, *Liberty and Justice for Some,* is much more balanced.

In 1983 the output of books on the New Right slowed appreciably, but the quality of the treatments improved markedly. Richard Rutyna and John Kuehl published *Conceived in Conscience,* the papers of a conference whose participants (including this writer) represented both sides of the controversy and considered matters from the perspective of contemporary church-state relations. My personal assessment of the religious right is contained in my paper and two other essays in 1983. George Marsden has written on the New Right in two 1983 collections, one edited by Mary Douglas and Steven Tipton and the other by Ronald Stone, that broadly reassess the role of religion in society and politics. *New Christian Politics,* edited by David Bromley and Anson Shupe, brings together the latest research on the New Right. Also significant is Robert Liebman and Robert Wuthnow, *The New Christian Right: Mobilization and Legitimation,* a compilation of twelve original essays that raise questions regarding the nature of religion and politics, the role of status groups, and contemporary American culture. British scholar Gillian Peale brings the unique perspective of an outside observer to her *Revival and Reaction: The Contemporary American Right,* an endeavor to explain the phenomenon to her countrymen. Philip Finch's journalistic piece on the really "hard" right, *God, Guts, and Guns,* suffers from some serious limitations but does give insights into the activities of the most far-out Christian rightists. In a book on the Jewish Holocaust, historian David Rausch includes a perceptive discussion of modern-day extremist "hate" groups and shows how they are a great threat to genuine Christianity.

WHITHER EVANGELICAL CONSERVATISM?

The issues that animate the New Christian Right are ones that appeal to a large segment of the evangelical community, not just a fringe of wild-eyed extremists. Thus substantial numbers of individuals and organizations sympathize with these concerns even though they may not be part of any old or new Christian rightist framework. Among the most burning matters are the role of religion in public life; freedom for Christian schools; the "family" issues of abortion, infanticide, homosexuality, women's liberation, divorce, and children's rights; and secular humanism. Lawyer John W. Whitehead stands in the forefront of the struggle against the Supreme Court's definition of strict separation of church and state, which has precluded state-prescribed prayer and Bible reading in the public schools, as one may see in his books *The Separation Illusion, The Second American Revolution,* and *The Stealing of America.* He can count on backing from the Christian Legal Society, the NAE Office of Public Affairs, yes, even President Reagan, in the campaign to "put God back in the schools" by means of a prayer amendment or some legislative device that would overturn the court rulings. Evangelical rightists contend that the state's alleged neutrality in religious matters is a fiction, and perhaps even revolutionary action may be required to get the nation back on the right track, as Francis Schaeffer intimates in *A Christian Manifesto*.

Abortion and other family issues have resulted in a published output so immense that another essay would be needed to assess it adequately. Such pieces as Carl Wilson, *Our Dance Has Turned to Death*, and Tim LaHaye, *The Battle for the Family*, have linked traditionalist views of the woman's role in the family with rightism. Landmark works in sensitizing evangelicals to the political implications of abortion include Francis Schaeffer and C. Everett Koop, *Whatever Happened to the Human Race?*, and Franky Schaeffer V, *A Time for Anger*. The Christian Action Council and a host of other organizations seek to draw moderate evangelicals into the pro-life movement, the net effect being the formation of coalitions with the rightist groups.

Secular humanism is a major obsession of the religious right. It is not clear when evangelicals first became concerned about the bogey of humanism, but their interest was undoubtedly given a substantial lift by the book and accompanying film series of Francis Schaeffer, *How Should We Then Live?* Emotive but facile tracts by Tim LaHaye, *The Battle for the Mind*, and Homer Duncan, *Secular Humanism*, helped to popularize the idea, and James Hitchcock gave it a more sophisticated twist in *What Is Secular Humanism?*

The New Christian Right propagates the vision of a Christian America that, although repugnant to evangelicals in other parts of the world, has a wide appeal here. It is an integral part of the Christian school textbooks of Rosalie Slater, Verna Hall, and Marshall Foster/Mary-Elaine Swanson, and was given wide currency in a classic piece of "holy history" by Peter Marshall and David Manuel, *The Light and the Glory*. The bicentennial observance in the mid-1970s further boosted the myth. It holds that America was founded as a Christian nation and flourished under the benevolent hand of divine providence. Our country had the mission to bear witness to the other nations of God's greatness and goodness and to serve as the base from which the gospel message went out into the world. It received the blessings of heaven as long as it remained faithful to the Creator and functioned as a "nation under God." But when a few decades ago Americans turned their backs on God, violated his laws, and gave themselves over to immoralities of all sorts, they began to feel his heavy hand of judgment. The nation will surely perish if our people do not return to God quickly.

Interestingly, it was a team of evangelical historians, Mark Noll, Nathan Hatch, and George Marsden, who finally laid the "Christian nation" thesis to rest. In *The Search for Christian America*, an incisive reassessment of how Christianity has and has not shaped the country, they examine the impact of Puritanism and show that there can be no Christian culture as such, re-evaluate the connections between the Great Awakening and the American Revolution and the role of Christians in the conflict, reflect on the myths of innocence and guilt in the American past, and demonstrate the hidden political agenda in the notion of a return to Christian America. Whether their ideas will find a firm lodging place in the Christian schools that populate the land is quite another question. Many of these function as agencies to inculcate an ideology of conservativism in the children, and any attempt to raise doubts about the nation's Christian origins and subsequent fall from the will of God may simply be rejected as another example of the all-pervasive secular humanist conspiracy.

Although many outside the evangelical orbit regard all rightists as ignorant reactionaries who wish to stifle the intellectual freedom of Americans, an idea rebutted in Cal Thomas's acerbic tome *Book Burning* but given the air of plausibility by the feisty textbook censors in Texas, Norma and Mel Gabler, there are in reality a number of academically trained and articulate evangelical conservatives who are writing today and whose work is overlooked because of the attention given the more extreme rightists. Although he does not hold an earned doctorate, theologian Francis Schaeffer enjoys considerable respect among rank-and-file evangelicals (less so among academics, who object to his tendency to oversimplify complex matters), and his ideas have greatly influenced rightist thinking in the past decade. Other evangelical conservatives who cannot be categorized as new rightists but have expressed themselves on political, social, and economic matters within the last few years include Ronald Nash, C. Gregg Singer, Harold O. J. Brown, Harold Lindsell, and most recently, Herbert Schlossberg.

The New Religious Right has deep roots in American evangelicalism, but it must now compete with other political stances for adherents. To be sure, the conservative tradition attracts many, but then, so do the more moderate, reformist, and radical positions. There is no longer an evangelical political consensus, and perhaps that is just as well.

NOTES

INTRODUCTION

1. Some of the most interesting discussions bearing on this theme are found in Mary Douglas and Steven M. Tipton, eds., *Religion and America* (Boston: Beacon Press, 1983).

2. An excellent discussion of this theme is found in James Davison Hunter, *American Evangelicalism: Conservative Religion and the Quandary of Modernity* (New Brunswick, N.J.: Rutgers University Press, 1983), esp. pp. 73–101. Cf. Richard Quebedeaux, *The Worldly Evangelicals* (San Francisco: Harper and Row, 1978). See also Nathan Hatch's discussion of this theme in this volume.

3. Smith and his students have been working on a major collective historical study with the working title "The Evangelical Mosaic."

4. Cf. Cullen Murphy, "Protestantism and the Evangelicals," *The Wilson Quarterly* V,4 (Autumn 1981): 105–16, an essay written in consultation with Timothy Smith which presents an admirable summary of this approach. Murphy describes evangelicalism as a "12-ring show" (p. 108). Robert E. Webber, *Common Roots: A Call to Evangelical Maturity* (Grand Rapids: Zondervan, 1978), 32, lists fourteen varieties of evangelicalism based on distinctive emphases rather than just on denominational differences.

5. Among Lutherans, "evangelical" has a more general meaning, roughly equivalent to "Protestant," and some neo-orthodox theologians have used it in its broad sense of "gospel-believer." The definition offered here, however, reflects the dominant Anglo-American usage.

6. For instance, of Americans who do not belong to, attend, or contribute to churches 64% say they believe Jesus is God or the Son of God, 68% believe in Jesus' resurrection, 40% say they have made a personal commitment to Jesus, 27% say the Bible is the actual word of God and "is to be taken literally, word for word," 25% claim to have been "born again." George Gallup, Jr. and David Poling, *The Search for America's Faith* (Nashville: Abingdon, 1980), 90–92. Also, 84% of Americans say the ten commandments are still valid for today, but only 42% know at least five of them. For those classed as "evangelicals," only 58% could name five of the commandments. James W. Reapsome, "Religious Values: Reflection of Age and Education," *Christianity Today*, 7 May 1980, 23–25.

7. James Hunter's *American Evangelicalism* presents some valuable analysis of the polling data but also illustrates the problem of conflating evangelicalism in its broad definitional sense with its other senses. For discussion of this point, see George Marsden, "Evangelicalism in the Sociological Laboratory," *The Reformed Journal* (June 1984).

8. Charles I. Foster, *An Errand of Mercy: The Evangelical United Front, 1790–1837* (Chapel Hill: University of North Carolina Press, 1960), 121.

9. Richard Lovelace aptly characterizes Jerry Falwell's activist fundamentalism as "really a sort of southern neo-evangelical reform movement." "Future Shock and Christian Hope," *Christianity Today*, 5 August 1983, 16.

CHAPTER ONE

1. Bruce Shelley, *Evangelicalism in America* (Grand Rapids: Eerdmans, 1967); Ronald H. Nash, *The New Evangelicalism* (Grand Rapids: Zondervan, 1963); and Donald G. Bloesch, *The Evangelical Renaissance* (Grand Rapids: Eerdmans, 1973) are evangelical accounts of this phenomenon; while Winthrop S. Hudson, *American Protestantism*

(Chicago: University of Chicago Press, 1961), 153–76; and Sydney E. Ahlstrom, *A Religious History of the American People* (New Haven: Yale University Press, 1972), 956–60, have made most note of it among the leading church historians.

2. On reductionist interpretations, see George M. Marsden, *Fundamentalism and American Culture: The Shaping of Twentieth-Century Evangelicalism, 1870-1925* (New York: Oxford University Press, 1980), 199–201; among current scholars, William G. McLoughlin, in his *Revivals, Awakenings and Reform: An Essay on Religion and Social Change in America, 1607-1977* (Chicago: University of Chicago Press, 1978); and his "The Illusions and Dangers of the New Christian Right," *Foundations* 25 (1982):128–43, argues most forcefully for the idea that fundamentalism is a passing, "nativist" reaction to modernity; while Martin E. Marty, "Religion in America Since Mid-century," *Daedalus* 111 (1982):149–64, and "Forward" and "The Revival of Evangelicalism and Southern Religion," in David Edwin Harrell, Jr., ed., *Varieties of Southern Evangelicalism* (Macon, Ga.: Mercer University Press, 1981), ix–xii, 7–22, insists that evangelicals have had a symbiotic relationship with modernity. The record of fundamentalism herein shows Marty to be more correct than is McLoughlin. For a fuller discussion of this theoretically induced myopia, see Grant Wacker's essay in this volume.

3. Ed., "The Sin of Timidity," *Revelation* 2 (December 1932): 489.

4. Ed., *Bibliotheca Sacra* 88 (October 1931): 385.

5. Ned B. Stonehouse, *J. Gresham Machen, A Biographical Memoir* (Grand Rapids: Eerdmans, 1954), 493–99, 500–05; George Hutchinson, *The History Behind the Reformed Presbyterian Church, Evangelical Synod* (Cherry Hill, N.J.: Mack Publishing, 1974), 215–70; George Marsden, "Perspectives on the Division of 1937," *Presbyterian Guardian* 29 (January–April 1964):5–8, 21–23, 27–29, 43–46, 54–56; William A. Bevier, "A History of the I.F.C.A." (Th.D. thesis, Dallas Theological Seminary, 1958); Robert Delnay, "A History of the Baptist Bible Union" (Th.D. diss., Dallas Theological Seminary, 1963); Joseph M. Stowell, *Background and History of the General Association of Regular Baptist Churches* (Haywood, Cal.: J.F. May Press, 1949); Patsy S. Ledbetter, "Crusade for the Faith: The Protestant Fundamentalist Movement in Texas" (Ph.D. diss., North Texas State University, 1975).

6. See, e.g., R.T. Ketcham, "An Open Letter to Dr. W.B. Riley from Dr. R.T. Ketcham," *Baptist Bulletin* 2 (November 1936):3–4; O.W. Van Osdel, "How About It?" *Baptist Bulletin* 1 (August 1933):2.

7. John W. Bradbury, "The N.B.C. Fundamentalists," *Watchman-Examiner* 25 (August 12, 1937):916–18.

8. "Notes on Open Letters: Dr. Riley and the Northern Baptists," *Sunday School Times* 79 (July 24, 1937):522.

9. Granville Hicks, "The Son of a Fundamentalist Prophet," *The Christian Register* CVI (March 10, 1927), 197–98; reprinted in *The Uncertain World of Normalcy: The 1920's*, ed. Paul A. Carter (New York: Pitman, 1971), 142–46; quotes: 143, 144.

10. For a fuller discussion of this development, see the author's "Fundamentalist Institutions and the Rise of Evangelical Protestantism, 1929–1942," *Church History* 49 (March 1980):62–75.

11. "What About Your Son or Daughter?" *Moody Monthly* 38 (July 1938): 560.

12. Advertisement, *Watchman-Examiner* 23 (April 25, 1933):476; "Wheaton College," *Bulletin of Wheaton College* 13 (June 1936):4.

13. Peter L. Berger, "A Sociological View of the Secularization of Theology," *Journal for the Scientific Study of Religion* (Spring 1967):11–12.

14. Ernest R. Sandeen, "Fundamentalism and American Identity," *Annals of the American Academy of Political and Social Sciences* 387 (January 1970):56–65; Sandeen, "The Problem of Authority in American Fundamentalism," *Review and Expositor* 75 (Spring 1978):211–17; George M. Marsden, "J. Gresham Machen, History, and Truth," *West-*

minster Theological Journal 42 (Fall 1979):157-75; Marsden, *Fundamentalism and American Culture,* esp. chs. XXII and XXV.

15. Walter Lippmann, *A Preface to Morals* (New York: Macmillan, 1929), 31-32; H.L. Mencken, "Doctor Fundamentalis," obituary of J. Gresham Machen in the *Baltimore Sun,* January 1937.
16. Robert S. and Helen Merrill Lynd, *Middletown in Transition: A Study in Cultural Conflicts* (New York: Harcourt, Brace and World, 1937), 491.
17. Richard H. Pells, *Radical Visions and American Dreams: Culture and Social Thought in the Depression Years* (New York: Harper and Row, 1973), is the best survey of the intellectual ferment of the era.
18. Warren Susman, "The Thirties," *The Development of an American Culture,* ed. Stanley Coben and Lorman Ratner (Englewood Cliffs, N.J.: Prentice-Hall, 1970), 179-218; Susman, ed., *Culture and Commitment, 1929-1945* (New York: George Braziller, 1973), 1-19.
19. Timothy P. Weber, *Living in the Shadow of the Second Coming: American Premillennialism, 1875-1925* (New York: Oxford University Press, 1979), 9-24, gives a concise explanation of premillennialism and dispensationalism; see also C. Norman Kraus, *Dispensationalism in America: Its Rise and Development* (Richmond: John Knox Press, 1958); for a helpful comparison of eschatological views, see Robert G. Clouse, ed., *The Meaning of the Millennium: Four Views* (Downers Grove, Ill.: Inter-Varsity Press, 1977).
20. Dwight Wilson, *Armageddon Now! The Premillenarian Response to Russia and Israel* (Grand Rapids: Baker Books, 1977), gives the best historical survey of fundamentalist prophetic speculation.
21. Barnhouse, "Russia Wins the War!" *Revelation* 9 (December 1939):477.
22. "Is Man Bound to Win?" *Sunday School Times* 75 (March 26, 1933):208; "Intellect a Failure," *Moody Monthly* 30 (September 1931):4; D.J. Fant, "This Machine Age," *Alliance Weekly* 67 (October 22, 1932):674-75; "God and Mammon," *Bibliotheca Sacra* 89 (July 1932):288; Kenneth Mackenzie, "Thanksgiving, 1932," *Alliance Weekly* 67 (November 19, 1932):744-45; E.P. Lipscomb, "Ominous Signs in American Life," *Watchman-Examiner* 23 (March 28, 1935):337-38; E.W. Crowell, "Why God Is Judging America," *Baptist Bulletin* 10 (May-June 1938):5-6, 11-12; P.B. Fitzwater, "America's Predicament—Why?" *Moody Monthly* 37 (November 1936):109.
23. "Is the Ship of State Drifting?" *Moody Monthly* 34 (June 1934):443; The Farm Mother (pseud.), "A Crop Survey," *Sunday School Times* 76 (July 28, 1934):481-82; editorial, *Bibliotheca Sacra* 93 (April-June 1936):130-31; "What Is Wrong?" *Bibliotheca Sacra* 94 (October 1937):383; Paul Rood, "On the Threshold of a New Year," *King's Business* 28 (January 1937):4; M.H. Duncan, "Trends Toward Liberalism in America," *Moody Monthly* 38 (November 1937):118; "Does It Matter?" *Revelation* (October 1940):444.
24. Judson E. Conant, *The Growing Menace of the "Social Gospel"* (Chicago: Bible Institute Colportage Association, 1937):8.
25. "Civilization's Peril," *Moody Monthly* 40 (July 1940):591.
26. "Unbelief and Its Fruit," *Moody Monthly* 42 (September 1941):4; see also "Evolution and This War," *Sunday School Times* 83 (August 2, 1941):4; W.W. Ayer, "The Pastor Says," *Calvary Pulpit* II:3 (1941):2; "Does Christianity Have Its Back to the Wall?" *Watchman-Examiner* 28 (June 13, 1940):664-65; "What Can Christians Do Now?" *Watchman-Examiner* 29 (August 21, 1941):880; "A Century of Despair," *Revelation* 13 (January 1943):6.
27. "It Must Not Happen Again," *Moody Monthly* 41 (August 1941):691-92.
28. Thomas M. Jacklin, "Mission to the Sharecroppers: Neo-Orthodox Radicalism and the Delta Farms Venture," *South Atlantic Quarterly* 78 (Summer 1979):302-16; Donald Meyer, *The Protestant Search for Political Realism, 1919-1941* (Berkeley and Los Angeles: University of California Press, 1960); Paul A. Carter, *The Decline and Revival of the*

Social Gospel: Social and Political Liberalism in American Protestant Churches, 1920-1940 (Hamden, Conn.: Anchor Books, 1971), 153-62, 213-19.

29. "The Church and Politics," *Revelation* 1 (June 1931):200.

30. Donald Grey Barnhouse, "The Mark for Commerce," *Revelation* 3 (August 1933):312; L. Sale-Harrison, "Mussolini and the Resurrection of the Roman Empire," *Moody Monthly* 29 (April 1929):386-87; Ralph C. Norton, "Mussolini's Place in Prophecy," *Sunday School Times* 75 (June 3, 1933):371; Walter P. Knight, "The Mark of the Beast, or Is Antichrist at Hand?" *Moody Monthly* 34 (July 1934):493.

31. Louis S. Bauman, "The Blue Eagle and Our Duty as Christians," *Sunday School Times* 75 (September 16, 1933):583-84; Barnhouse, "The Mark for Commerce," cited above; "The Blue Eagle," *Revelation* 3 (September 1933):329; "An Age of Dictators," *Moody Monthly* 33 (July 1933):480.

32. "Human Interests," *Moody Monthly* 35 (August 1935):553.

33. Marsden, *Fundamentalism and American Culture*, 206-11; Richard Hofstadter, *Anti-Intellectualism in American Life* (New York: Alfred Knopf, 1962), 135; *The Paranoid Style in American Politics and Other Essays* (New York: Random House, 1963), 29.

34. "Running True to Form," *Bibliotheca Sacra* 96 (January-March 1939):4; Barnhouse, "The Mark for Commerce," cited above; Barnhouse, "The Civil War in Spain," *Revelation* 7 (February 1937):78; Louis S. Bauman, "When Russia's Bear Meets Judah's Lion," *Sunday School Times* 74 (April 16, 1932):207, 210; Bauman, "I Believe in the Resurrection of the Empire," *Sunday School Times* 81 (December 2, 1939):886-88; Bauman, "The Red Dragon and the Woman's Child—in 1934," *King's Business* 25 (March 1934):94.

35. Ralph L. Roy, *Apostles of Discord: A Study of Organized Bigotry and Disruption on the Fringes of Protestantism* (Boston: Beacon Press, 1953); Erling Jorstad, *The Politics of Doomsday: Fundamentalists on the Far Right* (Nashville: Abingdon, 1970); Robert E. Wenger, "Social Thought in American Fundamentalism, 1918-1933" (Ph.D. diss., University of Nebraska, 1973), 271-81.

36. "The Red Menace," *Moody Monthly* 31 (August 1931):582-83; "The Soviets and the United States," *Moody Monthly* 32 (September 1931):5-6; W.B. Riley, "Modernist Preachers Propagating Communism," *The Pilot* 14 (March 1934):171; John Robertson Macartney, "The Spread of Communism in Our Land," *Moody Monthly* 35 (May 1935):414; R.T. Ketcham, "The Case Against the American Baptist Home Mission Society," *Baptist Bulletin* 1 (August-September 1935):2-11; Harold Lord Varney, "Radicals in Our Churches," *Revelation* 8 (May 1938):193, 226-27.

37. Ed., "Words of Comfort for Dark Days," *Sunday School Times* 77 (June 8, 1935):385; ed., "A Sure Cure for Depression," *Revelation* 2 (January 1932):10; ed., "Who Are Now the Pessimists?" *Moody Monthly* 32 (February 1932):280; James M. Gray, "Drawing Out Our Fear," *Moody Bible Institute Bulletin* 12 (January 1933):3-4; "A Crop Survey," cited above; ed., "Nearing the Crisis?" *Moody Monthly* 36 (December 1935):165; ed., "Is Peace Possible Today?" *Sunday School Times* 81 (June 10, 1939):393-94; ed., "A Time To Look Up," *Sunday School Times* 83 (December 20, 1941):1033.

38. Malcolm Cowley, *The Dream of the Golden Mountains: Remembering the 1930's* (New York: Penguin Books, 1981), 31-45, 171-75.

39. *Fundamentalism and American Culture*, 6-8, 43-49. The quote is the title of chapter IV.

40. "The Year Closes," *Moody Monthly* 39 (December 1938):171.

41. "The Sunday School Times Radio Directory," *Sunday School Times* 73 (May 30, 1931):313; "A Directory of Evangelical Radio Broadcasts," *Sunday School Times* 74 (January 23, 1932):44-45.

42. "Notes on Open Letters: Do People Want Gospel Radio Broadcasts?" *Sunday School Times* 74 (January 23, 1932):42.

43. "Salvation by Radio," *Moody Bible Institute Bulletin* 10 (November 1930):4.

44. *Annual Report of the Broadcasting Station of the Moody Bible Institute of Chicago*, for the year ending April 30, 1930, pp. 6-7, 13, 15, 21. This and other reports are on file at Station WMBI, Chicago.
45. See, for example, "Social Reform and Revival," *Moody Monthly* 38 (February 1938):296-98; "The Hope of the Church," *Moody Monthly* 38 (August 1938):607.
46. "Great Revival Due Soon Moody Successor Certain," *Toronto Daily Star*, 13 February 1937, cited in Wilbur M. Smith, *A Watchman On the Wall: The Life Story of Will H. Houghton* (Grand Rapids: Eerdmans, 1951), 191; *ibid.*, 128-30; "Report of the President for the Business Division," *Moody Bible Institute Bulletin* 19 (March 31, 1939):3, 8.
47. Smith, *Watchman*, 130-31.
48. "The Year Closes," *Moody Monthly* 39 (December 1938):171; "Again America Hears," *Moody Monthly* 40 (September 1939):2-3; Smith, *Watchman*, 130-31.
49. "Report of the Business Division for the Fiscal Year 1939-40," *Moody Bible Institute Bulletin* 20 (October 1940):7; *Annual Report of the Station WMBI . . . March 31, 1940*, 2; "Hear WMBI Favorites Over Your Station," *Moody Monthly* 41 (September 1940):31; *Annual Report . . . March 31, 1942*, 13; "Miracles and Melodies," *Moody Monthly* 42 (April 1942):497.
50. Fuller, *Give the Winds a Mighty Voice: The Story of Charles E. Fuller* (Waco, Tex.: Word Books, 1972), 144; *A Quick Glance Back over the 1941 Trail* (N.E.F.) (Boston: n.p., n.d.), 31.
51. Advertisement, *Moody Monthly* 42 (January 1942):307.
52. Wright, "A Few Observations," *New England Fellowship Monthly* 35 (April 1937):8-9.
53. J. Elwin Wright, "An Historical Statement of Events Leading up to the National Conference in St. Louis," *Evangelical Action!* (Boston: Evangelical Press, 1942), 5-7; form letter from Temporary Committee for United Action Among Evangelicals per R. T. Davis, Secretary, March 2, 1942, received by Herbert J. Taylor, Herbert J. Taylor Papers, collection 20, Box 65, folder 16, Archives of the Billy Graham Center, Wheaton, Illinois; cited hereafter as H.J. Taylor papers.
54. J. Elwin Wright to Herbert J. Taylor, July 2, 1942 (H.J. Taylor Papers).
55. Wright, "An Historical Statement," cited above; Minutes of the Committee for United Action Among Evangelicals, October 27-28, 1941, Chicago, Illinois, Records of the Africa Inland Mission, collection 81, box 14, folder 27, Archives of the Billy Graham Center, Wheaton, Illinois; cited hereafter as AIM Records.
56. *Ibid.*
57. "An Historical Statement," 13-14.
58. Carl McIntire, *Twentieth Century Reformation* (Collingswood, N.J.: Christian Beacon Press, 1944), 186-98; R.T. Ketcham, "J. Elwin Wright on Separation," *Baptist Bulletin* 11 (October 1945):10-12; Carl McIntire and associates kept a running debate with the NAE's statements and actions in the weekly *Christian Beacon*. For representative pieces through the early years of the controversy, see McIntire, "The NAE and 'Separation,'" *Christian Beacon* 13 (October 7, 1948):4-5; "NAE Leader Defends Communist-Front Preachers," *Christian Beacon* 14 (April 7, 1949):5; Carl McIntire, "Cooperation Without Compromise," *Christian Beacon* 14 (May 26, 1949):1-2, 4-5, 8.
59. NAE defenders responded to the separatists: Ockenga, "Can Fundamentalism Win America?" *Christian Life and Times* 2 (June 1947):13-15; Stephen W. Paine, "The NAE and 'Separation,'" *United Evangelical Action* (September 15, 1948):11, 22-23; Carl F.H. Henry, *The Uneasy Conscience of Modern Fundamentalism* (Grand Rapids: Eerdmans, 1947). Separatists' chorus of denunciation surged again in reaction to Billy Graham's ecumenical revivalism and the "New Evangelical" theological movement: William A. Ashbrook, "Evangelicalism: The New Neutralism," *The Voice* (October 1956):6-7, 13; part two (November 1956), 6-7, 11; Carl McIntire, "The Bible, Christ's Commands, and Separation," *Christian Beacon* 22 (January 30, 1957):1-2, 4-5; Alva J. McClain, "Is

Theology Changing In the Conservative Camp?" *The Sword of the Lord* 28 (April 5, 1957):1, 12. Robert L. Sumner, *Man Sent From God: A Biography of Dr. John R. Rice* (Grand Rapids: Eerdmans, 1959), 199–220, explains Rice's critical position toward Graham.

Meanwhile, the "new evangelicals" considered themselves to have advanced beyond fundamentalism: Edward John Carnell, "Post-fundamentalist Faith," *The Christian Century* 76 (August 26, 1959):971; "Theology, Evangelism, Ecumenism," *Christianity Today* 2 (January 20, 1958):20–23; "Is Evangelical Theology Changing?" *Christian Life* 9 (March 1956):16–19. See also Carnell, *The Case for Orthodox Theology* (Philadelphia: Westminster Press, 1959), where he castigates fundamentalism as "orthodoxy gone cultic" (pp. 120–21).

60. This feeling is portrayed poignantly in Carl McIntire, "NAE, Fuller Seminary, Championed by Ockenga," *Christian Beacon* (May 10, 1951), 1, 4, 5, 8, in which McIntire accuses Ockenga and other nonseparating Presbyterians such as Wilbur M. Smith of having sold out to the modernists. Robert T. Ketcham expresses the same sense of having "counted the cost" while others compromised themselves to gain security in his taped correspondence with Virgil Bopp (undated) on file at the Ketcham Library, Grand Rapids Baptist College. Robert T. Ketcham, "A New Peril in Our Last Days," *Christian Beacon* 21 (May 17, 1956), 2, 6, 7; Charles J. Woodbridge, *The New Evangelicalism* (Greenville, S.C.: Bob Jones University Press, 1969); William E. Ashbrook, *The New Neutralism* (Columbus, Ohio: n.p., 1969).

61. George W. Dollar, *A History of Fundamentalism in America* (Greenville, S.C.: Bob Jones University Press, 1973), 187–289; Jerry Falwell *et al.*, eds., *The Fundamentalist Phenomenon: The Resurgence of Conservative Christianity* (Garden City, N.Y.: Doubleday, 1981), 143–85; Frances Fitzgerald, "A Disciplined, Charging Army," *New Yorker*, 18 May 1981, 53–54 ff., through 126.

62. James DeForest Murch, *Cooperation Without Compromise: A History of the National Association of Evangelicals* (Grand Rapids: Eerdmans, 1956), 196, 202–3.

63. For suggestions of this, see Marsden, *Fundamentalism and American Culture*, 202–5; "From Fundamentalism to Evangelicalism: A Historical Analysis," *The Evangelicals*, eds., David F. Wells and John D. Woodbridge (Nashville: Abingdon, 1975), 130–31.

64. Joel A. Carpenter, "Fundamentalism and the Swedish Baptists' Search for Identity," paper presented at the Trinity College Conference on American Religious History, April 19, 1980. Other Scandinavian groups that entered fundamentalist circles include both the Swedish and Norwegian Evangelical Free Churches. Hints of their transition appear in H. Wilbert Norton, Olai Urang, Roy A. Thompson, and Mel Larson, *The Diamond Jubilee Story* (Minneapolis: Free Church Publications, 1959).

65. Rodney J. Sawatasky, "History and Ideology, Mennonite Identity Definition through History" (Ph.D. diss., Princeton University, 1977), chs. 6–8; Joseph H. Hall, "The Controversy over Fundamentalism in the Christian Reformed Church, 1915–1966" (Th.D. diss., Concordia Theological Seminary, 1974); James D. Bratt, "Dutch Calvinism in Modern America: The History of a Conservative Subculture" (Ph.D. diss., Yale University, 1978), 269–74, 278–80.

66. Milton L. Rudnick, *Fundamentalism and the Missouri Synod: A Historical Study of their Interaction and Mutual Influence* (St. Louis: Concordia Press, 1966), 84–90; Theodore Graebner, *The Problem of Lutheran Union and Other Essays* (St. Louis: Concordia, 1935), 50–52, 62–66, 70–72; F.E. Mayer, *The Religious Bodies of America* (St Louis: Concordia, 1954), 419–26, 480–81; Theodore Engelder, "Dispensationalism Disparaging the Gospel," *Concordia Theological Monthly* 8 (September 1937):649–66.

67. Timothy L. Smith, "Religion and Ethnicity in America," *American Historical Review* 83 (December 1978):1155–85, illuminates this tension and the role religion played in it.

68. Fundamentalist activity in the Southern Baptist Convention and the resulting tensions

are discussed in Walter B. Shurden, *Not A Silent People: Controversies That Have Shaped Southern Baptists* (Nashville: Broadman Press, 1972); Patsy Ledbetter, "Crusade for the Faith: The Protestant Fundamentalist Movement in Texas," cited above; Kenneth C. Hubbard, "Anti-Conventionism in the Southern Baptist Convention, 1940-1960" (Th.D. diss., Southwestern Baptist Theological Seminary, 1968); C. Allyn Russell, "J. Frank Norris, Violent Fundamentalist," *Voices of American Fundamentalism: Seven Biographical Studies* (Philadelphia: Westminster Press, 1976), 20-46; Robert A. Baker, "Premillennial Baptist Groups," *Encyclopedia of Southern Baptists II* (Nashville: Broadman, 1958), 1111; William Owen Carver, *Out of His Treasure* (Nashville: Broadman, 1956), 76-81, 96-97; and James J. Thompson, Jr., *Tried As by Fire: Southern Baptists and the Religious Controversies of the 1920's* (Macon, Ga.: Mercer University Press, 1982), 137-65.

Fundamentalist activity among southern Presbyterians is recorded in Ernest Trice Thompson, *Presbyterians in the South, Volume Three: 1840-1972* (Richmond: John Knox Press, 1973), 266-73, 302-39, 486-503, 552-53; on fundamentalist institutions and leaders influencing southern Presbyterianism, see R. Arthur Mathews, *Towers Pointing Upward* (Columbia, S.C.: Columbia Bible College, 1973), 10-22; Rudolph A. Renfer, "A History of Dallas Theological Seminary" (Ph.D. diss., University of Texas, 1959), 56-57, 97-100, 134-38, 189, 215, 219, 264, and Table VI; Marguerite C. McQuilkin, *Always in Triumph: The Life of Robert O. McQuilkin* (Columbia, S.C.: Columbia Bible College, 1956); John C. Pollack, *A Foreign Devil in China: The Story of Dr. L. Nelson Bell, An American Surgeon* (Grand Rapids: Zondervan, 1971), 227-34, 242-46.

69. Timothy L. Smith, *Called Unto Holiness, The Story of the Nazarenes: The Formative Years* (Kansas City: Nazarene Publishing, 1962), 298-315; Paul Merritt Bassett, "The Fundamentalist Leavening of the Holiness Movement, 1914-1940; The Church of the Nazarene: A Case Study," *Wesleyan Theological Journal* 13 (Spring 1978):65-91; Arthur O. Roberts, *The Association of Evangelical Friends: The Story of Quaker Renewal in the Twentieth Century* (Newberg, Ore.: Barclay Press, 1975), 4-5; Roberts, "Significant Trends Affecting Friends," *Report of the Fourth Triennial Conference of Evangelical Friends, July 11-15, 1956,* Denver, Colorado, pp. 10-11; Edward Mott, *The Friends Church in the Light of Its Recent History* (Portland, Ore.: n.p., [1936]). On fundamentalism in holiness-tinged Anabaptist churches, see Stanley Nussbaum, "Ye Must Be Born Again" (mimeographed study of the Evangelical Mennonite Church, 1976), 32-33, 36-38, 47-48; Walter H. Lugibihl and Jared F. Gerig, *The Missionary Church Association* (Berne, Ind.: Economy Printing, 1950), 122-30, 138.

70. Robert Mapes Anderson, *Vision of the Disinherited: The Making of American Pentecostalism* (New York: Oxford University Press, 1979), 5, 149; William W. Menzies, "Non-Wesleyan Origins of the Pentecostal Movement," *Aspects of Pentecostal-Charismatic Origins,* ed. Vinson Synan (Plainfield, N.J.: Logos, 1975), 84-85.

71. Anderson, *Vision,* 147-52; William W. Menzies, *Anointed to Serve: The Story of Assemblies of God* (Springfield, Mo.: Gospel Publishing, 1971), 180-81.

72. Menzies, 184-89; "Basic Unity of Evangelical Christianity," *Pentecostal Evangel,* 19 June 1943, 8.

73. O.W. Taylor, "Meeting of Evangelicals in St. Louis," *Baptist and Reflector* 106 (February 8, 1942):2-3; Hall, "The Controversy over Fundamentalism in the Christian Reformed Church," cited above, 94-118; Karl Olsson, *By One Spirit* (Chicago: Covenant Press, 1962), 641-42; *Annual Conference of the Evangelical Covenant Church of America,* Rockford, Illinois, June 16-20, 1943, 180-81; F.E. Mayer, "Two Councils Organized in Opposition to Federal Council," *Concordia Theological Monthly* 14 (February 1943):143-46.

74. "Youth for Christ Expands in Continent," *United Evangelical Action* 4 (January 1,

1946):9; "The History of Youth for Christ," *Christian Life and Times* 1 (July 1946):61; William F. McDermott, "Bobby-Soxers Find the Sawdust Trail," *Collier's Magazine* 115 (May 26, 1945):22–23. For general accounts of the movement, see Mel Larson, *Youth For Christ: Twentieth Century Wonder* (Grand Rapids: Zondervan, 1947); and James Hefley, *God Goes to High School* (Waco, Tex.: Word, 1970).

75. Richard Pells, *Radical Visions and American Dreams,* cited above, 114–50, 358–61; Charles C. Alexander, *Nationalism in American Thought, 1930-1945* (Chicago: Rand McNally, 1969), 155–56, 223–24, 229; Nathan Glazer, *American Judaism* (Chicago: University of Chicago Press, 1957; rev. ed., 1972), 108; Reinhold Niebuhr, *The Children of Light and the Children of Darkness: A Vindication of Democracy and a Critique of Its Traditional Defense* (New York: Scribners, 1944); Donald B. Meyer, *The Protestant Search for Political Realism, 1919-1941,* cited above.

76. Alexander, *Nationalism,* 223–24; Geoffrey Perrett, *Days of Sadness, Years of Triumph: the American People, 1939-1945* (New York: Penguin Books, 1973), 384–85; Lewis Gannett, "Books," and Bosley Crowther, "The Movies," in *While You Were Gone: A Report of Wartime Life in the United States,* ed. Jack Goodman (New York: Simon and Schuster, 1946), 455, 516.

77. Perrett, *Days of Sadness,* 238–40, 385–87, 394–95; Anna W.M. Wolf and Irene Simonton Black, "What Happened to the Younger People," *While You Were Gone,* cited above, 78–85; Agnes E. Meyer, *Journey Through Chaos* (New York: Harcourt, Brace and Co., 1944), 6, 60–65, 209–13, 250.

78. Perrett, *Days of Sadness,* 347–50.

79. Bob Bahr, *Man With a Vision: The Story of Percy Crawford* (Chicago: Moody Press, n.d.); Forrest Forbes, *God Hath Chosen: The Story of Jack Wyrtzen and the Word of Life Hour* (Grand Rapids: Zondervan, 1948); for leaders' backgrounds, see Frank Mead, "Apostle to Youth," *Christian Herald* 68 (September 1945):15–16; Mel Larson, *Youth for Christ,* 106–07, 112–13; Torrey Johnson and Robert Cook, *Reaching Youth for Christ* (Chicago: Youth Publications, 1944), 15, 18.

80. "Bobby-Sox Hit Sawdust Trail," *News-Views: The Chicago Daily News Pictorial Section,* 3 February 1945, 2; Clarence Woodbury, "Bobby Soxers Sing Hallelujah," *American Magazine* 141 (March 1946):26–27, 121, 123, 124; "Youth For Christ," *Time,* 4 February 1946, 46–47; "Wanted: A Miracle of Good Weather and 'Youth for Christ' Rally Got It," *Newsweek,* 11 June 1945, 84.

81. J. Elwin Wright, "Youth for Christ," *United Evangelical Action* 6 (February 15, 1945):8; Larson, *Youth for Christ,* 84–94, 90–91, 94–95; "Youth for Christ Expands in Continent," *United Evangelical Action* 4 (January 1, 1946):9. James Hefley, *God Goes to High School,* 38–49, 69.

82. "Five YFC Leaders Will Fly to Europe," *United Evangelical Action* 5 (March 1946):10; "G.I. Missionaries to Manila," *Sunday* 7 (February 1946):26–29, 49–52; Larson, 20–23, 60–63, 69–71, 80–81, 92–93; Hefley, 29–30, 34–40.

83. Hefley, 55–65.

84. Ibid., 66–68; J. Herbert Kane, *Faith, Mighty Faith: A Handbook of the Interdenominational Foreign Missions Association* (New York: I.F.M.A., 1956), 64–65, 76–78; Paul W. Freed, *Towers to Eternity: The Story of Trans-World Radio* (Waco, Tex.: Word Books, 1968).

85. Ralph D. Winter, *The Twenty-Five Unbelievable Years, 1945-1969* (South Pasadena, Calif.: Institute of Church Growth, 1970), 47–51.

86. Harry S. Truman, "The Need for Moral Analyzing," *New York Times,* 6 March 1946, 11; "Honoring Evangelical Chaplains of Our Armed Forces," *New York Times,* 25 April 1946, 5.

87. Billy Graham, "Report of the Vice President At Large," cited above, 36, 41; Larson, 29; Hefley, 13.

88. See, e.g., Mathews, *Towers Pointing Upward,* cited above, 143–45; "Philadelphia Bible

Institute Alumni Activities, Class of 1942 to 1953, inclusive," unpublished paper in Alumni Office files, The Philadelphia College of the Bible, Philadelphia, Pa.; "Enrollments," typescript table from file drawer G, Moodyana Room, Moody Bible Institute.

89. On Fuller Theological Seminary, see Daniel P. Fuller, *Give the Winds a Mighty Voice*, cited above, 193–217; Wilbur M. Smith, *Before I Forget* (Chicago: Moody Press, 1971), 283–95. On the idea of a Christian University, see "An Evangelical Manifesto: Issued by the Plymouth Conference for the Advancement of Evangelical Scholarship, Plymouth, Mass., August 18," *United Evangelical Action* 6 (September 15, 1945):4; "An American Christian University," *United Evangelical Action* 6 (May 2, 1945):7; Edwin H. Rian, "The Plight of Protestantism in Education," *Moody Monthly* 46 (October 1945):76, 110–11; "Planning Curriculum for New University," *United Evangelical Action* 5 (May 1, 1946):9; Rudolph L. Nelson, "Fundamentalism at Harvard: The Case of Edward John Carnell," *Quarterly Review* 2 (Summer 1982):79–98.

CHAPTER TWO

1. See, e.g., Jerry Falwell *et al.*, eds., *The Fundamentalist Phenomenon: The Resurgence of Conservative Christianity* (Garden City: Doubleday, 1981), 12–26; James M. Wall, "What Future for the New Right?" *Christian Century*, 25 November 1981, 1219; Theodore Roszak, "In Search of the Miraculous," *Harper's* (January 1981):54–62; David Martin, "Revived Dogma and New Cults," *Daedalus* 111 (1982):54; and Dean M. Kelley, *Why Conservative Churches Are Growing: A Study in Sociology of Religion* (New York: Harper and Row, 1972), 99, 110–11. Like many observers, Kelley assumes but does not prove that a demonstrable decline in the numerical strength of the mainline denominations is causally linked with a concurrent increase in the numerical strength of the conservative denominations.

2. Richard Lovelace, *Renewal* 2 (October 1982):7–8. For impressionistic yet informed descriptions of the Evangelical Left, see Timothy L. Smith, "Protestants Falwell Does Not Impress," *New York Times*, 22 October 1980, op ed page, and Richard Quebedeaux, *The Young Evangelicals: Revolution in Orthodoxy* (New York: Harper and Row, 1974), 99–135. For a quantitative profile, see James Davison Hunter, "The New Class and the Young Evangelicals," *Review of Religious Research* 22 (1980):160–63; Hunter, *American Evangelicalism: Conservative Religion and the Quandary of Modernity* (New Brunswick: Rutgers University Press, 1983), 56, 107–12, 118; Seymour Martin Lipset and Earl Raab, "The Election and the Evangelicals," *Commentary* (March 1981):25–26.

3. The complexity of the factors involved in church growth and decline is described in Dean R. Hoge, "A Test of Theories of Denominational Growth and Decline," in *Understanding Church Growth and Decline: 1950-1978*, ed. Hoge and David A. Roozen (New York: Pilgrim Press, 1979), 182–97. For the steady growth since the early 1950s of most major evangelical groups (as well as nonevangelical conservatives like Mormons), see Kelley, *Conservative Churches*, 24, 27–31, and Jackson W. Carroll *et al.*, *Religion in America: 1950 to the Present* (San Francisco: Harper and Row, 1979), 14–15, 23. The growth of some conservative groups has tapered off since 1980, but overall there is little change. In 1976 Gallup indicated 18% of the adult population was evangelical; in 1980, 19%; in 1982, 17%. Princeton Religious Research Center, *Religion in America 1982: The Gallup Report* (Reports #201–202, June-July 1982), 31.

4. Luther P. Gerlach and Virginia H. Hine, *People, Power, Change: Movements of Social Transformation* (Indianapolis: Bobbs-Merrill, 1970), 84–87. C. Kirk Hadaway, "Changing Brands: Denominational Switching and Membership Change," in *Yearbook of the American and Canadian Churches 1980*, ed. Constant H. Jacquet, Jr. (Nashville: Abingdon Press, 1980), 264–67. Reginald W. Bibby and Merlin B. Brinkerhoff, "The Circulation of the Saints: A Study of People Who Join Conservative Churches," *Journal for*

the Scientific Study of Religion 12 (1973):273–83. Reginald W. Bibby, "Why Conservative Churches *Really* Are Growing: Kelley Revisited," *Journal for the Scientific Study of Religion* 17 (1978):132–33; Wade Clark Roof and Christopher Kirk Hadaway, "Denominational Switching in the Seventies: Going Beyond Stark and Glock," *Journal for the Scientific Study of Religion* 18 (1979):363–79. The Gerlach/Hine study shows that conversions result principally from positive pre-existing personal relationships. The other studies deal with switching from liberal to conservative groups (including but not restricted to evangelical groups). The Bibby and Bibby/Brinkerhoff studies minimize the significance of liberal to conservative switching as a factor in the latter's growth. The Hadaway and Roof/Hadaway studies do see liberal to conservative switching as a significant factor in the growth of some very conservative bodies, but they do not show that this accounts for more than a small fraction of the overall expansion of the evangelical movement. Moreover, the evidence offered by Roof/Hadaway (374, Table 4, "New Morality") actually suggests that liberal to conservative switchers do not measurably differ from mainline Protestants on key questions like abortion and legalization of marijuana.

5. Neil Smelser, *Theory of Collective Behavior* (New York: Free Press, 1962); John Wilson, *Introduction to Social Movements* (New York: Basic Books, 1973), esp. chs. 1–3; Kenelm Burridge, *New Heaven, New Earth: A Study of Millenarian Activities* (New York: Schocken Books, 1969).

6. Perry Miller, *The New England Mind: From Colony to Province* (Boston: Beacon Press, 1961 [1953]), 484–85; Robert H. Wiebe, "Modernizing the Republic, 1920 to the Present," in *The Great Republic: A History of the American People*, 2 vols., ed. Bernard Bailyn *et al.* (Lexington, Mass.: D.C. Heath, 1981 [1977]), II:930. For the social and cultural consequences of modernization, especially in the United States since World War II, see Wiebe, "Modernizing the Republic," 857–77; Richard D. Brown, *Modernization: The Transformation of American Life, 1600-1865* (New York: Hill and Wang, 1976), chs. 1, 8. For a lucid discussion of the way that modernization—commonly defined as "technologically induced economic growth"—has altered and structured modern consciousness, see Peter L. Berger *et al., The Homeless Mind: Modernization and Consciousness* (New York: Random House, 1973), esp. chs. 1–4. Berger's notions have been imaginatively used to interpret contemporary evangelicals by Hunter, *American Evangelicalism,* and nonevangelicals by James G. Moseley, *A Cultural History of Religion in America* (Westport, Conn.: Greenwood Press, 1981), ch. 8. See also Daniel Bell, *The Cultural Contradictions of Capitalism* (New York: Basic Books, 1976), 3–84, 146–71. The idea that social modernization is the vehicle of cultural modernity has not gone uncriticized, to say the least. See, for example, Mary Douglas, "The Effects of Modernization on Religious Change," *Daedalus* 111 (1982):1–20.

7. For a general discussion of the relation of phenomenological, reductionist, and functionalist models to the study of religion, see John H. Schütz, "Introduction," in Gerd Theissen, *The Social Setting of Pauline Christianity: Essays on Corinth,* ed. and trans. John H. Schütz (Philadelphia: Fortress Press, 1982), 15–20. For a general discussion of systemic analysis in history, and mechanistic (reductionist) and organic (funtionalist) models therein, see Robert F. Berkhofer, Jr., *A Behavioral Approach to Historical Analysis* (New York: Free Press, 1969), chs. 8, 9.

8. William G. McLoughlin, *Revivals, Awakenings, and Reform: An Essay on Religion and Social Change in America, 1607-1977* (Chicago: University of Chicago Press, 1978), esp. chs. 1, 5–6. Quotation in next paragraph is on p. 10. For earlier formulations of the argument see McLoughlin, "Revivalism," in Edwin S. Gaustad, ed., *The Rise of Adventism: Religion and Society in Mid-Nineteenth Century America* (New York: Harper and Row, 1974), 119–53, and "Is There a Third Force in Christendom?" in *Religion in America,* eds. McLoughlin and Robert N. Bellah (Boston: Beacon Press, 1966), 45–72.

"Effluvia" is on p. 47. For the most recent formulation of the argument, essentially unchanged, see McLoughlin, "The Illusions and Dangers of the New Christian Right," *Foundations* 25 (1982):128-43.

9. Martin E. Marty, "Religion in America Since Mid-century," *Daedalus* 111 (1982):149-64, and "Forward" and "The Revival of Evangelicalism and Southern Religion," in *Varieties of Southern Evangelicalism,* ed. David Edwin Harrell, Jr. (Macon: Mercer University Press, 1981), ix-xii, 7-22, respectively. Quotation is on p. 9. See also Marty, *The Public Church: Mainline—Evangelical—Catholic* (New York: Crossroad, 1981), 11-12, 81, and *passim;* and Marty, *A Nation of Behavers* (Chicago: University of Chicago Press, 1976), ch. 4, esp. 105.

10. Gilman M. Ostrander, *American Civilization in the First Machine Age: 1890-1940* (New York: Harper and Row, 1970), 1-27, 237-74.

11. Martin, "Revived Dogma and New Cults," 59; John Crothers Pollock *et al., The Connecticut Mutual Life Report on American Values in the '80s: The Impact of Belief* (Hartford, Conn.: Ct Mutual Life Ins. Co., 1981), 9. More generally, see Robert T. Handy, "Protestant Patterns in Canada and the United States: Similarities and Differences," in *In the Great Tradition: In Honor of Winthrop S. Hudson: Essays on Pluralism, Voluntarism, and Revivalism,* eds. Joseph D. Ban and Paul R. DeKar (Valley Forge: Judson Press, 1982), 33-52; George M. Marsden, "Fundamentalism as an American Phenomenon: A Comparison with English Evangelicalism," *Church History* 46 (1977):215-32.

12. Berger, *Homeless Mind,* chs. 5-6. Laurence Veysey, "The Autonomy of American History Reconsidered," *American Quarterly* 31 (1979):455-77, esp. 473; John Kenneth Galbraith, *The New Industrial State* (Boston: Houghton Mifflin, 1967), 339; Daniel Bell, *The Coming of Post-Industrial Society: A Venture in Social Forecasting* (New York: Basic Books, 1973), x, 41, 99, 112-14. See also the review of the literature in Richard D. Brown, "Modernization and the Modern Personality in Early America, 1600-1865: A Sketch of a Synthesis," *Journal of Interdisciplinary History* 2 (1971/1972):201-3.

13. The diversity and complexity of religious traditionalism (or apparent traditionalism) in nations like Iran make comparative generalizations with American evangelicalism virtually useless. See, for example, Edward Said, *Covering Islam: How the Media and the Experts Determine How We See the Rest of the World* (New York: Pantheon Books, 1981), 53-64, 94, 106; Michael M. J. Fischer, "Islam and the Revolt of the Petit Bourgeoisie," *Daedalus* 111 (1982):101-25.

14. John Winthrop, *A Modell of Christian Charity,* in *American Christianity,* 2 vols., eds. H. Shelton Smith *et al.* (New York: Charles Scribner's Sons, 1960), I:97-102. For Penn, Jefferson, and civil religion, see Winthrop S. Hudson, ed., *Nationalism and Religion in America: Concepts of American Identity and Mission* (New York: Harper and Row, 1970), 138-52. See also Hudson, *The Great Tradition of the American Churches* (New York: Harper and Row, 1953); Edwin S. Gaustad, "The Great Tradition and the Coercion of Voluntarism," in *Great Tradition,* eds. Ban and DeKar, 161-72. The literature describing the custodial tradition is extensive. Good introductions to different dimensions of the tradition include Elwyn A. Smith, "The Voluntary Establishment of Religion," in *The Religion of the Republic,* ed. Smith (Philadelphia: Fortress Press, 1971), 154-82; Robert D. Linder, "Civil Religion in Historical Perspective: The Reality that Underlies the Concept," *Journal of Church and State* 17 (1975):399-421; and Mark DeWolfe Howe, *The Garden and the Wilderness: Religion and Government in American Constitutional History* (Chicago: University of Chicago Press, 1965). It is almost needless to add that modern proponents of civil religion would not want to be uncritically linked with the custodial tradition. See, for example, Robert N. Bellah and Phillip E. Hammond, *Varieties of Civil Religion* (San Francisco: Harper and Row, 1980).

15. *Cambridge Platform,* in *American Christianity,* eds. Smith *et al.,* I:128-39. For the extensive literature on the plural tradition, the best place to start is Elwyn A. Smith,

Religious Liberty in the United States (Philadelphia: Fortress Press, 1972), esp. part 3. For the relation between diversity and pluralism, see Martin E. Marty, "Interpreting American Pluralism," in Carroll *et al.*, *Religion in America*, 78–90. More generally, see Edwin Scott Gaustad, *Dissent in American Religion* (Chicago: University of Chicago Press, 1973).

16. For the link between evangelicalism and the custodial tradition, see George M. Marsden, *Fundamentalism and American Culture: The Shaping of Twentieth-Century Evangelicalism, 1870-1925* (New York: Oxford University Press, 1980), esp. chs. 4 and 15. For the demonstrably adversarial nature of the relationship between the two traditions in contemporary America, see *Connecticut Mutual Life Report*, 86–87, 252.

17. Berger, *Homeless Mind*, 79–80. Although the changes of the last twenty years have not been as radical as many people assume, the balance has unquestionably shifted toward an amplification of personal freedom. Sydney E. Ahlstrom, "The Traumatic Years: American Religion and Culture in the '60s and '70s," *Daedalus* 107 (1978):13–29; Daniel Yankelovich, *New Rules: Searching for Self-Fulfillment in a World Turned Upside Down* (New York: Random House, 1981). For statistical documentation of growing religious pluralism, see Beth Spring, "The Changing Face of American Religion," *Christianity Today*, 22 October 1982, 64. To say that modernization has spurred pluralism is one thing, but to say that it has spurred secularization is quite another. For a critique of the latter assumption, see Talcott Parsons, "Christianity and Modern Industrial Society," in *Religion, Culture and Society*, ed. Louis Schneider (New York: John Wiley and Sons, 1964), 273–98.

18. Samuel S. Hill and Dennis E. Owen, *The New Religious Political Right* (Nashville: Abingdon Press, 1982); Wade Clark Roof, "America's Voluntary Establishment: Mainline Religion in Transition," *Daedalus* 111 (1982):168–69.

19. John Murray Cuddihy, *No Offense: Civil Religion and Protestant Taste* (New York: Seabury Press, 1978). For impressionistic yet informed descriptions of the status hungry, upwardly mobile, stable working, or lower middle class position of evangelicals, see Martin E. Marty, *Nation of Behavers*, ch. 4, esp. p. 104; Richard Quebedeaux, *The Worldly Evangelicals* (San Francisco: Harper and Row, 1978); Quebedeaux, *By What Authority: The Rise of Personality Cults in American Christianity* (San Francisco: Harper and Row, 1982), ch. 3. For quantitative data that strongly support this conclusion, see Hunter, *American Evangelicalism*, 46, 53–56, 117. For a sophisticated analysis of structural reasons why the Evangelical Right—and, by implication, the evangelical movement as a whole—is a potent force in the social system, see Michael Lienesch, "Right-Wing Religion: Christian Conservatism as a Political Movement," *Political Science Quarterly* 97 (1982):403–25; see also McLoughlin, "Christian Right," 140–41.

20. For the ambivalence of the Evangelical Left, see Richard Lovelace, "Renewal and the Moral Majority," *Renewal* 1 (September 1981):5–12. One 1982 poll of evangelical college students indicated that 57% believed that "people should be free to follow life-styles very different from their own." On the surface, at least, this suggests that more than two-fifths of evangelical college students would *not* allow alternative life-styles for others. *Pentecostal Evangel*, 13 March 1983, 25.

21. For the demographic shifts of the postwar period, and their cultural consequences, see Godfrey Hodgson, *America in Our Time: From World War II to Nixon* (New York: Random House/Vintage Books, 1978 [1976]), 54–64; Winthrop S. Hudson, *Baptists in Transition: Individualism and Christian Responsibility* (Valley Forge: Judson Press, 1979), 119. For the extraordinary economic and demographic growth of the South since 1940 and especially since 1970, and its impact upon the North and West, see Robert Estall, "The Changing Balance of the Northern and Southern Regions of the United States," *Journal of American Studies* 14 (1980):365–86; Carl Abbott, *The New Urban America: Growth and Politics in Sunbelt Cities* (Chapel Hill: University of North Carolina Press,

1981), 15-20. The assumption, evident in this paragraph, that culture is "the forms of things that people have in mind, their models for perceiving, relating, and otherwise interpreting them" is drawn from Ward H. Goodenough, "Cultural Anthropology and Linguistics," in *Language in Culture and Society: A Reader in Linguistics and Anthropology,* ed. Dell Hymes (New York: Harper and Row, 1964), 36.

22. Harrell, *Southern Evangelicalism,* 1-5. William Martin, "Billy Graham," *Southern Evangelicalism,* 71-88. For a survey of the rapidly expanding literature on Southern religion, and especially Southern evangelicalism, see John B. Boles, "Religion in the South: Recent Historiography," *Journal of Southern History* (forthcoming).

23. Wayne Flynt, "One in the Spirit: Many in the Flesh," in *Southern Evangelicalism,* 23-44; John P. McDowell, *The Social Gospel in the South: The Woman's Home Mission Movement in the Methodist Episcopal Church, South, 1886-1939* (Baton Rouge: Louisiana State University Press, 1982); Charles Reagan Wilson, *Baptized in Blood: The Religion of the Lost Cause, 1865-1920* (Athens, Ga.: University of Georgia Press, 1980); John R. Earle et al., *Spindles and Spires: A Re-Study of Religion and Social Change in Gastonia* (Atlanta: John Knox Press, 1976); Donald G. Mathews and Jane DeHart Mathews, "The Cultural Politics of ERA's Defeat," *OAH Newsletter* (November 1982):13-15. Robert F. Martin, "Critique of Southern Society and Vision of a New Order: The Fellowship of Southern Churchmen, 1934-1957," *Church History* 52 (1983):66-80.

24. John Shelton Reed, *The Enduring South: Subcultural Persistence in Mass Society* (Chapel Hill: University of North Carolina Press, 1974), 69-72, and *One South: An Ethnic Approach to Regional Culture* (Baton Rouge: Louisiana State University Press, 1982), 49-51, 54-55, 171-73. Conal Furay, *The Grass-Roots Mind in America: The American Sense of Absolutes* (New York: Franklin Watts/New Viewpoints, 1977), 90-92. Samuel S. Hill, "The South's Two Cultures," in *Religion and the Solid South,* ed. Hill (Nashville: Abingdon Press, 1972), 24-56. Grace Ann Emerson, "Jimmy Carter and Tension in the American Religious Dichotomy" (senior honor thesis, Department of Religion, University of North Carolina at Chapel Hill, 1983).

25. Alexis de Tocqueville, *Democracy in America,* ed. Phillips Bradley, 2 vols. (New York: Random House/Vintage Books, 1945 [1835]), I:317; Hudson, ed., *Nationalism and Religion,* chs. 2 and 3; Robert T. Handy, *A Christian America: Protestant Hopes and Historical Realities* (New York: Oxford University Press, 1971), esp. chs. 3, 4; Nathan O. Hatch and Mark A. Noll, eds., *The Bible in America: Essays in Cultural History* (New York: Oxford University Press, 1982), 39-78.

26. Wilbur J. Cash, *The Mind of the South* (1941), 46, and William Faulkner, both quoted (the latter without attribution) in Furay, *Grass-Roots Mind,* 89, 94 respectively. "Bulwark," etc. in Reed, *Enduring South,* 57. For the main point of the paragraph, see Wilson, *Baptized in Blood;* Samuel S. Hill, Jr., *The South and the North in American Religion* (Athens, Ga.: University of Georgia Press, 1980), 90-106; C. Vann Woodward, *The Burden of Southern History* (Baton Rouge: Louisiana State University Press, 1960), ch. 8.

27. The recent evangelical formulation of the Christian America myth is described and critiqued in Mark A. Noll et al., *The Search for Christian America* (Westchester, Ill.: Crossway Books, 1983). See also Hill and Owen, *New Religious Political Right,* 109-13; George M. Marsden, "America's 'Christian' Origins: Puritan New England as a Case Study," in *John Calvin: His Influence in the Western World,* ed. W. Stanford Reid (Grand Rapids: Zondervan, 1982), 241-60, 386-87.

28. Reed, *One South,* 135.

CHAPTER THREE

1. Frank Kermode, *The Sense of Ending: Studies in the Theory of Fiction* (Oxford: Oxford University Press, 1967).

2. For the 1960s as representing "a fundamental shift in American moral and religious attitudes," see Sydney E. Ahlstrom, "The Radical Turn in Theology and Ethics: Why It Occurred in the 1960s," *Annals of the American Academy of Political and Social Science* 387 (January 1970):1–13.

3. Martin E. Marty, *The Fire We Can Light* (Garden City, N.Y.: Doubleday & Company, 1973), 19–20.

4. Quoted in Daniel Dervin, "Trashing the Sixties: Defensive Reactions Within Psycho-analysis," *Journal of Psychohistory* 9 (Fall 1981):187.

5. In this paper I shall be developing and refining a tip from Martin E. Marty, who has argued that "a generational shift appears to separate the period from roughly the end of World War II (or the beginning of the Eisenhower Era) through the mid-sixties, from the late sixties into the 1980s" in "Religion in America since Mid-century," *Daedalus* 111 (Winter 1982):151.

6. John F. Kennedy, quoted in William E. Leuchtenburg, *A Troubled Feast: American Society Since 1945* (rev. ed.; Boston: Little, Brown & Co., 1979), 130.

7. For the concept of the "expressive ethic," see Steven M. Tipton, *Getting Saved from the Sixties* (Berkeley: University of California Press, 1982).

8. Peter Berger, "A Call for Authority in the Christian Community," *Christian Century* 98 (27 October 1981): 1257.

9. Benton Johnson, "Taking Stock: Reflections on the End of Another Era," *Journal for the Scientific Study of Religion* 21 (1982): 189-200.

10. Those who accent the 1960s "crisis of authority" include Leonard Krieger, "The Idea of Authority in the West," *American Historical Review* 82 (April 1977); Richard Quebe-deaux, *By What Authority: The Rise of Personality Cults in American Christianity* (San Francisco: Harper and Row, 1982); Richard Sennett, *Authority* (New York: Alfred Knopf, 1980). Philip Gleason warns against the careless use of the concept of "identity" in historical analysis at the same time that he admits the "aptness" of the term in understanding how the 1960s "brought about a re-examination on a massive scale of the relationship between the individual and society." See Gleason, "Identifying Identity: A Semantic History," *Journal of American History* 69 (March 1983):910-31.

11. Roland Robertson, "Aspects of Identity and Authority in Sociological Theory," in *Identity and Authority: Exploration in the Theory of Society,* eds. Roland Robertson and Burkhart Holzner (New York: St. Martin's Press, 1979), 218.

12. Robert E. Fitch, "The Protestant Sickness," *Religion in Life* 35 (Autumn 1966): 503.

13. For the antinomian temper of the 1960s, see Daniel Bell, "Religion in the Sixties," *Social Research* 38 (Autumn 1971): 447–97.

14. Joseph Fletcher, *Situation Ethics: The New Morality* (Philadelphia: Westminster Press, 1966), 45.

15. The 1965 study by Charles Glock and Rodney Stark of church members in Northern California revealed that over two-thirds of those polled thought they had been in the presence of God. Glock and Stark were shocked: "There are few clues in the culture which would lead an observer to predict so high a rate of supernaturalism in what seems to be an increasingly modern, scientific and secularized society." Charles Glock and Rodney Stark, *Religion and Society in Tension* (Chicago: Rand McNally, 1965), 158. See also the 1968 Gallup poll survey on religion in the *New York Times,* 26 December 1968. One of the few interpreters who got it right was Guy E. Swanson, "Modern Secularity," in *The Religious Situation: 1968,* ed. Donald R. Cutler (Boston: Beacon Press, 1968), 813–14.

16. Harvey Cox, *The Secular City* (New York: Macmillan, 1965).

17. Bernard E. Meland, "A New Morality—But to What End?" *Religion in Life* 35 (Spring 1966):195.

18. Harvey Cox, "The Place and Purpose of Theology," *Christian Century* 83 (January 1966):7.

19. In speaking of the "levelling" of "hippie *cum* military surplus" styles of clothing, William L. O'Neil argues that "it gave the ugly parity with the beautiful for the first time in modern history." See his *Coming Apart: An Informal History of America in the 1960s* (Chicago: Quadrangle Books, 1971), 249.

20. Jacquetta Hawkes, "Nine Tantalizing Systems of Nature," *New York Times Sunday Magazine,* 7 July 1957, 5.

21. Even Norman Vincent Peale publicly acknowledged some of the religious shallowness of the 50s and his complicity in it in "Can Protestantism Be Saved?" *Reader's Digest* 81 (September 1962):49–54. See also Donald T. Miller, "Popular Religion of the 1950's: Norman Vincent Peale and Billy Graham," *Journal of Popular Culture* 9 (Summer 1975):66–76.

22. For media coverage of "the problem of God," see *Time,* 9 March 1962, 77; *Time,* 7 May 1965, 68, 70; *Time,* 23 December 1966, 61. See also J.A.T. Robinson, *Honest to God* (Philadelphia: Westminster Press, 1963).

23. William Hamilton's call for obedience to Jesus can be found in "The Shape of Radical Theology," *Christian Century* 82 (October 1965):1221. For the importance of Jesus to death-of-God theologians, see John W. Rathbun, "God is Dead: Avant-garde Theology for the Sixties," *Canadian Review of American Studies* V (Fall 1974):177–80.

24. John H. Schaar's summary of Fromm's position is on p. 125 of his *Escape from Authority: The Perspective of Erich Fromm* (New York: Basic Books, 1961).

25. Norman Pittenger, "American Theology Today: Impressions on Revisiting America," *Religion in Life* 42 (Spring 1973):267.

26. Thomas J. Altizer, *The Gospel of Christian Atheism* (Philadelphia: Westminster Press, 1966).

27. William Hamilton, "Thursday's Child," in *Radical Theology and the Death of God,* eds. Altizer and Hamilton (Indianapolis: Bobbs-Merrill, 1966), 87–90.

28. Winthrop S. Hudson, *Religion in America* (3rd ed.; New York: Charles Scribner's Sons, 1980), 415. See also Irving Howe's "The Decade that Failed," *New York Times Magazine* 19 (September 1982):42–43, 78–84.

29. Leuchtenburg, *A Troubled Feast,* 129–283; Henry F. May, "The Free Speech Movement at Berkeley: A Historian's View," in *Ideas, Faiths, and Feelings: An American Intellectual and Religious History 1952-1982* (New York: Oxford University Press, 1983), 103.

30. Richard Flacks, "The Liberated Generation: An Exploration of the Roots of Student Protest," in his *Conformity, Resistance, and Self-Determination: The Individual and Authority* (Boston: Little, Brown, 1973), 110.

31. Although I have major disagreements with various features of the "narcissistic" argument, see Simon Sobo's "Narcissism as a Function of Culture," in *The Psychoanalytic Study of the Child* annual for 1977; Christopher Lasch, "The Narcissistic Personality of Our Time," *Partisan Review* 44 (No. 1, 1977): 9–19.

32. Erich Fromm, *The Art of Loving* (New York: Harper and Brothers, 1956), 57–63.

33. Harvey Cox, *On Not Leaving it to the Snake* (New York: Macmillan, 1967).

34. Roszak, *Making of a Counter Culture.* For the Jesus People, see Ronald M. Enroth, "The Jesus People," in *The Role of Religion in American Life: An Interpretive Historical Anthology,* ed. Robert R. Mathisen (Washington, D. C.: University Press of America, 1982), 394–406.

35. See Philip Rieff, *The Triumph of the Therapeutic* (New York: Harper and Row, 1966).

36. Guy E. Swanson, "A Basis of Authority and Identity in Post-Industrial Society," in *Identity and Authority,* eds. Robertson and Holzner, 190–217.

37. *Ibid.,* 204–5.

38. Ralph H. Turner, "The Theme of Contemporary Social Movements," *British Journal of Sociology* 20 (December 1969):390–405.

39. Erik H. Erikson, *Identity and the Life Cycle* (New York: International Universities Press, 1959).

40. Barbara Hall and Richard Shaull, "From Somewhere Along the Road," *Theology Today* 29 (April 1972):90.

41. This is the thesis of William Braden, *The Private Sea: LSD and the Search for God* (Chicago: Quadrangle Books, 1967).

42. See Leonard I. Sweet, "Not All Cats are Gray: Beyond Liberalism's Uncertain Faith," *Christian Century* 99 (23–30 June 1982):221–25.

43. Quoted in Arianna Stassinopoulos, *After Reason* (New York: Stein and Day, 1978), 149.

44. For the generational conflict, see Joseph Anthony Amato II, *Guilt and Gratitude: A Study of the Origin of Contemporary Conscience* (Westport, Conn.: Greenwood Press, 1982), 150–85.

45. Hall and Shaull, "From Somewhere Along the Road," 89–90.

46. Billy Graham, *Peace with God* (Garden City, N.Y.: Doubleday, 1953), 222. In the very first issue of the evangelical periodical *Christianity Today,* Billy Graham called for those searching for "authority, finality, and conclusiveness" in their faith to rally behind the magazine. See 15 October 1956 editorial, as reprinted in Frank E. Gaebelein, ed., *A Christianity Today Reader* (Westwood, N.Y.: Spire Books, 1968), 13–16.

47. For the political equivalent of this argument that nothing fails like success, see John Frederick Martin, *Civil Rights and the Crisis of Liberalism: The Democratic Party 1945–1976* (Boulder, Colo.: Westview Press, 1979).

48. James Davison Hunter, *American Evangelicalism: Conservative Religion and the Quandary of Modernity* (New Brunswick, N.J.: Rutgers University Press, 1983), 84–97.

49. Richard G. Hutcheson, Jr., *Mainline Churches and the Evangelicals: A Challenging Crisis?* (Atlanta: John Knox Press, 1981), 115.

CHAPTER FIVE

1. There is no way, of course, to measure the number of fundamentalists for these reasons: a) the distinction between fundamentalist and evangelical is too blurry; b) very few church bodies are constituted around the name fundamentalism; c) many fundamentalists are in church bodies that are not technically fundamentalist; d) many people who might be classified as fundamentalists are not necessarily to be located on any church rolls at all. Gallup polls of the late 1970s made some efforts to assess evangelical sympathies, "evangelical" and "born again" being terms the Gallup people used to encompass fundamentalism as well. At that time, 60% of the public claimed to be Protestant; 48% of the Protestants claimed a "born again" experience; and 35% of the Protestants considered themselves "evangelical." It does not take much reckoning to find 10 million Americans out of this sector who could safely be described—or are self-described—as "fundamentalist." See the *Gallup Opinion Index* No. 145, American Institute of Public Opinion, Princeton, N. J., 1978.

2. Many sociologists of religion have pointed to the phenomenon of privatization; the most systematic account is Thomas Luckmann, *The Invisible Religion* (New York: Macmillan, 1967).

3. We now fortunately possess twin volumes that describe these polarities and parties: William R. Hutchison, *The Modernist Impulse in American Protestantism* (New York: Oxford University Press paperback edition, 1982 [first published in 1976]) and George M. Marsden, *Fundamentalism and American Culture: The Shaping of Twentieth-Century Evangelicalism, 1870-1925* (New York: Oxford University Press, 1982 [first published in 1980]).

4. See Patricia Barrett, *Religious Liberty and the American Presidency* (New York: Herder and Herder, 1963).

5. In February 1981, an inclusive conference on this subject was held; proceedings are in Dean M. Kelley, ed., *Government Intervention in Religious Affairs* (New York: Pilgrim, 1982).

6. Definitions of politics on which I am here relying are elaborated upon in Bernard Crick, *In Defence of Politics* (Baltimore: Penguin, 1962), 15 ff.

7. Martin E. Marty, *Righteous Empire: The Protestant Experience in America* (New York: Dial, 1970); see esp. ch. 17, "The Two-Party System," 177 ff.

8. Timothy Smith, *Revivalism and Social Reform in Mid-Nineteenth Century America* (Nashville: Abingdon, 1957).

9. Donald W. Dayton, *Discovering an Evangelical Heritage* (New York: Harper and Row, 1976), is a popular account; see ch. 2, pp. 15-24 on Finney.

10. Details of the concept of the public are in Parker J. Palmer, *The Company of Strangers: Christians and the Renewal of American Public Life* (San Francisco: Harper and Row, 1981).

11. See Timothy Weber, *Living in the Shadow of the Second Coming* (New York: Oxford University Press, 1981).

12. The first account of the second rise of fundamentalism was Louis Gasper, *The Fundamentalist Movement* (The Hague: Mouton, 1963); see also Joel A. Carpenter, "Fundamentalist Institutions and the Rise of Evangelical Protestantism, 1929-1942," *Church History* 49 (March 1980): 62-75.

13. Jerry Falwell, *Listen, America!* (New York: Bantam Books, 1981), outlines the program.

14. For a theoretical description of antimodernity in action, see John Murray Cuddihy, *The Ordeal of Civility* (New York: Basic, 1974), 9-10.

15. An excellent description is Harold R. Isaacs, *Idols of the Tribe: Group Identity and Political Change* (New York: Harper and Row, 1975).

16. A doomsday scenario with a socialist tinge is in Robert L. Heilbroner, *Business Civilization in Decline* (New York: Norton, 1976), 119-20.

17. A characteristic plea for "believers' rights" is to be found in Lynn R. Buzzard and Samuel Ericsson, *The Battle for Religious Liberty* (Elgin, Ill.: David C. Cook, 1982).

CHAPTER SIX

1. Laurence Veysey, "Continuity and Decline in American Religion Since 1900," Kaplan Lecture, University of Pennsylvania, 1980. The Gallup figures are taken from *Religion in America 1979-80* (The Princeton Religion Research Center, Princeton, N.J., 1980).

2. David Martin, *A General Theory of Secularization* (New York, 1978).

3. *Ibid.*, 28, 35. "The clergy [in America] are assimilated to the concept of rival entrepreneurs running varied religious series on a mixed laissez-faire and oligopolistic model: their status usually is not high. Religious styles constantly adapt and accept vulgarization in accordance with the stylistic tendencies of their varied markets, sometimes in such a way as to weaken content and intellectual articulation."

4. The process of democratization in religion I have described in "The Christian Movement and the Demand for a Theology of the People," *Journal of American History* 67 (December 1980).

5. Martin E. Marty, *Righteous Empire: The Protestant Experience in America* (New York, 1970), 57.

6. Sydney E. Ahlstrom, *A Religious History of the American People* (New Haven, 1972), 385.

7. Alexis de Tocqueville, *Democracy in America*, trans. Henry Reeve (New York, 1945), I: 313, 317.

8. Harry S. Stout, "Religion, Communications, and the Ideological Origins of the American Revolution," *William and Mary Quarterly*, 3rd ser., 34 (October 1977):525.

9. See Frederick Dreyer, "Faith and Experience in the Thought of John Wesley," *American Historical Review* 88 (February 1983).

10. See E.P. Thompson, *The Making of the English Working Class* (New York, 1966); Rhys Isaac, "Evangelical Revolt: The Nature of the Baptists' Challenge to the Traditional Order in Virginia, 1765 to 1775," *William and Mary Quarterly*, 3rd ser., 31 (July 1974).

11. On these developments generally, see Gordon S. Wood, "The Democratization of Mind in the American Revolution," *Leadership in the American Revolution* (Washington, D.C., 1974), 68–89; "Evangelical America and Early Mormonism," *New York History* 61 (1980).

12. See Stanley N. Gundry, *Love Them In: The Proclamation Theology of D.L. Moody* (Chicago, 1976).

13. Charles G. Finney, *Lectures on Revivals of Religion*, ed. William G. McLoughlin (Cambridge, Mass., 1960), 181.

14. *Ibid.*, 199, 210–11. "Wherever the Methodists have gone," Finney said admiringly, "their plain, pointed and simple, but warm and animated mode of preaching has always gathered congregations" (p. 273).

15. James F. Findlay, Jr., *Dwight L. Moody: American Evangelist, 1837-1879* (Chicago, 1969), 223, 225.

16. Gordon S. Wood, "The Democratization of Mind in the American Revolution," 64.

17. On the tradition of commonsense realism in America, see George M. Marsden, "Everyone One's Own Interpreter?: The Bible, Science, and Authority in Mid-Nineteenth-Century America," in *The Bible in America: Essays in Cultural History*, eds. Nathan O. Hatch and Mark A. Noll (New York, 1982), 79–100.

18. See Nathan O. Hatch, "The Christian Movement and the Demand for a Theology of the People."

19. Benjamin Austin, Jr., *Constitutional Republicanism in Opposition to Fallacious Federalism* (Boston, 1803), 212.

20. Alexis de Tocqueville, *Democracy in America*, I:269–80.

21. *Ibid.*, 277.

22. See Niebuhr's brilliant essay, "The Protestant Movement and Democracy in the United States," in *The Shaping of American Religion*, eds. James W. Smith and A. Leland Jamison (Princeton, 1961), 20–71, quote on p. 42.

23. See Sidney E. Mead, "The Rise of the Evangelical Conception of the Ministry," in *The Ministry in Historical Perspective*, eds. H. Richard Niebuhr and Daniel D. Williams (New York, 1956), 218.

24. De Tocqueville, *Democracy in America*, I:317.

25. Luther P. Gerlach and Virginia H. Hine, *People, Power, Change: Movements of Social Transformation* (Indianapolis, 1970), 69.

26. On Lincoln, see William J. Wolf, *The Almost Chosen People: A Study in the Religion of Abraham Lincoln* (Garden City, N.Y., 1969).

27. David Martin, *A General Theory of Secularization*, 36.

28. Gerlach and Hine, *People, Power, Change*, 33–78.

29. Hugh McLeod, *Religion and the People of Western Europe, 1789-1970* (London, 1981); Alan D. Gilbert, *Religion and Society in Industrial England: Church, Chapel and Social Change, 1740-1914* (London, 1976).

30. De Tocqueville, *Democracy in America*, I:321, 325.

31. See the superb study by Virginia Lieson Brereton, "Protestant Fundamentalist Bible Schools, 1882-1940" (Ph.D. diss., Columbia University, 1981).

32. Harry Stout made this point about Deism in "Religion, Communications, and the Ideological Origins of the American Revolution," 532.

33. On Simpson, Gordon, and Torrey, see Brereton, "Protestant Fundamentalist Bible Schools"; on Fuller and Ockenga, Daniel P. Fuller, *Give the Winds a Mighty Voice: The Story of Charles E. Fuller* (Waco, Tex., 1972).

34. This was the focus of the Berlin Congress on Evangelism in 1966 and subsequent international congresses of evangelicals held in Switzerland and Thailand. Evangelism is also the principal subject that evangelicals bring to discussions in the World Council of Churches.

35. Virginia Lieson Brereton, "Protestant Fundamentalist Bible Schools," 149.

36. See the advertisement for the study Bible on the back cover of *Christianity Today,* 4 March 1983. Such an emphasis can produce a lay audience that is surprisingly sophisticated in its theological knowledge and capable of significant self-education. Virginia Brereton's experience with respect to this point is instructive. She recounts in "Protestant Fundamentalist Bible Schools" (pp. 59–60): "A few years ago, on a flight to Chicago, the writer met an accountant from Wisconsin. The man had spent most of the trip intently revising numerous pages of closely written prose in a notebook he balanced on his knee. It turned out that he and a fellow layman in his independent Baptist congregation were waging a friendly theological battle, each turning out pages of arguments supporting his position as against the position of the other. The point in contention was whether 'the rapture' would happen before or after the Great Tribula- tion. One disputant was an earnest pretribulationist, the other an equally fervent posttribulationist. This encounter contained a couple of lessons. First, it drove home the fact that details in the dispensationalist scheme are hardly viewed by dispensation- alists as 'academic' matters. Second, it taught that lay people in the evangelical churches of the present energetically involve themselves in theological matters, and in the process carry on a remarkable activity of self-education."

37. Rudolph L. Nelson, "Fundamentalism at Harvard: The Case of Edward John Carnell," *Quarterly Review* 2 (Summer 1982), 79–98. Carnell was probably the exception to the point being made here. His orientation was more to the broader world of scholarship.

38. William R. Hutchison, *The Modernist Impulse in American Protestantism* (Cambridge, Mass., 1976), 196–99.

39. For fascinating insights on the limitations of substantive political debate in a democ- racy, see Gordon S. Wood, "The Democratization of Mind in the American Revolution."

40. For a superb discussion of how nineteenth-century religious periodicals easily drifted into becoming submissive to popular taste, see John C. Nerone, "The Press and Popular Culture in the Early Republic: Cincinnati, 1793–1848" (Ph.D. diss., University of Notre Dame, 1982), 178–234.

41. Compare Daniel Yankelovich, *New Rules: Searching for Self-fulfillment in a World Turned Upside Down* (New York, 1981), and Robert H. Schuller, *Self Esteem: The New Refor- mation* (Waco, Tex., 1982).

42. See Robert H. Schuller, *Self Esteem,* and Charles H. Kraft, *Christianity in Culture: A Study in Dynamic Biblical Theologizing in Cross-Cultural Perspective* (Maryknoll, N.Y., 1979).

43. *Facts on File* 40 (May 30, 1980): 413, quoted in Brereton, "Protestant Fundamentalist Bible Schools," 2.

44. Charles Malik, *The Two Tasks* (Westchester, Ill., 1980), 32.

CHAPTER SEVEN

1. J. Gresham Machen, *Christianity and Liberalism* (Grand Rapids: Eerdmans, 1968).

2. Examples within evangelicalism abound, but few are as strident and as unabashed as Robert Schuller's *Self-Esteem: The New Reformation* (Waco, Tex.: Word, 1982). Poor self- image is what constitutes original sin (p. 67), and changing that image is what is

conversion (p. 68). Christian life, he claims, is a divinely sanctioned "ego-trip" (p. 74). Pride is a virtue and humility a vice, for God's purpose in the resurrection is to symbolize that his work is now in our hands (p. 99). Schuller's theology is little else than humanism employing the language of the self-movement. The parallels with Harry Emerson Fosdick's *On Being a Real Person* indicate how close Schuller is to liberalism and how far he is from evangelicalism.

3. Kenneth Cauthen, *The Impact of American Religious Liberalism* (New York, 1962), 26-37.

4. The linchpin of the liberal perception, as Karl Barth and Emil Brunner argued so fiercely, was that of divine immanence. See Alexander V. G. Allen, "The Continuity of Christian Thought," in *American Protestant Thought: The Liberal Era*, ed. William R. Hutchison (New York, 1968), 56-68. Reinhold Niebuhr countered that "the adjustment of modern religion to the 'mind' of modern culture inevitably involved capitulation to its thin 'soul'" (*Reflections on the End of an Era* [New York, 1934], ix). The issues are broadly presented and assessed in Richard J. Coleman, *Issues of Theological Warfare: Evangelicals and Liberals* (Grand Rapids, 1972).

5. Frank Hugh Foster, *A Genetic History of the New England Theology* (Chicago, 1907), 543. This school of thought is also sympathetically discussed by George Nye Boardman, *A History of New England Theology* (New York, 1899).

6. Joseph Haroutunian, *Piety Versus Moralism: The Passing of the New England Theology* (New York, 1970), 281.

7. See George M. Marsden, *Fundamentalism and American Culture: The Shaping of Twentieth Century Evangelicalism, 1870-1925* (New York, 1980), 109-18.

8. Charles Hodge, *Systematic Theology* (3 vols.; New York, 1929), I:21. See also John C. Vander Stelt, *Philosophy and Scripture: A Study in Old Princeton and Westminster Theology* (Marlton, N.J., 1978).

9. L.S. Chafer, *Systematic Theology* (8 vols.; Dallas, 1947), I:5.

10. E.H. Bancroft, *Christian Theology: Systematic and Biblical* (Johnson City, 1925), 13.

11. H.O. Wiley, *Christian Theology* (3 vols., Kansas City, 1940), I:16.

12. J.T. Mueller, *Christian Dogmatics* (St. Louis, 1934), 15.

13. Chafer, 5.

14. F. Pieper, *Christian Dogmatics* (3 vols., St. Louis, 1950), I:154.

15. J. Oliver Buswell, *A Systematic Theology of the Christian Religion* (3 vols.; Grand Rapids, 1962), I:19.

16. William Shedd, *Dogmatic Theology* (3 vols., Grand Rapids, 1888-94), I:25.

17. Bancroft, 16.

18. Buswell, I:15.

19. A.H. Strong, *Systematic Theology* (3 vols.; Philadelphia, 1907), I:10.

20. *Ibid.*

21. The Consultation issued in summary form its findings in *The Willowbank Report*. This report, together with the papers presented, may be found in John R.W. Stott and Robert Coote, eds., *Down to Earth: Studies in Christianity and Culture* (Grand Rapids, 1980).

22. Cf. David Kelsey, *The Uses of Scripture in Recent Theology* (Philadelphia, 1975).

23. Bruce J. Nicholls, *Contextualization: Gospel and Culture* (Downers Grove, 1979), 24-36.

24. Rudolf Bultmann, in fact, argues that the world view that a person adopts is not a matter of choice but is prescribed for him or her by the age in which that person lives. See, for example, his book, jointly authored with Karl Jaspers, entitled *Myth and Christianity: An Inquiry into the Possibility of Religion Without Myth* (New York, 1958), 3-10.

25. Cf. David Willis, "In Quest of Context," *Theology Today* 29 (April 1972):10-12; Paul Lehrmann, "Contextual Theology," *Theology Today* 29 (April 1972):3-8.

26. See Dale Vree, "Ideology versus Theology: Case Studies of Liberation Theology and

the Christian New Right," in *Christianity Confronts Modernity*, eds. Peter Williamson and Kevin Perrotta (Ann Arbor, 1981), 57–85; Gabriel Fackre, *The Religious Right and Christian Faith* (Grand Rapids, 1982), 31–35.

27. Cf. John W. Montgomery, "Toward a Christian Philosophy of History," in *Jesus of Nazareth, Saviour and Lord*, ed. Carl F. H. Henry (Grand Rapids, 1966), 227–40.

28. For a presentation of the hermeneutical issues by advocates of the new approach, see James M. Robinson and John B. Cobb, eds., *The New Hermeneutic* (New York, 1964). This approach is sharply rebutted by Cornelius Van Til, *The New Hermeneutic* (Philadelphia, 1974).

29. Krister Stendahl, "Biblical Theology, Contemporary," in *Interpreter's Dictionary of the Bible* (5 vols.; New York, 1962), I:419–20.

30. T. B. Bottomore, ed., *Karl Marx: Selected Writings in Sociology and Social Philosophy* (London, 1963), 83–92.

31. Cf. Peter Berger, *Pyramids of Sacrifice: Political Ethics and Social Change* (New York, 1974), 30. Charles H. Kraft has examined this theme at length in his *Christianity in Culture: A Study in Dynamic Biblical Theologizing in Cross-Cultural Perspective* (New York, 1979). Kraft contributes helpful insights from his expertise in anthropology, but at times seems to surrender the full meaning of an authoritative Bible in contextualization. See also David J. Hesselgrave, *Communicating Christ Cross-Culturally* (Grand Rapids, 1978).

32. Despite Carl Henry's vigorous defense of propositional revelation, he still argues for the fallibility of the interpreter. The Reformation principle of *sola scriptura* means, he asserts, that all interpretations must be kept open to the reforming, correcting work of God's revelation in Scripture. See his *God, Revelation and Authority* (4 vols.; Waco, Tex., 1979), IV:296–352.

CHAPTER EIGHT

1. This theme is discussed in detail in Mark A. Noll, Nathan O. Hatch, and George M. Marsden, *The Search for Christian America* (Westchester, Ill.: Crossway Books, 1983).

2. Cf. fuller discussions of these themes in George M. Marsden, *Fundamentalism and American Culture* (New York: Oxford University Press, 1980) and in Mary Douglas and Steven M. Tipton, eds., *Religion and America: Spirituality in a Secular Age* (Boston: Beacon Press, 1983).

3. See *Fundamentalism and American Culture*, esp. 48–55, 62–71.

4. John Ngusha Orkar, "Patterns of Assimilation of the Tiv," paper presented to the Centre for African Studies, Dalhousie University, 1983.

5. G. Aiken Taylor, "Francis Schaeffer: America's Historical Underpinnings," *The Presbyterian Journal*, 2 March 1983, 7.

6. Frederick Dreyer, "Faith and Experience in the Thought of John Wesley," *American Historical Review* 88 (February 1983): 12–30.

7. This phrase and its application are suggested by Michael A. Cavanaugh, "A Sociological Account of Scientific Creationism: Science, True Science, Pseudoscience" (Ph.D. diss., University of Pittsburgh, 1983).

8. Cf. "Dispensationalism and the Baconian Ideal," in *Fundamentalism and American Culture*, 55-62.

9. I am indebted to Grant Wacker for clarifying this point that the view of history was the central challenge to evangelical thinking in the early twentieth century. See, for instance, his "The Demise of Biblical Civilization," in *The Bible in America: Essays in Cultural History*, eds. Nathan O. Hatch and Mark A. Noll (New York: Oxford University Press, 1982), 121–38.

10. Carl Sagan, *Cosmos* (New York: Random House, 1980), 4.

11. Richard B. Gaffin, Jr., "Old Amsterdam and Inerrancy?" *Westminster Theological Journal* 44 (1982):250–89.

CHAPTER NINE

1. As an evangelical who believes that Scripture constitutes a revelation from God, I am not in a position to write on this subject either disinterestedly or dispassionately. Nonetheless, I hope that enough of the research lying behind this essay shows through to make it useful even for those who do not share either my evangelical standpoint or my specific views about evangelical study of the Bible. This paper has benefited greatly from the criticism that an earlier version received from more than a dozen professional Bible scholars.

2. On Stuart, see Herbert Hovenkamp, *Science and Religion in America, 1800-1860* (Philadelphia: University of Pennsylvania Press, 1978), 62–68; and on the general story, Jerry Wayne Brown, *The Rise of Biblical Criticism in America, 1800-1870: The New England Scholars* (Middletown, Conn.: Wesleyan University Press, 1969).

3. On the great change in higher education, see Richard Hofstadter, "The Revolution in Higher Education," *Paths of American Thought*, eds. A. M. Schlesinger, Jr., and Morton White, (Boston: Houghton Mifflin, 1963), 269–90; Edward Shils, "The Order of Learning in the United States: The Ascendancy of the University," in *The Organization of Knowledge in Modern America, 1860-1920*, eds. Alexandra Oleson and John Voss (Baltimore: Johns Hopkins, 1979), 19-50; and Mark A. Noll, "Christian Thinking and the Rise of the American University," *Christian Scholar's Review* 9 (1979): 3–16.

4. Ernest W. Saunders, *Searching the Scriptures: A History of the Society of Biblical Literature, 1880-1980* (Chico, Cal.: Scholar's Press, 1982), 84.

5. See George M. Marsden, *Fundamentalism and American Culture: The Shaping of Twentieth-Century Evangelicalism, 1870-1925* (New York: Oxford, 1980), 212–21.

6. See Rudolph L. Nelson, "Fundamentalism at Harvard: The Case of Edward John Carnell," *Quarterly Review* 2 (Summer 1982): 79–98, where the careers of fifteen such fundamentals are discussed, including at least five who studied either New or Old Testament. Kenneth Kantzer recently reflected on the process that led him to Harvard: "I began my own advanced study for the ministry when I graduated from college in the 1930's. I sought an accredited school committed to a consistent biblical theology, with a scholarly faculty, a large library, and a disciplined intellectual atmosphere. I couldn't find any. . . . So I chose two schools: the first, a rather typical fundamentalist school so new the ink was barely dry on its articles of incorporation; and the second, a liberal school with a solid reputation for academic excellence." "Documenting the Dramatic Shift in Seminaries from Liberal to Conservative," *Christianity Today*, 4 February 1983, 10.

7. Quotation is from the preface, as cited by Moises Silva, "Ned B. Stonehouse and Redaction Criticism," *Westminster Theological Journal* 40 (Fall 1977, Spring 1978): 77–88, 281–303 (quotation p. 81). This entire essay is a valuable overview of recent evangelical reactions to critical study of the New Testament.

8. Ladd's open, yet cautious approach to the study of Scripture received its fullest exposition in *The New Testament and Criticism* (Grand Rapids: Eerdmans, 1967).

9. A forthcoming study of the Christian Reformed Church by James Bratt (University of Pittsburgh), revised from his Yale dissertation, presents a fine general picture of how this confessional denomination with strong European ties was led to seek wider contacts with American evangelicals in the days after World War II (Grand Rapids: Eerdmans, 1984).

10. One of these was won by Merrill Tenney, a graduate of Gordon College and Harvard

University and a teacher at Wheaton College, for his book *John: The Gospel of Belief: An Analytic Study of the Text,* published in 1948.

11. The thirteen authors of the NICNT volumes currently in print include two from the United States (one of whom did graduate work in Scotland), two from Holland, two from South Africa, one from Australia, and six from the United Kingdom (some of whom held or hold positions in the United States).

12. See I. Howard Marshall, "F. F. Bruce as a Biblical Scholar," *Journal of the Christian Brethren Research Fellowship* 22 (1971): 5-12 (distributed with TSF Newsletter, Spring 1975); R. T. France, "The Tyndale Fellowship—Then and Now," *TSF Bulletin* (January/February 1982): 12-13; and F. F. Bruce's own reflections on the importance of these institutions, *In Retrospect: Remembrance of Things Past* (Grand Rapids: Eerdmans, 1980), 110-11, 122-29.

13. Bruce, *The New Testament Documents—Are They Reliable?* (first published in America by Fleming Revell, 1943, and in many editions by other publishers thereafter).

14. Wheaton College catalogues.

15. *Word Biblical Commentary in 52 volumes: A Prospectus* (Waco, Texas: Word, 1983).

16. The program of the 1982 annual meeting of the SBL listed 472 participants, of whom I was able to identify 48 as evangelical from their institutional identifications or through personal information.

17. For the *Journal of Biblical Literature,* 1978-80, at least 9 or 10 of the 141 authors were from evangelical institutions or were known to me personally as evangelicals. Using the same criteria, I found 19 of 170 authors in *New Testament Studies* for 1977-79 and 1981 to be evangelicals.

18. The Institute for Biblical Research was founded by Prof. E. Earle Ellis of New Brunswick Theological Seminary; Prof. Clark Pinnock, then of Regent College in Vancouver and now at McMaster Divinity College, led in the establishment of the North American TSF.

19. Geerhardus Vos, *Notes on Biblical Theology* (Grand Rapids: Eerdmans, 1948); and George Eldon Ladd, *A Theology of the New Testament* (Grand Rapids: Eerdmans, 1974).

20. See the helpful summaries on evangelical commentaries in Mark Lau Branson, TSF General Secretary, *The Reader's Guide to the Best Evangelical Books* (San Francisco: Harper & Row, 1982); and Grant Osborne, ed., *An Annotated Bibliography on the Bible and the Church* (Deerfield, Ill: Trinity Evangelical Divinity School, 1982).

21. So serious are anomalies in the evangelical study of the Bible that even an evangelical can be tempted to go partway with James Barr's evaluation published in 1977 under the title *Fundamentalism* (Philadelphia: Westminster). That book excoriated the evangelical study of Scripture as puerile, self-contradictory, anti-intellectual, naive, polemical, and nearly worse than worthless. As the more perceptive evangelical reviewers pointed out at the time, Barr's book gratuitously minimized the presumptuous character of much secular treatment of Scripture and grossly maximized the extent of evangelical follies. Yet such reviewers also admitted that Barr's shafts struck uncomfortably close to home. See David F. Wright, in *Themelios* 3 (April 1978):86-89; and George M. Marsden, in *Theology Today* 35 (January 1979): 520-22.

22. Robert K. Johnston, *Evangelicals at an Impasse: Biblical Authority in Perspective* (Atlanta: John Knox, 1979), vii-viii.

23. For brief indications, see Mark A. Noll, *Christians in the American Revolution* (Grand Rapids: Eerdmans/Christian University Press, 1977), 49-78; David Brion Davis, ed., *The Fear of Conspiracy: Images of Un-American Subversion from the Revolution to the Present* (Ithaca, N.Y.: Cornell, 1971); Ray A. Billington, *The Protestant Crusade, 1800-1860: A Study of the Origins of American Nativism* (New York: Macmillan, 1938).

24. Quoted in Johnston, *Evangelicals at an Impasse,* 160 n.5.

25. F. F. Bruce, *The English Bible: A History of Translations from the earliest English Versions to*

the New English Bible (rev. ed.; New York: Oxford, 1970), 194–209; Bruce M. Metzger, "The Revised Standard Version," in The Word of God: A Guide to English Versions of the Bible, ed. Lloyd R. Bailey (Atlanta: John Knox, 1982), 33–34; Gerald A. Larue, "Another Chapter in the History of Bible Translation," Journal of Bible and Religion 31 (1963):301–10.

26. It is worth observing that the committee of translation for the New English Bible included several scholars with evangelical connections, including R. V. G. Tasker, Donald Coggan, and C. F. D. Moule, while, with the exception of Bruce Metzger, there were few similarly connected individuals on the committees of translation for the RSV. Along with the fact that the RSV was sponsored by the National Council of Churches, which evangelicals mistrusted, this may be one reason why British evangelicals reacted more cordially to the NEB than Americans did to the RSV. Lists of translators for these two versions are found in Bailey, ed., The Word of God, 42–44, 62.

27. Robert G. Bratcher, "The New International Version," in ibid., 165.

28. Sales of the Living Bible had reached 25 million by 1981, with sales of the RSV by that time at about 50 million, of the NEB, NASB, and Good News Bible between 12–15 million each, and of the NIV (published only in 1978) already over 3 million. For a compilation of figures and sources, see Nathan O. Hatch and Mark A. Noll, "Introduction," The Bible in America: Essays in Cultural History (New York: Oxford, 1982), 14–15 n.21.

29. To be sure, the story on translations is not entirely ironic and paradoxical, for evangelicals in recent years have been busy publishing balanced works themselves on matters of the ancient texts and modern translations. See D. A. Carson, The King James Version Debate (Grand Rapids: Baker, 1978); Jack P. Lewis, The English Bible from KJV to NIV (Grand Rapids: Baker, 1981); Eugene H. Glassman, The Translation Debate (Downers Grove, Ill.: InterVarsity Press, 1981).

30. Robert H. Gundry, Matthew: A Commentary on His Literary and Theological Art (Grand Rapids: Eerdmans, 1982); on the discussion of this volume at the 1982 annual meetings of the ETS and the SBL, see Grant R. Osborne, "Studies in Matthew: Professional Societies Evaluate New Evangelical Directions," and "Evangelical Theological Society: 1982 Annual Meeting," TSF Bulletin (March/April 1983): 14–15, which reports also that the ETS executive committee rejected a proposal at that annual gathering to remove Gundry from the society.

31. James D. G. Dunn, "The Authority of Scripture According to Scripture," Churchman 96:2, 3 (1982):104–22; 201–25, with quote from p. 118.

32. Bernard Ramm, After Fundamentalism: The Future of Evangelical Theology (San Francisco: Harper & Row, 1983), esp. 101–15, "The Humanity of Holy Scriptures."

33. "The Issue of Biblical Authority Brings a Scholar's Resignation," Christianity Today, 15 July 1983, 35–38.

34. Geoffrey W. Bromiley, "Evangelicals and Theological Creativity," Themelios 5 (September 1979):49.

35. John R. W. Stott, Between Two Worlds: The Art of Preaching in the Twentieth Century (Grand Rapids: Eerdmans, 1982), 87.

36. See the forceful exposition of this assertion in D. A. Carson, "Redaction Criticism: On the Legitimacy and Illegitimacy of a Literary Tool," in Scripture and Truth, eds. Carson and John D. Woodbridge (Grand Rapids: Zondervan, 1983).

37. Wright, review of Barr's Fundamentalism, in Themelios 3 (April 1978):88.

38. Ramm, After Fundamentalism, 34.

39. A partial list would include the following: William J. Abraham, The Divine Inspiration of Holy Scripture (New York: Oxford, 1981); Abraham, Divine Revelation and the Limits of Historical Criticism (New York: Oxford, 1982); Gleason L. Archer, Encyclopedia of Bible Difficulties (Grand Rapids: Zondervan, 1982); Paul J. Achtemeier, The Inspiration

of Scripture: Problems and Proposals (Philadelphia: Westminster, 1980); James Barr, *The Scope and Authority of the Bible* (Philadelphia: Westminster, 1980); Harry R. Boer, *The Bible and Higher Criticism* (rev. ed.; Grand Rapids: Eerdmans, 1981); James M. Boice, ed., *The Foundations of Biblical Authority* (Grand Rapids: Zondervan, 1977); Russ Bush and Tom J. Nettles, *Baptists and the Bible* (Chicago: Moody, 1980); D. A. Carson and John Woodbridge, eds., *Scripture and Truth* (Grand Rapids: Zondervan, 1983); Richard J. Coleman, *Issues of Theological Conflict* (rev. ed.; Grand Rapids: Eerdmans, 1979); Jack Cottrell, *The Authority of the Bible* (Grand Rapids: Baker, 1979); Stephen T. Davis, *The Debate About the Bible: Inerrancy Versus Infallibility* (Philadelphia: Westminster, 1977); Norman L. Geisler, ed., *Biblical Errancy: An Analysis of its Philosophical Roots* (Grand Rapids: Zondervan, 1979); Geisler, *Decide for Yourself: How History Views the Bible* (Grand Rapids: Zondervan, 1982); Robert K. Johnston, *Evangelicals at an Impasse: Biblical Authority in Perspective* (Atlanta: John Knox, 1979); Gordon Lewis and Bruce Demerest, eds., *Challenges to Inerrancy* (Chicago: Moody, forthcoming); Harold Lindsell, *The Battle for the Bible* (Grand Rapids: Zondervan, 1976); Lindsell, *The Bible in the Balance: A Further Look at the Battle for the Bible* (Grand Rapids: Zondervan, 1979); I. Howard Marshall, *Biblical Inspiration* (Grand Rapids: Eerdmans, 1982); Donald K. McKim, ed., *The Authoritative Word: Essays on the Nature of Scripture* (Grand Rapids: Eerdmans, 1983); Ronald H. Nash, *The Word of God and the Mind of Man: The Crisis of Revealed Truth in Contemporary Theology* (Grand Rapids: Zondervan, 1982); Roger R. Nicole and J. Ramsey Michaels, eds., *Inerrancy and Common Sense* (Grand Rapids: Baker, 1980); J. I. Packer, *Beyond the Battle for the Bible* (Westchester, Ill.: Crossway, 1980); Earl D. Radmacher, ed., *Hermeneutics: The Papers of the 1982 ICBI Summit Conference* (Grand Rapids: Zondervan, forthcoming); Jack Rogers and Donald McKim, *The Authority and Interpretation of the Bible: An Historical Approach* (San Francisco: Harper & Row, 1979); Francis L. Schaeffer, *No Final Conflict: The Bible Without Error in All That It Affirms* (Downers Grove, Ill.: InterVarsity, 1975); and John D. Woodbridge, *Biblical Authority: A Critique of the Rogers/McKim Proposal* (Grand Rapids: Zondervan, 1982).

40. *Christianity Today,* 21 December 1979, 13-15.

41. As examples, of the 27 United States-born contributors to the *Word Biblical Commentary,* 19 did the first part of their graduate education at evangelical institutions before going on to finish at universities (4 did all of their graduate education at evangelical seminaries, 2 did all of their graduate work at universities, and 2 attended nonevangelical seminaries before proceeding to the university). Of these 19 United States scholars, 15 now teach or work in evangelical institutions, as do 6 of those who did not have the predominant evangelical-then-university pattern of graduate education. Only 3 of the 27 teach at universities or nonevangelical universities or colleges (Western Kentucky, St. Xavier in Chicago, Wycliffe College of the University of Toronto).

By contrast, of the 19 contributors from the British Commonwealth, 13 did all of their graduate training (and often undergraduate as well) at research universities, while only 6 did even part of their work at theological colleges or seminaries (and some of these had been undergraduates at the research universities). Of these 19, 9 teach or taught at research universities in England or Canada (3 at Manchester, 1 each at Cambridge, Nottingham, Oxford, Sheffield, Calgary, and Toronto).

42. Some of the interpretations that support this view of American religious history, often with references to further such interpretations, are George M. Marsden, *The Evangelical Mind and the New School Presbyterian Experience* (New Haven: Yale University Press, 1970), esp. 31-58 and 230-44; Marsden, *Fundamentalism and American Culture,* esp. 221-28, "Fundamentalism as an American Phenomenon"; David Martin, *A General Theory of Secularization* (New York: Harper & Row, 1978); Martin E. Marty, *Righteous*

Empire: The Protestant Experience in America (New York: Dial, 1970); Henry May, *The Enlightenment in America* (New York: Oxford, 1976); Sidney E. Mead, *The Lively Experiment: The Shaping of Christianity in America* (New York: Harper & Row, 1963); Perry Miller, *The Life of the Mind in America from the Revolution to the Civil War* (New York: Harcourt, Brace & World, 1965), "Book One: The Evangelical Basis"; H. Richard Niebuhr, *The Kingdom of God in America* (New York: Harper & Row, 1959 [orig. 1937]); Gordon S. Wood, "Evangelical America and Early Mormonism," *New York History* 61 (October 1980):359-86.

43. For example, Paul Althaus, *The Theology of Martin Luther* (Philadelphia: Fortress, 1966), 294-322.

44. Quotations from John Adams and Tom Paine.

45. See Nathan O. Hatch, "*Sola Scriptura* and *Novus Ordo Seclorum*," in *The Bible in America,* 59-78; and "The Christian Movement and the Demand for a Theology of the People," *Journal of American History* 67 (1980):545-66.

46. See George M. Marsden, "Everyone One's Own Interpreter? The Bible, Science, and Authority in Mid-Nineteenth-Century America," in *The Bible in America,* esp. 81-84, "The Prevailing Solution: Common Sense and Baconian Science"; and for the most complete treatment to date of the academic use of commonsense philosophy in biblical interpretation, Theodore Dwight Bozeman, *Protestants in an Age of Science: The Baconian Ideal and Antebellum American Religious Thought* (Chapel Hill: University of North Carolina, 1977).

47. John Higham, *History* (Englewood Cliffs, N.J.: Prentice-Hall, 1965), 143.

48. For excellent treatments of this subject, from sociological and biblical perspectives respectively, see Edward Shils, *Tradition* (Chicago: University of Chicago Press, 1981); and F.F. Bruce, *Tradition, Old and New* (Grand Rapids: Zondervan, 1970).

49. This adopts a definition of ideology by George M. Frederickson, cited in Nathan O. Hatch, *The Sacred Cause of Liberty: Republican Thought and the Millennium in Revolutionary New England* (New Haven: Yale University Press, 1977), 9 n.14.

50. It is important to at least note—though it is a theme for an entire essay of its own— that a similar kind of ideological intolerance occurs when other scholars write off without argument the evidence for "virgin" in Isaiah 7:14 or other conservative arguments on debated questions of biblical meaning.

51. It is significant in this regard that theologically conservative British Protestants never underwent a fundamentalist phase as did Americans; see George M. Marsden, "Fundamentalism as an American Phenomenon: A Comparison with English Evangelicalism," *Church History* 46 (June 1977):215-32.

52. See, for one example of this recognition, the kindly but patronizing review by B. B. Warfield of R. A. Torrey's *What the Bible Teaches* (1898) in *The Presbyterian and Reformed Review* 39 (July 1899):562-64, which praises Torrey for trusting in Scripture for theological insight, but which questions whether a simple "Bible-reading" is able to go very far into the depths of biblical theology.

53. See Timothy P. Weber, "The Two-Edged Sword: The Fundamentalist Use of the Bible," in *The Bible in America,* 101-20.

54. For a sketch of Warfield's biography, a sampling of his work, and a bibliography of critical studies, see Mark A. Noll, ed., *The Princeton Theology* (Grand Rapids: Baker, 1983), 15-16, 241-316, 327-28, 333.

55. See the exhaustive list of citations in John E. Meeter and Roger Nicole, *A Bibliography of Benjamin Breckinridge Warfield, 1851-1921* (Nutley, N.J.: Presbyterian and Reformed, 1974).

56. The depth and range of Warfield's interests are suggested in the ten volumes of his collected works (New York: Oxford, 1927-1932; reprint edition, Grand Rapids: Baker,

1981) and in a two-volume compilation of *Selected Shorter Writings of Benjamin B. Warfield*, ed. John E. Meeter (Nutley, N.J.: Presbyterian and Reformed, 1970, 1973).

57. Warfield, "On the Antiquity and the Unity of the Human Race," *Princeton Theological Review* 9 (1911):1-25; reprinted in *Studies in Theology* (New York: Oxford, 1932), quote p. 235.

58. Warfield, "Calvin's Doctrine of Creation," *Princeton Theological Review* 13 (1915); reprinted in *Calvin and Calvinism* (New York: Oxford, 1931).

59. *Ibid.*; see also Warfield, "The Divine and Human in the Bible," *Presbyterian Journal*, 3 May 1894; reprinted in *Selected Shorter Writings of Benjamin B. Warfield*, II: 546-48.

60. James D. G. Dunn's assertion that "the supporters of inerrancy have not paid sufficient heed to the question of the biblical author's *intention*" ("The Authority of Scripture," p. 110) may have some contemporary validity. But it has nothing to say to Warfield, who in 1880 grounded his view of inspiration on the biblical writers' "professions and intentions," and who maintained just this position in his work thereafter. See Warfield, "Inspiration and Criticism" (Inaugural Address delivered at induction as New Testament Professor, Western Theological Seminary, 1880), reprinted in *Revelation and Inspiration* (New York: Oxford, 1927), 420; and for Warfield's specific attention to authorial intent in the discussion of the age of the earth, "On the Antiquity and the Unity of the Human Race," in *Studies in Theology*, 237.

CHAPTER TEN

1. *Woman in Christian Tradition* (Notre Dame, Ind.: Notre Dame University Press, 1973), 185, *passim*.

2. See George M. Marsden, "From Fundamentalism to Evangelicalism: A Historical Analysis," in *The Evangelicals*, eds. David F. Wells and John D. Woodbridge (Nashville: Abingdon Press, 1975), 122-42.

3. Ethelbert D. Warfield, "May Women Be Ordained in the Presbyterian Church?" *The Presbyterian* 99 (November 14, 1929):6; Walden Howard, "Are You Man or Molly-Coddle?" *Moody Monthly* 48 (July 1948):793-94.

4. Clarence Macartney, "Shall We Ordain Women as Ministers and Elders?" *Presbyterian* 99 (November 7, 1929):7.

5. Inez Cavert, *Women in American Church Life: A Study Prepared Under the Guidance of a Counseling Committee of Women Representing National Interdenominational Agencies* (New York: Friendship Press, 1949), 10; "Women's Status in Protestant Churches," *Information Service* 19 (November 16, 1940):3.

6. For statistics, see *Religious Bodies, 1916. Part I: Summary and General Tables* (Washington, D.C., 1919), 40-41; *Religious Bodies, 1936. Volume I: Summary and Detailed Tables* (Washington, D.C., 1941), 23, 35, 850-53. *28th Issue-Annual. Edition for 1960, Yearbook of American Churches, Information on All Faiths in the United States of America*, ed. Benson Y. Landis (New York: National Council of Churches, 1960), 282.

7. *Annual Address of Miss Frances E. Willard, President, Before the 19th National W.C.T.U. Convention, Denver, Co., U.S.A., 1892* (Chicago, 1892), 6.

8. Rev. D. Sherman, "Woman's Place in the Gospel," in *The Harvest and the Reaper, Reminiscences of Revival Work of Mrs. Maggie N. Van Cott, The First Lady Licensed to Preach in the Methodist Episcopal Church in the United States* (New York, 1883), xxxv; Mrs. W. E. Boardman, *Who Shall Publish the Glad Tidings?* (Boston, 1875), 39; Kate Tannatt Woods, "Women in the Pulpit," in *Transactions of the National Council of Women in the United States*, ed. Rachel Foster Avery (Philadelphia, 1891), 287.

9. Cavert, *Women in American Church Life*, 60-82; *Journal of the 31st Delegated General Conference of the Methodist Episcopal Church, Held in Atlantic City, N.J., May 2-May 25, 1932* (New York, Cincinnati, Chicago: The Methodist Book Concern, 1932), 1627.

10. "Woman's Place in Missions Fifty Years Ago and Now," *Missionary Review of the World* 50 (December 1927):909. For a more detailed account of denominational reorganization as it affected women's groups, see Virginia Lieson Brereton and Christa Ressmeyer Klein, "American Women in Ministry: A History of Protestant Beginning Points," in *Women in American Religion,* ed. Janet Wilson James (Philadelphia: University of Pennsylvania Press, 1980), 171-90.

11. Peabody, "Woman's Place in Missions," 909.

12. "Women's Meetings in St. Paul. The Second Biennial," *Women and Missions* 6 (July 1929):126.

13. Katherine Bennett and Margaret Hodge, "Open Letter to Presbyterian Women," *Women and Missions* 6 (September 1929):232; "Conference of One Hundred Women," *Women and Missions* 6 (July 1929):129.

14. For a more detailed account, see Elizabeth Howell Verdesi, *In But Still Out: Women in the Church* (Philadelphia: Westminster Press, 1976).

15. Jesse M. Bader, "Conference of Jews and Christians," *The Church Woman* 4 (February 1938):5-6.

16. Gladys Gilkey Calkins, *Follow Those Women: Church Women in the Ecumenical Movement* (New York: National Council of Churches, 1961), 19.

17. Elizabeth Rice Achtemeier, *The Feminine Crisis in Christian Faith* (Nashville: Abingdon Press, 1965), 14, 17.

18. Cavert, *Women in American Church Life,* 38-39.

19. Brereton and Klein, "American Women in Ministry," 172, 187.

20. *A Map of the New Country: Women and Christianity* (London and Boston: Routledge and Kegan Paul, 1983), 103.

21. Quoted in "God's Word on Femininity," *Moody Bible Institute Magazine* 31 (June 1931):486; D. L. Peters, "The Preservation of American Womanhood," *Moody Bible Institute Magazine* 31 (January 1931):253; Kenneth S. Wuest, "The Adornment of the Christian Woman," *Moody Monthly* 40 (May 1940):481; E. Myers Knoth, "Woman's Rebellion and Its Consequences," *Moody Bible Institute Magazine* 34 (October 1933):55. See also David S. Smith, "The Dating of the American Sexual Revolution: Evidence and Interpretation," in *The American Family in Social-Historical Perspective,* ed. Michael Gordon (2nd ed.; New York: St. Martin's Press, 1978), which dates the sexual revolution from the late nineteenth century, but notes its appearance among college women in the 1920s.

22. See, for example, P. E. Kretzmann, "The Position of the Christian Woman, Especially as Worker in the Church," *Concordia Theological Monthly* 1 (1930):351-60.

23. Alan Graebner, *Uncertain Saints: The Laity in the Lutheran Church—Missouri Synod, 1900-1970* (Westport, Conn.: Greenwood Press, 1975), 139.

24. Ruth Fritz Meyer, *Women on a Mission: The Role of Women in the Church from Bible Times Up To and Including a History of the Lutheran Women's Missionary League During Its First Twenty-Five Years* (St. Louis: Concordia Publishing House, 1967), 201.

25. C. R. Daley, "Women as Baptist Leaders," *Baptist Standard* 81 (February 26, 1969):7; Norman H. Letsinger, "The Status of Women in the Southern Baptist Convention in Historical Perspective," *Baptist History and Heritage* 12 (January 1977):37-44.

26. "Statement Made by Miss Burroughs at the Close of Her Annual 'Report to Women's Convention, at St. Louis,'" September 8, 1938, 3, in Nannie Helen Burroughs Papers, Manuscript Division, Library of Congress, Washington, D.C.

27. John R. Seeley, R. Alexander Sim, and Elizabeth W. Loosley, *Crestwood Heights: A Study of the Culture of Suburban Life* (New York: Basic Books, 1956), 167.

28. David R. Mace, "Equality in Marriage," *Home Life* (August 1959):8; Rhoda Bacmeister, *All In the Family* (New York: Appleton-Century-Crofts, 1951), 234.

29. Henry A. Bowman, *Marriage for Moderns* (4th ed.; New York: McGraw-Hill, 1960), 23.

30. Donald Dayton notes that the nineteenth-century Princeton theologians, whose influence was crucial in the rise of fundamentalism, held an unusually restrictive view of the Genesis curse as a normative pattern, unaffected by the work of Christ. "The Social and Political Conservatism of Modern American Evangelicalism: A Preliminary Search for the Reasons," *Union Seminary Quarterly Review* 32 (Winter 1977):71–80.

31. "The Orders of Creation—Some Reflections on the History and Place of the Term in Systematic Theology," *Concordia Theological Monthly* 43 (March 1972):165–78. Franklin Sherman also notes that Karl Barth espoused a hierarchical view of sexuality in his discussion of marriage as well, although this was "a concept that Barth otherwise rejects." See his introduction to Karl Barth, *On Marriage* (Philadelphia: Fortress Press, 1968), iv; and George Tavard's similar analysis in *Woman in Christian Tradition,* 179–81.

32. *The Place of Women in the Church* (2nd ed.; Chicago: Moody Press, 1968), 68.

33. *Let Me Be a Woman: Notes on Womanhood for Valerie* (Wheaton: Tyndale, 1976), 132–33.

34. Quoted in Larry and Nordis Christenson, *The Christian Couple* (Minneapolis: Bethany Fellowship, 1977), 124.

35. *Ibid.,* 133.

36. Virginia Ramey Mollenkott, "Evangelicalism: A Feminist Perspective," *Union Seminary Quarterly Review* 32 (Winter 1977):95.

37. "Women and Evangelical Christianity," in *The Cross and the Flag,* eds. Robert G. Clouse *et al.,* (Carol Stream, Ill.: Creation House, 1972), 69.

38. Walter C. Hobbs, "Jesus and Women in a Male-Dominated Society," *Eternity* 24 (January 1973):20; G. William Carlson, "ERA: Fairness or Fraud?" *Eternity* 26 (November 1975):30.

39. *All We're Meant to Be: A Biblical Approach to Women's Liberation* (Waco, Tex.: Word Books, 1974), 169.

40. John and Judy Alexander, "Who Cleans the Toilets?" *Eternity* 26 (March 1975):38; Carlson, "ERA: Fairness or Fraud?" 31.

41. John Alexander, "Are Women People?" in *What You Should Know About Women's Lib,* ed. Miriam G. Moran (New Canaan, Conn.: Keats Publishing, Inc., 1974), 31, 33.

42. A. Duane Litfin, "Evangelical Feminism: Why Traditionalists Reject It," *Bibliotheca Sacra* 136 (July–September 1979):267.

43. *The Worldly Evangelicals* (San Francisco: Harper and Row, 1978), 126.

CHAPTER ELEVEN

1. Nathaniel Hawthorne, *Tales and Sketches* (New York: The Library of America, 1982), 746. All further page references will be to this edition and will be cited in parentheses within the text.

2. "The Stolen Child," in *Selected Poems and Two Plays of William Butler Yeats,* ed. M. L. Rosenthal (New York: Collier Books, 1966), 3.

3. I. M. Haldeman, *The Signs of the Times* (5th ed.; New York: Charles C. Cook, 1914), 69, 72.

4. Wesley Ingles, "Art as Incarnation," *Christianity Today,* 1 March 1963, 15.

5. "A Model of Christian Charity," in *The Norton Anthology of American Literature,* eds. Ronald Gottesman *et al.* (New York: W. W. Norton, 1979), I:19.

6. "Letter III: What is an American?" in *Letters From an American Farmer and Sketches of 18th-Century America* (New York: Penguin, 1981), 70. On the subject of America as

Eden or the New Jerusalem, see, among many other studies, Henry Nash Smith, *Virgin Land: The American West as Symbol and Myth* (Cambridge: Harvard University Press, 1950); R. W. B. Lewis, *The American Adam: Innocence, Tragedy, and Tradition in the Nineteenth Century* (Chicago: University of Chicago Press, 1953); Perry Miller, *Errand into the Wilderness* (Cambridge: Belknap Press, 1956).

7. *Walden and Other Writings of Henry David Thoreau,* ed. Brooks Atkinson (New York: The Modern Library, 1937), 10.

8. *Fundamentalism and American Culture* (New York: Oxford University Press, paper ed., 1982), 225-28.

9. Dorothy Sayers, *The Mind of the Maker* (London: Methuen & Co., 1941). For a discussion of the romantic roots of this analogy, see M. H. Abrams, *The Mirror and the Lamp: Romantic Theory and the Critical Tradition* (New York: Oxford University Press, paper ed., 1971), 256-62.

10. Ingles, 11.

11. Harold Best, "Christian Responsibility in Music," in *The Christian Imagination: Essays on Literature and the Arts,* ed. Leland Ryken (Grand Rapids: Baker, 1981), 404, 407.

12. Harold Bloom, *The Anxiety of Influence* (New York: Oxford University Press, 1973).

13. *Natural Supernaturalism: Tradition and Revolution in Romantic Literature* (New York: W. W. Norton & Company, Norton Library, 1973). See also Abrams, *The Mirror and the Lamp,* 252-62; Ernest Tuveson, *The Imagination as a Means of Grace: Locke and the Aesthetics of Romanticism* (Berkeley: University of California Press, 1960); and Jerome J. McGann, *The Romantic Ideology: A Critical Investigation* (Chicago: University of Chicago Press, 1983).

14. *Hyperion* III, 113-18, in *The Poems of John Keats,* ed. Jack Stillinger (Cambridge: The Belknap Press, 1978), 355-56.

15. "The American Scholar," in *Selections from Ralph Waldo Emerson,* ed. Stephen E. Whicher (Boston: Houghton Mifflin Company, 1957), 75.

16. "The Divinity School Address," in *Selections from Emerson,* 104.

17. *Shelley's Poems* (London: J. M. Dent & Sons, 1907), 331.

18. As quoted in Marsden, *Fundamentalism,* 76.

19. "Arts and Religion: They Need Not Clash," *Christianity Today,* 21 January 1966, 9.

20. "Self-Reliance," in *Selections from Emerson.*

21. "Prospectus" to *The Excursion,* in Abrams, *Natural Supernaturalism,* 467.

22. *Walden* in *Walden and Other Writings,* ed. Atkinson, 275.

23. *The Feminization of American Culture* (New York: Avon Books, A Discus Book, 1978), 17-93.

24. Marsden, *Fundamentalism,* 11, 17.

25. "The Demise of Biblical Civilization," in *The Bible in America,* eds. Nathan O. Hatch and Mark A. Noll (New York: Oxford University Press, 1982), 121-38.

26. *Christ and Culture* (New York: Harper & Row, 1951), 81-82.

27. For example, it is difficult to find any treatment of the arts in issues of the *Christian Fundamentalist* from the early 1930s. But when one picks up a copy of, say, *Christian Life* from the late 1940s, one discovers a marked increase of interest in the arts. The treatment, however, remains quite suspicious of them. The July 1948 issue, for example, contains several letters that doubt whether non-Christian actors can accurately portray Christians in the many evangelistic films beginning to appear at that time. This particular issue also contains two Christian short stories written according to predetermined formulas of the victorious life.

28. This is an implicit or explicit theme in many of the essays appearing in the past several decades in periodicals such as *Eternity* and *Christianity Today.*

29. "Hawthorne and His Mosses," in *The Portable Melville,* ed. Jay Leyda (New York: The Viking Press, 1952), 406.

30. *Christ and Time,* trans. Floyd Filson (Philadelphia: The Westminster Press, 1964).
31. *The Burden of Southern History* (New York: Vintage Books, 1961), 170–71.
32. *The Eclipse of Biblical Narrative* (New Haven: Yale University Press, 1974).
33. *Art in Action* (Grand Rapids: Wm. B. Eerdmans, 1980), 11.
34. *Ibid.*
35. *Ibid.,* 4–5.
36. *After Virtue* (Notre Dame: University of Notre Dame Press, 1981), 197.
37. *Testament of Vision* (Grand Rapids: Wm. B. Eerdmans, 1958), 44.
38. *Ibid.,* 50.
39. *Ibid.,* 51.
40. *The Last Year of the War* (New York: Harper & Row, 1978), 4.
41. *Ibid.,* 155.

CHAPTER TWELVE

1. Claude E. Stipe, "Does the ASA Take a 'Position' on Controversial Issues?" *Journal of the American Scientific Affiliation* 29 (March 1977):4, quoting from the ASA statement of belief.
2. Bernard Ramm, *The Christian View of Science and Scripture* (Grand Rapids: Eerdmans, 1954), 180.
3. Harold W. Clark to G. M. Price, September 12, 1937, Price Papers, Andrews University, Berrien Springs, Mich. On Higley, see *National Cyclopedia of American Biography,* 43:363.
4. Clark to Price, September 12, 1937.
5. Walter E. Lammerts, "The Creationist Movement in the United States: A Personal Account," *Journal of Christian Reconstruction* 1 (1974):54; F. Alton Everest, "The American Scientific Affiliation—The First Decade," *JASA* 3 (September 1951):33–38.
6. Cordelia Erdman, "Stratigraphy and Paleontology," *JASA* 5 (March 1953):3–11.
7. Russell L. Mixter, "An Evaluation of the Fossil Record," *JASA* 11 (December 1959):24–26; J. Frank Cassel, "The Evolution of Evangelical Thinking on Evolution," *JASA* 11 (December 1959):27.
8. Irving A. Cowperthwaite, "Some Implications of Evolution for A.S.A.," *JASA* 12 (June 1960):12.
9. Russell L. Mixter, ed., *Evolution and Christian Thought Today* (Grand Rapids: Eerdmans, 1959), 67, 188; Walter R. Hearn, "Origin of Life," *JASA* 13 (June 1961):38.
10. Cassel, "Evolution of Evangelical Thinking," 27.
11. J. Frank Cassel, "The Origin of Man and the Bible," *JASA* 12 (June 1960):13.
12. Ramm, *Christian View of Science,* esp. 9.
13. Cassel, "Origin of Man," 15.
14. *JASA* 31 (December 1979).
15. Cassel, "Evolution of Evangelical Thinking," 27.
16. Philip B. Marquart, Letter to the Editor, *JASA* 15 (September 1963):100. See also V. Elving Anderson, "The Goals of the ASA—a Personal View," *JASA* 17 (June 1965):35.
17. Henry M. Morris, *The Twilight of Evolution* (Grand Rapids: Baker, 1963), 93.
18. Quoted in Richard H. Bube, *The Human Quest: A New Look at Science and the Christian Faith* (Waco, Tex.: Word, 1971), 180.
19. See, e.g., V. Elving Anderson and David O. Moberg, "Christian Commitment and Evolutionary Concepts," *JASA* 15 (September 1963):69–70.
20. See, e.g., Walter R. Hearn, "Biological Science," in *The Encounter between Christianity*

and Science, ed. Richard H. Bube (Grand Rapids: Eerdmans, 1968), 100, 220. Regarding the fundamentalist heritage, see "Doctrinal Statement," *JASA* 7 (March 1955):2.

21. "The Christianity Today—Gallup Poll: An Overview," *Christianity Today,* 21 December 1979, 14.

22. Davis A. Young, *Christianity and the Age of the Earth* (Grand Rapids: Zondervan, 1982), 10.

23. William D. Sisterson, quoted in Arnold D. Ehlert, "The Literature of Scientific Creationism and Anti-Evolution Polemic," *Proceedings, 31st Annual Conference of the American Theological Library Association* (June 20-24, 1977):154.

24. Russell L. Mixter, "Developmentalism?" *JASA* 23 (December 1971):142.

25. "What Christian Colleges Teach about Creation," *Christianity Today,* 17 June 1977, 8.

26. D. Gareth Jones, "Evolution: A Personal Dilemma," *JASA* 29 (June 1977):76. On evangelical attitudes toward creation and evolution, see also George M. Marsden, "Creation versus Evolution: No Middle Way," *Nature* 305 (1983):571-74; and Marsden, "Understanding Fundamentalist Views of Science," in *Science and Creationism,* ed. Ashley Montagu (New York: Oxford University Press, 1984), 95-116.

CHAPTER THIRTEEN
WORKS CITED

ABRAMS, RAY H. *Preachers Present Arms.* Rev. ed. Scottdale, Penn.: Herald Press, 1969.

ALLEN, ROBERT L. *Reluctant Reformers: Racism and Social Reform Movements in the United States.* Washington, D.C.: Howard University Press, 1974.

ANDERSON, JOHN B. *Between Two Worlds: A Congressman's Choice.* Grand Rapids: Zondervan, 1970.

————. *Vision and Betrayal in America.* Waco, Tex.: Word Books, 1975.

BELL, DANIEL, ed. *The Radical Right.* Garden City, N.Y.: Doubleday, 1963.

BILLINGTON, RAY A. *Protestant Crusade, 1800-1960: A Study in the Origins of American Nativism.* New York: Macmillan, 1938.

BISNOW, MARK. *Diary of a Dark Horse: The 1980 Anderson Presidential Campaign.* Carbondale: Southern Illinois University Press, 1983.

BOLLIER, DAVID. *Liberty and Justice for Some: Defending Free Society from the Radical Right's Holy War on Democracy.* New York: Frederick Ungar, 1983.

BOWDEN, HENRY WARNER. *American Indians and Christian Missions: Studies in Cultural Conflict.* Chicago: University of Chicago Press, 1981.

BROMLEY, DAVID G. and ANSON D. SHUPE, eds. *New Christian Politics.* Macon, Ga.: Mercer University Press, 1984.

BROWN, HAROLD O. J. *Christianity and the Class Struggle.* New Rochelle, N.Y.: Arlington House, 1970.

————. *The Reconstruction of the Republic.* New Rochelle, N.Y.: Arlington House, 1977.

CHALMERS, DAVID M. *Hooded Americanism: The History of the Ku Klux Klan.* Rev. ed. New York: Franklin Watts, 1981.

CHERRY, CONRAD, ed. *God's New Israel: Religious Interpretations of American Destiny.* Englewood Cliffs, N.J.: Prentice-Hall, 1971.

CLABAUGH, GARY K. *Thunder on the Right: The Protestant Fundamentalists.* Chicago: Nelson-Hall, 1974.

CLOUSE, ROBERT G., ROBERT D. LINDER, and RICHARD V. PIERARD, eds. *The Cross and the Flag.* Carol Stream, Ill.: Creation House, 1972.

————. *Protest and Politics: Christianity and Contemporary Affairs.* Greenwood, S.C.: Attic Press, 1968.

CONWAY, FLO and JIM SIEGELMAN. *Holy Terror: The Fundamentalist War on America's Freedoms in Religion, Politics and Our Private Lives.* Garden City, N.Y.: Doubleday, 1982.

COOPER, JOHN CHARLES. *Religious Pied Pipers: A Critique of Radical Right Religion.* Valley Forge, Penn.: Judson Press, 1981.

COTHAM, PERRY C. *Politics, Americanism, and Christianity.* Grand Rapids: Baker Book House, 1976.

CRAWFORD, ALAN. *Thunder on the Right: The "New Right" and the Politics of Resentment.* New York: Pantheon, 1980.

DATA CENTER, THE. *The New Right: Readings and Commentary.* 464 19th St., Oakland, CA 94612, 1982.

DAYTON, DONALD W. *Discovering an Evangelical Heritage.* New York: Harper & Row, 1976.

DOUGLAS, MARY and STEVEN M. TIPTON, eds. *Religion and America: Spirituality in a Secular Age.* Boston: Beacon Press, 1983.

DUNCAN, HOMER. *Secular Humanism: The Most Dangerous Religion in America.* Lubbock, Tex.: Missionary Crusader, 1979.

DUNN, JAMES M., ed. *Politics: A Guidebook for Christians.* Dallas: Christian Life Commission, 1970.

EELS, ROBERT, with BARTELL NYBERG. *Lonely Walk: The Life of Senator Mark Hatfield.* Chappaqua, N.Y.: Christian Herald Books, 1979.

ERICSON, EDWARD L. *American Freedom and the Radical Right.* New York: Frederick Ungar, 1982.

FACKRE, GABRIEL. *The Religious Right and Christian Faith.* Grand Rapids: Eerdmans, 1982.

FALWELL, JERRY. *Listen, America!* Garden City, N.Y.: Doubleday, 1980.

————, with ED DOBSON and ED HINDSON. *The Fundamentalist Phenomenon: The Resurgence of Conservative Christianity.* Garden City, N.Y.: Doubleday, 1981.

FINCH, PHILIP. *God, Guts, and Guns: A Close Look at the Radical Right.* New York: Putman, 1983.

FORSTER, ARNOLD and BENJAMIN R. EPSTEIN. *Danger on the Right.* New York: Random House, 1964.

FOSTER, MARSHALL and MARY–ELAINE SWANSON. *The American Covenant: The Untold Story.* Thousand Oaks, Cal.: Foundation for Christian Self-Government, 1981.

FOWLER, ROBERT BOOTH. *A New Engagement: Evangelical Political Thought, 1966–1976.* Grand Rapids: Eerdmans, 1983.

FRAZIER, CLAUDE A., ed. *Politics and Religion Can Mix!* Nashville: Broadman Press, 1974.

FURNESS, CHARLES Y. *The Christian and Social Action.* Old Tappan, N.J.: Revell, 1972.

GEDRAITIS, ALBERT F. *Worship and Politics.* Toronto: Wedge, 1972.

GOODMAN, WILLIAM R., JR. and JAMES J. H. PRICE. *Jerry Falwell: An Unauthorized Profile.* 510 Rolfe Ave., Lynchburg, VA 24503, 1981.

GRANT, DANIEL R. *The Christian and Politics.* Nashville: Broadman, 1968.

GRIFFIN, CLIFFORD S. *Their Brothers' Keepers: Moral Stewardship in the United States, 1800–1865.* New Brunswick, N.J.: Rutgers University Press, 1960.

GROUNDS, VERNON C. *Evangelicalism and Social Responsibility.* Scottdale, Penn.: Herald Press, 1969.

GRUBB, NORMAN P. *Modern Viking: The Story of Abram Vereide, Pioneer in Christian Leadership.* Grand Rapids: Zondervan, 1961.

HADDEN, JEFFREY and CHARLES E. SWANN. *Prime-Time Preachers: The Rising Power of Televangelism.* Reading, Mass.: Addison-Wesley, 1981.

HALL, VERNA M. *The Christian History of the American Revolution.* San Francisco: Foundation for American Christian Education, 1976.

HARRELL, DAVID EDWIN, ed. *Varieties of Southern Evangelicalism.* Macon, Ga.: Mercer University Press, 1981.

HATFIELD, MARK O. *Between a Rock and a Hard Place.* Waco: Word Books, 1976.

———. *Conflict and Conscience.* Waco: Word Books, 1971.

———. *Not Quite So Simple.* New York: Harper & Row, 1968.

HAYS, BROOKS. *Politics Is My Parish.* Baton Rouge: Louisiana State University Press, 1981.

———. *A Southern Moderate Speaks.* Chapel Hill: University of North Carolina Press, 1959.

HEDSTROM, JAMES A. "Evangelical Program in the United States, 1945–1980: The Morphology of Establishment, Progressive, and Radical Platforms." Ph.D. diss., Vanderbilt University, 1982.

HEFLEY, JAMES C. and EDWARD G. PLOWMAN. *WASHINGTON: Christians in the Corridors of Power.* Wheaton, Ill.: Tyndale House, 1975.

HENRY, CARL F. H. *Aspects of Christian Social Ethics.* Grand Rapids: Eerdmans, 1964.

———. *A Plea for Evangelical Demonstration.* Grand Rapids: Baker, 1971.

———. *The Uneasy Conscience of Modern Fundamentalism.* Grand Rapids: Eerdmans, 1947.

HENRY, PAUL B. *Politics for Evangelicals.* Valley Forge, Penn.: Judson Press, 1974.

HIGHAM, JOHN. *Strangers in the Land: Patterns of American Nativism, 1860–1925.* New Brunswick, N.J.: Rutgers University Press, 1955.

HILL, SAMUEL S. and DENNIS E. OWEN. *The New Religious-Political Right in America.* Nashville: Abingdon, 1982.

HITCHCOCK, JAMES. *What Is Secular Humanism? Why Humanism Became Secular and How It Is Changing Our World.* Ann Arbor, Mich.: Servant Books, 1982.

HOFSTADTER, RICHARD. *Anti-Intellectualism in American Life.* New York: Knopf, 1963.

———. *The Paranoid Style in American Politics, and Other Essays.* New York: Knopf, 1965.

JORSTAD, ERLING. *Evangelicals in the White House: The Cultural Maturation of Born Again Christianity 1960–1981.* Lewiston, N.Y.: Edwin Mellen Press, 1981.

———. *The Politics of Doomsday: Fundamentalists of the Far Right.* Nashville: Abingdon, 1970.

———. *The Politics of Moralism: The New Christian Right in American Life.* Minneapolis: Augsburg, 1981.

KATER, JOHN L., JR. *Christians on the Right: The Moral Majority in Perspective.* New York: Seabury, 1982.

KINZER, DONALD L. *An Episode in Anti-Catholicism: The American Protective Association.* Seattle: University of Washington Press, 1964.

KOLKEY, JONATHAN M. *The New Right, 1960-1968: With Epilogue, 1969-1980.* Lanham, Md.: University Press of America, 1983.

LAHAYE, TIM. *The Battle for the Family.* Old Tappan, N.J.: Revell, 1981.

————. *The Battle for the Mind.* Old Tappan, N.J.: Revell, 1980.

LAZAR, ERNIE. *Bibliography on Conservative and Extreme Right Thought and Activity in the U.S. since 1960.* 495 Ellis St., #1753, San Francisco, CA 94102, 1982; 1984.

LIEBMAN, ROBERT C. and ROBERT WUTHNOW. *The New Christian Right: Mobilization and Legitimation.* Hawthorne, N.Y.: Aldine, 1983.

LINDER, ROBERT D. and RICHARD V. PIERARD. *Politics: A Case for Christian Action.* Downers Grove, Ill.: InterVarsity, 1973.

————. *Twilight of the Saints: Biblical Christianity and Civil Religion in America.* Downers Grove, Ill.: InterVarsity, 1978.

LINDSELL, HAROLD. *Free Enterprise: Judeo-Christian Defense.* Wheaton, Ill.: Tyndale House, 1982.

LIPSET, SEYMOUR MARTIN and EARL RABB. *The Politics of Unreason: Right-wing Extremism in America, 1790-1970.* New York: Harper & Row, 1970.

LITTELL, FRANKLIN H. *Wild Tongues: A Handbook of Social Pathology.* New York: Macmillan, 1969.

MCINTYRE, THOMAS J. *The Fear Brokers.* New York: Pilgrim, 1979.

MAGNUSON, NORRIS. *Salvation in the Slums: Evangelical Social Work, 1865-1920.* Metuchen, N.J.: Scarecrow Press, 1977.

MAGUIRE, DANIEL. *The New Subversives: Anti-Americanism of the Religious Right.* New York: Continuum, 1982.

MARCUS, SHELDON. *Father Coughlin: The Tumultuous Life of the Priest of the Little Flower.* Boston: Little, Brown, 1973.

MARSDEN, GEORGE M. *Fundamentalism and American Culture: The Shaping of Twentieth-Century Evangelicalism, 1870-1925.* New York: Oxford University Press, 1980.

————. "Preachers of Paradox: The Religious New Right in Historical Perspective." In *Religion and America: Spirituality in a Secular Age,* edited by Mary Douglas and Steven M. Tipton. Boston: Beacon Press, 1983.

————. "Understanding Fundamentalist Views of Society." In *Reformed Faith and Politics,* edited by Ronald H. Stone. Washington: University Press of America, 1983.

MARSHALL, PETER and DAVID MANUEL. *The Light and the Glory.* Old Tappan, N.J.: Revell, 1977.

MARTY, MARTIN E. *The Public Church: Mainline, Evangelical, Catholic.* New York: Crossroad, 1981.

MOBERG, DAVID O. *The Great Reversal: Evangelism Versus Social Concern.* Philadelphia: Lippincott, 1972.

————. *Inasmuch: Christian Social Responsibility in the Twentieth Century..* Grand Rapids: Eerdmans, 1965.

MONSMA, STEPHEN V. *The Unraveling of America.* Downers Grove, Ill.: InterVarsity, 1974.

MOTT, STEPHEN C. *Biblical Ethics and Social Change.* New York: Oxford University Press, 1982.

MOUW, RICHARD J. *Called to Holy Worldliness.* Philadelphia: Fortress, 1980.

———. *Political Evangelism.* Grand Rapids: Eerdmans, 1973.

———. *Politics and the Biblical Drama.* Grand Rapids: Eerdmans, 1976.

MURCH, JAMES DEFOREST. *Co-operation without Compromise: A History of the National Association of Evangelicals.* Grand Rapids: Eerdmans, 1956.

MYERS, GUSTAVUS. *History of Bigotry in the United States.* Rev. ed. New York: Capricorn Books, 1960.

NASH, RONALD. *Social Justice and the Christian Church.* Milford, Mich.: Mott Media, 1983.

NOLL, MARK A., NATHAN O. HATCH, and GEORGE M. MARSDEN. *The Search for Christian America.* Westchester, Ill.: Crossway Books, 1983.

OVERSTREET, HARRY and BONARO. *The Strange Tactics of Extremism.* New York: Norton, 1964.

PEALE, GILLIAN. *Revival and Reaction: The Contemporary American Right.* Oxford: Oxford University Press, 1984.

PERKINS, JOHN. *With Justice for All.* Ventura, Cal.: Regal Books, 1982.

PIERARD, RICHARD V. "Billy Graham and the U.S. Presidency." *Journal of Church and State* 22 (Winter 1980): 107–27.

———. "The Christian Right: Suggestions for Further Reading." *Foundations* 25 (April–June 1982): 212–27.

———. "The New Religious Right: A Formidable Force in American Politics." *Choice* 19 (March 1982): 863–79.

———. "One Nation under God: Judgment or Jingoism?" In *Christian Social Ethics: Perspectives and Problems,* edited by Perry C. Cotham. Grand Rapids: Baker Book House, 1979, 81–103.

———. "Religion and the New Right in Contemporary American Politics." In *Religion and Politics,* edited by James E. Wood, Jr. Waco, Tex.: Baylor University Press, 1983, 59–81.

———. *The Unequal Yoke: Evangelical Christianity and Political Conservatism.* Philadelphia: Lippincott, 1970.

———, and ROBERT G. CLOUSE. "What's New About the New Right?" *Contemporary Education* 54 (Spring 1983): 194–200.

PIPPERT, WESLEY G. *Faith at the Top.* Elgin, Ill.: David C. Cook, 1973.

———. *The Spiritual Journey of Jimmy Carter.* New York: Macmillan, 1978.

RAUSCH, DAVID. *A Legacy of Hatred: Why Christians Must Not Forget the Holocaust.* Chicago: Moody Press, 1984.

REDEKOP, JOHN H. *The American Far Right: A Case Study of Billy James Hargis and Christian Crusade.* Grand Rapids: Eerdmans, 1968.

RIBUFFO, LEO P. *The Old Christian Right: The Protestant Far Right from the Great Depression to the Cold War.* Philadelphia: Temple University Press, 1983.

ROY, RALPH LORD. *Apostles of Discord: A Study of Organized Bigotry and Disruption on the Fringes of Protestantism.* Boston: Beacon, 1953.

ROZEK, EDWARD J., ed. *Walter H. Judd: Chronicles of a Statesman.* Denver: Grier, 1980.

RUTYNA, RICHARD A. and JOHN W. KUEHL, eds. *Conceived in Conscience*. Norfolk, Va.: Donning, 1983.

SCHAEFFER, FRANCIS A. *A Christian Manifesto*. Westchester, Ill.: Crossway Books, 1981.

———. *How Should We Then Live? The Rise and Decline of Western Thought and Culture*. Old Tappan, N.J.: Revell, 1976.

———, and C. EVERETT KOOP. *Whatever Happened to the Human Race?* Old Tappan, N.J.: Revell, 1979.

SCHAEFFER, FRANKY V. *A Time for Anger: The Myth of Neutrality*. Westchester, Ill.: Crossway Books, 1982.

SCHLOSSBERG, HERBERT. *Idols for Destruction: Christian Faith and Its Confrontation with American Society*. Nashville: Nelson, 1983.

SHRIVER, PEGGY. *The Bible Vote: Religion and the New Right*. New York: Pilgrim, 1981.

SHUPE, ANSON and WILLIAM STACEY. *Born Again Politics and the Moral Majority: What Social Surveys Really Show*. Lewiston, N.Y.: Edwin Mellen Press, 1982.

SIDER, RONALD J., ed. *The Chicago Declaration*. Carol Stream, Ill.: Creation House, 1974.

SINGER, C. GREGG. *A Theological Interpretation of American History*. Rev. ed. Phillipsburg, N.J.: Presbyterian and Reformed, 1981.

SKILLEN, JAMES W., ed. *Christian Politics: False Hope or Biblical Demand*. Indiana, Penn.: Jubilee Enterprises, 1976.

———. *Christians Organizing for Political Service*. Washington, D.C.: Association for Public Justice, 1980.

SLATER, ROSALIE J. *Teaching and Learning America's Christian History*. San Francisco: Foundation for American Christian Education, 1965.

SMITH, TIMOTHY L. *Revivalism and Social Reform: American Protestantism on the Eve of the Civil War*. New ed. Baltimore: Johns Hopkins University Press, 1980.

SMYLIE, JOHN E. "Protestant Clergymen and America's World Role 1865–1900." Th.D. diss. Princeton Theological Seminary, 1959.

STAUFFER, VERNON. *New England and the Bavarian Illuminati*. New York: Columbia University Press, 1918.

STEWART, JAMES BREWER. *Holy Warriors: The Abolitionists and American Slavery*. New York: Hill and Wang, 1976.

STONE, RONALD H., ed. *Reformed Faith and Politics*. Washington, D.C.: University Press of America, 1983.

STREIKER, LOWELL D. and GERALD S. STROBER. *Religion and the New Majority: Billy Graham, Middle America, and the Politics of the 70s*. New York: Association Press, 1972.

STROBER, GERALD and RUTH TOMSCZAK MCCLELLAN. *The Jerry Falwell Story*. Dunmore, Penn.: Ibex Publishing Co., 1982.

TARRANTS, THOMAS A., III. *The Conversion of a Klansman*. Garden City, N.Y.: Doubleday, 1979.

THAYER, GEORGE. *The Farther Shores of Politics: The American Political Fringe Today*. New York: Simon & Shuster, 1968.

THOMAS, CAL. *Book Burning*. Westchester, Ill.: Crossway Books, 1983.

TULL, CHARLES J. *Father Coughlin and the New Deal*. Syracuse: Syracuse University Press, 1965.

TUVESON, ERNEST LEE. *Redeemer Nation: The Idea of America's Millennial Role.* Chicago: University of Chicago Press, 1968.

VALENTINE, FOY. *Citizenship for Christians.* Nashville: Broadman, 1965.

———. *The Cross in the Marketplace.* Waco, Tex.: Word Books, 1966.

VAUGHN, WILLIAM P. *The Antimasonic Party in the United States, 1826-1843.* Lexington: University of Kentucky Press, 1983.

VETTER, HERBERT F., ed. *Speak Out Against the New Right.* Boston: Beacon Press, 1982.

VIGUERIE, RICHARD A. *The New Right: We're Ready to Lead.* Falls Church, Va.: Caroline House, 1981.

WALKER, BROOKS R. *The Christian Fright Peddlers.* Garden City, N.Y.: Doubleday, 1964.

WALLIS, JIM. *Agenda for Biblical People: A New Focus for Developing A Life-Style of Discipleship.* New York: Harper & Row, 1976.

———. *The Call to Conversion.* San Francisco: Harper & Row, 1981.

———, and WES MICHAELSON. "The Plan to Save America." *Sojourners* 5 (April 1976): 5-12.

WALTERS, RONALD G. *American Reformers 1815-1860.* New York: Hill and Wang, 1978.

WEBBER, ROBERT E. *The Moral Majority—Right or Wrong?* Westchester, Ill.: Crossway Books, 1981.

———. *The Secular Saint: A Case for Evangelical Social Responsibility.* Grand Rapids: Zondervan, 1979.

WEBER, TIMOTHY P. *Living in the Shadow of the Second Coming: American Premillennialism, 1875-1925.* New York: Oxford University Press, 1979.

WELLS, RONALD A., ed. *The Wars of America: Christian Views.* Grand Rapids, Eerdmans, 1981.

WERSICH, RÜDIGER BERND. *Zeitgenössischer Rechtsextremismus in den Vereinigten Staaten: Organisation, Ideologie, Methoden und Einfluss, dargestellt unter besonderer Berücksichtigung der John Birch Society.* Munich: Minerva Publikation, 1978.

WHITEHEAD, JOHN W. *The Second American Revolution.* Elgin, Ill.: David C. Cook, 1982.

———. *The Separation Illusion: A Lawyer Examines the First Amendment.* Milford, Mich.: Mott Media, 1977.

———. *The Stealing of America.* Westchester, Ill.: Crossway Books, 1983.

WILLOUGHBY, WILLIAM. *Do We Need the Moral Majority?* Plainfield, N.J.: Logos Haven Books, 1981.

WILSON, CARL W. *Our Dance Has Turned to Death: But We Can Renew the Family and Nation.* Wheaton, Ill.: Tyndale House, 1979.

WIRT, SHERWOOD ELIOT. *The Social Conscience of the Evangelical.* New York: Harper & Row, 1968.

WYATT-BROWN, BERTRAM. *Lewis Tappan and the Evangelical War Against Slavery.* Cleveland: Case Western Reserve University Press, 1969.

YODER, JOHN HOWARD. *The Politics of Jesus.* Grand Rapids: Eerdmans, 1972.

YOUNG, PERRY DEANE. *God's Bullies: Power Politics and Religious Tyranny.* New York: Holt, Rinehart and Winston, 1982.

ZWIER, ROBERT. *Born-Again Politics: The New Christian Right in America.* Downers Grove, Ill.: InterVarsity, 1982.

INDEX

280.4
M 364e

69773